DIGITAL LEGEND AND BELIEF

DIGITAL LEGEND AND BELIEF

The Slender Man, Folklore, and the Media

Andrew Peck

THE UNIVERSITY OF WISCONSIN PRESS

The University of Wisconsin Press
728 State Street, Suite 443
Madison, Wisconsin 53706
uwpress.wisc.edu

Gray's Inn House, 127 Clerkenwell Road
London ECIR 5DB, United Kingdom
eurospanbookstore.com

Printed in the United States of America
This book may be available in a digital edition.

Library of Congress Cataloging-in-Publication Data

Names: Peck, Andrew, 1985- author.
Title: Digital legend and belief : the Slender Man, folklore, and the media / Andrew Peck.
Description: Madison, Wisconsin : The University of Wisconsin Press, 2023. | Includes bibliographical references and index.
Identifiers: LCCN 2022045685 | ISBN 9780299343408 (hardcover)
Subjects: LCSH: Slender Man (Legendary character) | Folklore and the Internet. | Communication in folklore. | Social media. | Digital media.
Classification: LCC GR44.E43 P43 2023 | DDC 363.1076/95073—dc24/eng/20221128
LC record available at https://lccn.loc.gov/2022045685

To

Bill Ellis,

who talked to me like I was somebody

even when I was nobody.

Contents

Illustrations

Acknowledgments

First and foremost, I'd like to thank my wife, Nicky Kurtzweil. When I started working on this book in August 2019, I had no idea how difficult the next several years would be, or that writing a book would often be the least of my worries. In the last three years, we've struggled together through a cancer diagnosis, multiple miscarriages, and a global pandemic. Throughout it all, her strength and perseverance have been nothing short of inspiring. I am humbled to be married to someone so brilliant and driven. Thank you for everything, Nicky. The future is always uncertain, but I wouldn't want to spend it with anyone else.

I also owe special thanks to the colleagues and mentors who provided direct input on this project. In particular, I would like to thank Ashley Hinck, Kathy German, Robert Glenn Howard, and Rosemary Pennington for the feedback they provided on various chapters of this book. Their ongoing support and encouragement mean the world to me. My thanks as well to those who provided advice, answered questions, and helped me talk through ideas: Ron Becker, Lydia Bringerud, Bill Ellis, Katie Day Good, Carey Hardin, Becca Keyel, Anna Morel, Emily Sauter, Casey Schmitt, and Jeff Tolbert. I'd also like to obliquely thank the Folklorists of Flavortown and the Mongeese—they know who they are. The feedback I received from all these individuals was invaluable in shaping this book, and I am unbelievably lucky to have found such a brilliant and supportive scholarly community.

My thanks as well to Amber Rose Cederström, my editor at the University of Wisconsin Press, for her faith in this project and for her keen editorial advice. I am similarly grateful to the scholars who reviewed this book for their kind encouragement and insightful criticism. This book has greatly benefited from the time and attention so generously given by my reviewers and editor. I am also indebted to the Department of Media, Journalism & Film and to the College of Arts and Science at Miami University for the support they provided, which allowed me to bring this project to fruition.

I would also like to acknowledge some of the mentors whose support was crucial to developing my identity as a scholar. Thank you to Steve Lucas for sparking my love of academia and for believing in me even when others did not. Thank you to Paul Stob, whose offhand compliment that I was the best writer in his class changed the course of my life. Thank you to Jon McKenzie for showing me that my work as a digital folklorist had broad, multidisciplinary appeal. Thank you to Jenell Johnson for teaching me to live in the present. And thank you to Rob Howard for absolutely everything.

I also owe thanks to all the folklorists who welcomed me into the field and encouraged my work on digital folklore over the last decade, especially Trevor Blank, Simon Bronner, Anthony Buccitelli, Coppélie Cocq, Tom DuBois, Bill Ellis, Russell Frank, Stefan Gelfgren, Andrea Kitta, Liisi Laineste, John Laudun, Jim Leary, Lynne McNeill, David Puglia, Tok Thompson, Jeff Tolbert, and Libby Tucker. Thank you for helping a media scholar learn the joy of calling himself a folklorist.

Finally, I wish to offer thanks to the friends and family who supported this project in various ways over the years. A heartfelt thanks goes out to my parents, who read *Scary Stories to Tell in the Dark* with me when I was a child. The series kindled a lifelong love of contemporary legends and, although I didn't know it at the time, introduced me to the work of several of the folklorists cited in this book. Thank you to my crewmates on the *Tibanna Valkyrie*—Jeramie Parenteau and Bennett Whelan—and to Kyle Bursaw for running our tabletop sessions, which provided a welcome (and often needed) distraction from this project over the last few years. Thank you to Hannah Lewis, Sarah Snyder, and Zoe Heller for their classroom assistance and moral support while I completed the final stages of this project. And thank you to all the friends I used to go on night drives and legend trips with back in high school (a few of whom even agreed to be interviewed for this book). My thanks to the original group—Stacey

Cain, Nicole Mamura, and Isaiah Waid—and to all those who joined us in the years that followed: Lindsey Bergin, Amber Cramer, Rob Finlayson, Jessica Gentry, Matt Gilbertson, Angie Janas, Ethan Jensen, Kirby Kirchgasler, Mallori Nentl, Natalie Remus, Julie Schadle, Neal Skoy, and Peter Snell. We had a lot of close calls, but it turns out the real horror was the friends we made along the way.

DIGITAL LEGEND AND BELIEF

Introduction

Folklore for the Digital Age

It was almost 11 p.m. when we reached the mouth of an unknown dirt road. I was driving, my friend Izzy was riding shotgun, and we weren't looking to get anywhere but lost.

We were bored high schoolers, looking to break up the humid doldrums of another Minnesota August by creating a maze from a multitude of impulsive turns down unlit highways and across silent country roads. We likened our lack of a map or cell phone to walking a high wire without a net. With our safe suburban upbringings, this endeavor seemed inherently dangerous, and like many teenagers, we reveled in this small act of rebellion.

The trees along the road were thick, forming a dense canopy and concealing the way forward. A small sign loomed near the edge of the highway that had brought us here, rusted from age and lack of care. We proceeded away from the highway, down "Old Game Farm Road."

The road was barely wider than my car, and the forest was black and starless in every direction. The dirt road twisted and dipped, only allowing us to travel at about fifteen miles per hour. As the highway behind us was swallowed up by trees, the gravity of our choice began to set in: the narrow road and surrounding terrain made turning around impossible, and the winding, uneven road prevented us from backing out. We had no idea how deep into the forest this road went, but now we had no choice but to find out.

The sounds of crickets and crunching gravel hung heavy in the air for several minutes before Izzy finally broke our silence.

"You ever hear the story about the two teenagers who parked their car in the woods?"

"Oh! The one with the escaped serial killer who has a hook for a hand?"

"No," he replied, "this is a different one." Izzy's voice went low, and he proceeded to tell a version of "The Boyfriend's Death," a contemporary legend about a young woman and her boyfriend who run out of gas while driving in a forest.[1] At the end of the story, when Izzy revealed that the boyfriend was killed shortly after he left the car to find help, I shivered and laughed.

"That's a good one," I said, "but it's not as good as the one about the scarecrow."

Izzy looked back at me expectantly and after a short pause I began telling my own story—a modified version of "Harold," from Alvin Schwartz's *Scary Stories to Tell in the Dark*—about an abused scarecrow coming to life and tormenting his creators.

After I finished, it was Izzy's turn again, and he told a folkloresque version of the movie *Cube*. I responded with a story about the curse that befell explorers who opened a pharaoh's tomb. He told me about a Rube Goldberg–style death in the vein of the *Final Destination* films. I shared a personal experience narrative based on rumors of a local cult. We swapped these stories for more than an hour—an expressive assemblage of popular culture, contemporary legends, short stories, movies, and our favorite horror tropes designed to simultaneously calm our nerves and keep our adrenaline pumping.

It was well past midnight when we finally saw another vehicle traversing that derelict road to nowhere. Our folk-pop bricolage stopped abruptly as we were returned to the reality of our situation. A windowless white van drove slowly in front of us, heading in the same direction. We knew we weren't supposed to be here, but neither were they. I slowed the car to below ten miles per hour. The van in front of us slowed too.

Soon we were going five miles per hour. Then four. Then barely a crawl. The van ahead was stopping, and we had nowhere to turn. Then, just as the van came to a final halt, its brake lights illuminated the start of a large circular clearing where the access road widened into a hub with spokes branching off in every direction. We passed the van and made a rapid U-turn, kicking up a cloud of dust and gravel as we accelerated back in the direction we entered. An hour of driving was condensed into twenty short minutes as we sped back toward the highway—a need for escape overwhelming any concerns about my car's suspension.

Despite our close call, these night drives became a tradition between the two of us. Izzy and I would go driving and storytelling about once a month when school was out and the weather was warm. Before long, we widened this tradition to include new passengers, and these drives became a sort of initiation ritual among our group of friends. Old Game Farm Road became one of our most frequent destinations, increasingly haunted with every retelling.

We didn't invent this tradition, but at the time it felt uniquely ours. Years later, I would come to understand that our small group tradition—a mix of legend telling and driving to find haunted places—was actually a fairly common practice among American adolescents (McNeill and Tucker 2018b). As Bill Ellis wrote the same year we found Old Game Farm Road, there is a pattern to these legend trips: "Teenagers gather together, tell spooky stories about a local site, and then travel by car to see the place for themselves" (2001a, 186).

The practices we were engaging in—from their folk roots to their mass media influences—were fairly common (Dégh 2001, 307–9), but at the time, we lacked the connective affordances to easily learn from others or to document and share our own experiences with a broader audience. Our small suburb limited us to dial-up internet connections that were shared by entire families, and our legend trips predated both Web 2.0 and the rise of social media. While legends certainly existed on the internet in the 1990s and early 2000s (Kinsella 2011), our technological limitations obfuscated and fragmented our sense of connection to these larger social processes. What happens, then, when people engaging in widespread expressive practices like legend telling and legend tripping encounter new media with built-in affordances that encourage ongoing interpersonal connection and the sharing of everyday communication?

In other words, what happens when legends go digital?

The Slender Man

The night drives stopped when I moved away to college in the fall of 2004 and quickly became one of the things that I missed most about home. On sleepless nights I'd often try to recapture the feelings these drives elicited by locating and reading a variety of "born-digital" legends, including Ted the Caver, Killswitch, and the Dionaea House.[2] In retrospect, many of these stories might be regarded as "folkloresque" (Foster and Tolbert 2016); that is, the authors had intentionally integrated many markings of contemporary legends into their stories, but these stories didn't change as they circulated. Many of them simply existed on static personal web pages or blogs—destinations that invited visitation but not participation.[3]

In the summer of 2009, I was passing another sleepless night by reading the Something Awful forums when a user made an offhand remark about something called the Slender Man. A quick search led me to a thread that had started a few weeks prior called "Create Paranormal Images." The thread had initially started as a joke—a photoshop contest to hoax paranormal-image discussion boards—but a few days in it had taken an odd turn. A user going by the name Victor Surge had posted a pair of images and a few lines of text that captured a creature he referred to as "the Slender Man." Victor Surge's creation was a tall, shadowy figure with long limbs and wispy black tendrils that lurked in the background of photographs. Other users were enamored with the creation and ran with it, creating dozens of variations over the course of just a few days.

The expressive dynamics in the thread felt immediately familiar. In many respects, Victor Surge's initial images resembled the singular, folkloresque legends I had become accustomed to seeing online. The difference was not in the original artifact but instead in the sense of open collaboration and variation that emerged in its wake. Whereas other digital legends had integrated the familiar text and tropes of legends, this thread also replicated the *experience* of legend telling. The collaborative spirit, the back-and-forth storytelling, the sense of friendly one-upmanship, and the communal suspension of disbelief that emerged in the thread all reminded me of driving down Old Game Farm Road with Izzy as a teenager. The Slender Man was almost certainly not the first example of such a digital phenomenon, but like our night drives, it felt special—a unique bit of cultural knowledge shared between users that became a marker of group identity and membership. And I wasn't alone in feeling this way.

At the time, I had no idea how widely the Slender Man legend would circulate in the coming decade. Within two weeks, another Something Awful user posted a series of found-footage videos based on the Slender Man to YouTube. The series, known as *Marble Hornets*, went on to garner over one hundred million views over the course of the next ten years and inspired a variety of imitators, ranging from Slender Man–centric blogs to video series like *EverymanHYBRID* and *TribeTwelve*. These media often encouraged further user interaction and discussion, providing clues for users to piece together and tacitly inviting users to collaboratively speculate about the true nature of the supernatural happenings contained therein (Curlew 2017; Kinsella 2011, 60).

By the early 2010s, the Slender Man had become a well-known subcultural reference across a variety of web spaces. It was rife enough to spawn popular parodies (such as Neil Cicierega's *Splendorman*) and homages in variety of media, from the video game *Minecraft* to the television show *Supernatural*. A series of Slender Man video games were published in 2012 and 2013 and gained significant traction on YouTube, where users frequently watched others play and react to the games' jump scares. A *Marble Hornets* movie was released in 2015, and another movie, simply titled *Slender Man*, was released in 2018. But, despite this preponderance of ongoing, collaborative expression and the increasing availability of commercial Slender Man media throughout the decade, it was a singular event in May 2014 that changed the Slender Man from a somewhat obscure digital cryptid to a folk devil of national interest.

On May 31, 2014, two twelve-year-old girls lured a friend and classmate into the woods near their home in Waukesha, Wisconsin. Once there, the two girls stabbed their friend nineteen times and left her to die. Their victim survived and the two girls were quickly apprehended by local authorities. When questioned about their heinous act, the girls claimed they had attempted the murder to appease the Slender Man and prevent it from harming their families. Their bizarre rationale sparked a flurry of reporting, news specials, and documentaries that tried to explain the danger of the Slender Man to worried parents. Users who were already familiar with the character met these reports with a mix of shock, ridicule, and disbelief. After all, the Slender Man in these reports differed so greatly from their own generic expectations for the creature that its link to any real, embodied form of violence seemed nothing less than surreal.

Suffice it to say, the Slender Man didn't just circulate widely; it also garnered many new meanings as it traveled across mediated spaces. Whereas I understood it as an inside joke among Something Awful users, I would later speak with several individuals (from children to college students) who would swear the character was real—a recent name for some elemental, ancient, and nameless horror (see also Kitta 2018b). Some claimed that it had been believed into existence, referencing the Buddhist spiritual concept of a *tulpa*. Even more people expressed uncertainty about the character's origins. Most understood that the Slender Man was not real but assumed it had more traditional folk roots, while others assumed it came from a video game or movie (see also Tolbert 2018a).[4] Often people I talked to doubted it in the same way that they might doubt the existence of Bloody Mary[5]—the Slender Man was almost certainly not real, but why turn off the lights, chant into the bathroom mirror, and tempt fate? When viewed in this way, it becomes apparent that what circulated was not only a digital legend cycle but also belief itself.

The case of the Slender Man can tell us a lot about the formation and circulation of belief in the digital age. Its expansive digital circulation illuminates how the affordances of a given network location influence factors like the creation, circulation, and variation of belief. Its appearance in a wide variety of commercial and news media demonstrates how belief flows across increasingly interconnected media environments as well as how those media not only influence each other but also feed back into the legend cycle itself. Despite its verifiable origins, the frequent uncertainty over its authenticity reveals how playful practices, once divorced from their original context and intention by networked circulation, may give way to sincerely held beliefs.

Accordingly, this book is about more than just the Slender Man. As one of the most visible digital legend cycles of the last decade, it would be easy to position the Slender Man as worthy of attention for being exceptional; instead, I contend that it merits further attention because of how *typical* it is as an example of contemporary, mediated folk expression. The scope of the Slender Man is large, but it is not unprecedented (Tucker 2020). My choice to focus on this case stems not from its expansive scale or from its brief role as a salacious national news item, but instead from how well digital networks have documented the origin, formation, circulation, commercialization, ostension, and amplification of the Slender Man legend cycle. Although it is unlikely that every element discussed in this book will resonate with every digitally mediated legend, it *is* likely that many of the same dynamics will resonate in various quantities for other contemporary legends, both online and off. A study of the Slender Man, then, is a study of the common expressive dynamics of digital legend performances and, consequently, a study of the nature of digitally networked belief.

The Purpose of This Book

This book uses legend as a way of understanding the nature of networked belief in the digital age. Digital media technologies—ranging from devices like smartphones to social media platforms like Instagram and Facebook to the internet itself—are increasingly integrated into the everyday lives of the folk. While these technologies offer users new potential for mediated connection and expression, their ubiquity also raises several questions about how they might extend traditional folk practices as well as their implications on belief.

How do digital media facilitate the creation and spread of contemporary legends? What does legend performance look like in digitally mediated spaces? What is the relationship between tradition and technology in shaping these expressive practices?

As these questions make clear, this book is about what happens when new media extend old practices. I want to be clear at the onset, however, about what I mean by "extend." I am not arguing that digital media create a totally new paradigm for folk culture; instead, I am arguing that new technologies build on existing practices in novel ways by enabling new possibilities for expression and connection. In other words, this book demonstrates how the affordances of digital media—the capabilities these technologies enable—extend the potential for connection, expression, and circulation.

Accordingly, this book is meant to extend both online and offline legend scholarship. As we shall later see, oral legends are still alive and well not only among adults and adolescents but also at sleepovers and on the playground. Indeed, many of these born-digital legends have found parallel lives in the rumors and whisperings of tweens and children. To a nine-year-old, the Slender Man and Bloody Mary might as well be kin. These forms of oral culture continue to exist alongside digital culture, influencing digital practices while, at the same time, being influenced by them. Therefore, the expressive digital dynamics discussed in this book are meant to supplement (and not supplant) current understandings of contemporary legend—to show how old practices resonate in new ways across both digital and non-digital spaces.

Making this intervention requires taking both the "digital" and "folklore" elements of this legend cycle seriously. Prior work on the Slender Man from media scholars has persuasively argued that the Slender Man constitutes a form of digital folklore but has struggled to meaningfully integrate current folklore scholarship in making that argument. Shira Chess and Eric Newsom (2015), for example, position the Slender Man as a form of digital folklore, but key terms like "legend," "myth," and "mythos" are often conflated and ill-defined in their work. The result, as Ian Brodie writes, is that the authors "talk around and around practices precisely because they do not have such concepts as 'ostension' or 'type and version' or 'legend cycle' or 'dynamism and conservatism' or even 'motif' to guide them" (2015, 133). Such media-based scholarship has tended to suffer from including only a superficial engagement with folklore scholarship and, as a result, lacks the rich and critical vocabulary developed by folklorists since the nineteenth century to explain and interrogate informal expressive practices.

In the last several years, a handful of folklorists have used the case of the Slender Man to explore how digital media extend concepts like emergent performance (Peck 2015b), legend cycles (Blank and McNeill 2018a), ostension (Manning 2018; Peck 2015a; Tolbert 2013; Tucker 2018a), and belief (Kitta 2018b; Tolbert 2018b), most notably in a special issue of *Contemporary Legend* and in a subsequent edited collection, *Slender Man Is Coming* (Blank and McNeill 2015, 2018b). While many of these studies offer more nuanced analyses of these expressive cultures and practices, they also tend to elide what the underlying technologies themselves are doing beyond broadly affecting transmission or creating informal archives.

In the following sections of this introduction, I begin to bridge these gaps and lay the groundwork for the chapters to come by arguing that the study of contemporary legends online—like the Slender Man—can help scholars understand the new potentialities for belief in the digital age. Belief, I argue, is best understood as epistemological and emergent, but these same qualities also make it a difficult object of study. Focusing on legends, then, is a useful way to provide insight into belief because legends function as a dialectic on belief. To understand how digital media extend the possibilities for legend performance and circulation, I utilize the concept of "technological affordances" to account for the reciprocal relationship between technology and those who use it. Having established the interrelationship between legend performance and technology, I conclude this introduction with an outline of the chapters that follow, which begins to build a case for the specific ways that digital networks extend these folk practices.

Belief

Belief is an unwieldy concept—it is simultaneously prevalent and elusive. It touches a wide variety of topics, ranging from the ideological to the cosmological and from the secular to the sacred (Mullen 2000, 120).

Many folklorists position belief as epistemological or phenomenological, a lived process of meaning-making and of knowing that is reciprocally personal and social (Hufford 1982; Motz 1998, 340; Mullen 2000, 138; O'Connor 1995, 7). Individual actions are influenced by established belief systems while also feeding back into those systems, maintaining and further forming them. Sabina Magliocco (2012) has called this capacity "participatory consciousness," whereas Robert Glenn Howard (2013) has offered the similar "aggregate volition" to describe not only the personal/social dynamics of belief but also its potential for discursive power by appealing to ideas like tradition, common knowledge, and vernacular authority.

On the individual level, this process of knowing and meaning-making is both contextual and emergent (Magliocco 2012). It exists in the mind as a nebulous reserve of potential, which is activated in certain moments to help deal with uncertainty, ambiguity, and other forms of chaos. Belief may emerge in moments of anxiety (praying for a sick loved one), play (suspending disbelief while listening to a campfire story), solemnity (narrativizing a destined path from arbitrary life choices), or inspiration (following a prophetic dream). What is common to belief in all these moments is a longing for meaning that encourages personal and social ways of giving structure to the world.

Therefore, belief can be viewed as a desire for meaning, however temporary or sincerely entertained. The word "desire" is fundamental here, as it elucidates a fundamental duality of belief—to make sense of things, things must first be unsettled or unknown. Even if certain ideas are taken as axiomatic in a belief system or by a believer (e.g., "a benevolent divine being exists"), belief emergently deploys those axiomatic ideas as a way of connecting facts and making meaning for an exigence provided by one's current situation (O'Connor 1995, 10–11). In this way, belief expresses a sort of dialectic tension between itself and the unsettled questions which call it into being. Belief is simultaneously a need to entertain "what if?" and to answer an elusive "why?"

I wish to be careful here and acknowledge that my use of belief in this book is not meant in a diminutive way, as if belief were an inferior or purely irrational form of knowledge. Knowledge entails belief and the two terms are often context-dependent—we tend to refer to our constructed certainties as knowledge while viewing the certainties of others as mere belief (Hufford 1982; see also O'Connor 1995, 7–8). This suggests that belief constitutes a culturally dependent way of determining justification and authority (O'Connor 1995, 8–9). For instance, believing in a process like the scientific method is still a type of belief—it vests certainty in a skeptical process of systematic observation, testing, and reproducibility for the purpose of generating both explicatable belief and further questions.

Similarly, while belief is frequently defined in opposition to rationality, this dichotomy is problematic because it assumes that many beliefs are the result of flawed thinking or a lack of reflection (Motz 1998; Goldstein 2007a). As Diane E. Goldstein argues, "Careful analysis of belief traditions reveal reasoned consideration and the testing of alternatives on the part of the percipients and narrators" (2007a, 67). Accordingly, this book is not concerned with proving the fact, fiction, or irrationality of belief; instead, it is concerned with how belief functions socially for those who engage with it and the implications of those functions for critical scholarship and analysis (Dégh 2001, 7; Goldstein 2007a).

So, if belief is fundamentally social and expressive, then this book examines what happens to belief when new forms of media allow individuals and groups to be social and expressive in new ways. The internet offers new affordances for making and maintaining social connections across space and over time, and social media thrive on a constant churn of expressive, user-generated content. These affordances—as well as the social norms that have grown alongside them—offer new potential for the creation, circulation, transformation, commodification, and amplification of belief. The resulting intersection of participatory culture and participatory consciousness creates the potential for visibility and transmission at unprecedented (and often unintended) speeds and scales. Put simply, this book explores the many ways that digital networks change how we come together and collaborate in communal forms of meaning-making.

The problem with studying belief—whether online or off—lies in its intangibility (Dégh 2001, 82). Belief is not a static thing; instead, it is a quality that emerges in expressive practices (Magliocco 2012). These expressive practices are not one-to-one maps of belief; instead, they give the researcher a fleeting glimpse into belief, facilitating scholarly understanding through participant observation and the aggregation of vernacular expression (Dégh 2001, 82). So while belief exists primarily in the abstract, its study requires looking at concrete practices and specific cultural expressions (Mullen 2000, 120). Folklorists who strive to better understand belief do so by looking at a variety of expressive genres, including studies of customs, rituals, superstitions, folk religion, omens, memorates, or—the focus of this book—legends.

Legend and Belief

Legends can help us understand belief because, at their core, legends are conversations about belief (Dégh 1996, 44; 2001, 97, 405). What is most quintessential about legends is that they locate themselves in the real, lived world while also stretching the boundaries of that world (Ellis 2001a, 11), functioning as a sort of dialectic between real and unreal, known and unknown, certain and uncertain (Dégh 2001, 97). In this way, legends are less about individual texts and more about communication. They function as a dialectic on belief—as a social and discursive way of simultaneously entertaining "what if?" and conjecting about an elusive "why?" (Dégh 2001, 98–99).

Although the most popular emic term for legends in modern contexts is "urban legend," folklore scholars tend to prefer the term "contemporary legend" for several reasons.[6] First, the shift in nomenclature from "urban" to "contemporary" reminds us that these practices are living, evolving cultural forms with long-standing roots in expressive oral tradition. Legends are not relics of a bygone past; instead, they are persistent and emergent practices that are continually updated by the culture that shares them—a present manifestation of a long-standing practice (Dégh 2001, 90–91). Second, a shift in terms helps us to decouple from the more limiting "paranormal" or "ghost story" meanings elicited by the popular understanding of "urban legend," and allows us to focus on legends as discursive practices as opposed to a more text-based understanding that relies on the presence of paranormal or horror tropes. Discursively stretching the boundaries of the lived, known world does frequently involve telling stories about ghosts, aliens, or cryptids, but it could also involve sharing narratives about unusual or unlikely occurrences.[7] Finally, folklorists generally prefer "contemporary legend" to "urban legend" because the former acknowledges that modern legends come from a variety of spaces and not just from urban environments. This final facet is especially well-suited to a study of digitally mediated legends because digital media often deemphasize the role of geographic space.

Like all legends, contemporary legends are emergent, meaning they "are subject to communal composition and performance" (Ellis 2001a, 9) and come into being in the moment as the result of an ongoing negotiation between teller and audience (R. Bauman 1984; Buccitelli 2012). When we think about contemporary legends, we often think about them strictly in terms of oral communication—as stories, tales, or narratives that lack centralized ownership and circulate informally from teller to teller. Like a nebulous game of telephone, each iteration of an orally told legend is a variation that is based on the myriad variants that came before it. Through this informal circulation, legends naturally vary and fragment, becoming localized to groups and personalized by tellers. Each legend-telling event is the result of a mix of social expectations, assumed knowledge, and personal expression (Tangherlini 1994, 11).

But legends are much more than just stories; legends can also emerge through the embodied action or practices they inspire, a process that folklorists call "ostension" (Dégh and Vázsonyi 1983). Ostensive actions describe real-life occurrences of events described in legends and include both conscious choices and unconscious behaviors that emerge from (and act out elements of) a known legend cycle (Lindahl 2005, 164). These actions range from playful to macabre, with the former category being significantly more common (Ellis 1989, 202; 2001a, 163; Lindahl 2005, 181n2). When legends inspire actions like donning a costume, traveling to a legend's location, hunting for supernatural creatures and experiences, pranking and hoaxing ("pseudo-ostension"), attributing natural phenomena to a known legend ("quasi-ostension"), creating personal experience narratives ("proto-ostension"), poisoning Halloween candy, xenophobic violence, or murder they are inspiring ostensive action (Bird 1994; Burger 2009; Dégh 1995; Ellis 1981, 1989, 2001a; Grider 1984; Kinsella 2011). Like oral performances, ostensive actions both express and construct the legend cycles that inspire them. These types of actions constitute modes of legend performance that offer an alternative focus beyond legends as narrative (Dégh and Vázsonyi 1983).

Digital media further complicate understanding legends as stories because they offer users new potential for multimedia expression. A legend online could take the form of an image, a video, written text, or a mixed modality including any of the above. Since digital legends often contain significant visual components, terms such as "storytelling" or "narration" do not quite capture these events, as they seem to privilege the use of language (written or oral) to convey meaning. To account for the challenges presented by the multiplicity of both digital and embodied legend expression, I use the term "performance" to refer to these communication events (Ellis 2001a, 10).[8]

A legend performance refers to any of the numerous narrative, ostensive, and multimedia possibilities for engaging with legends in the digital age. For the purposes of this book, those who tell stories, engage in discussions, draw pictures, manipulate images, wear costumes, go on legend trips, and engage in other similar social methods of creative expression are said to "perform" the Slender Man legend. Accordingly, when I refer to Slender Man legend performance, I am referring to the ways in which individuals, acting as part of a networked group, use the character as a resource for creative expression and discourse that "*challenges accepted definitions of the real world and leaves itself suspended, relying for closure on each individual's response*" (Ellis 2001a, 60).

Digital Legend and Belief

Understanding legend performances requires understanding not just the artifacts themselves but also their performative context (Dégh 2001, 112–13; Ellis 2001a, 12). As Ellis writes, "It makes little sense to consider the legend a text apart from its performance. . . . By observing and comparing the way legends are performed in groups, and especially by observing the ways in which points are verbalized or negotiated, the folklorist can identify concepts central to the group's definition of cultural reality" (2001a, 12). It then follows that to fully understand the context of digital contemporary legends (as well as their implications for belief), scholars need to attend to not only the social context but also the technological context that guides the emergent performance and circulation of those legends.

The new potential for legend performance offered by digital communication technologies should not be viewed as an absolute or as a determinant; instead, it would be more accurate to regard the relationship between technology and society as a mutually constitutive feedback loop in which neither force is solely dominant and each is continually influencing the other. This perspective—commonly called the "social shaping of technology"—suggests that technologies exist in a state of "interpretive flexibility," providing users with structure while also leaving potential for individualization and variation inside that structure (Baym 2010; MacKenzie and Wajcman 1999; McNeill 2012).[9]

We can understand the structure provided by digital communication technologies in terms of their affordances. "Affordances" refers to the capabilities that a technology enables. In line with the social shaping perspective, the idea of technological affordances suggests that technologies have certain preferred uses designed into them while also understanding that people frequently use technologies in modified or unexpected ways (Baym 2010, 44–45). For the purpose of this book, these affordances are very often the social or communicative capabilities enabled by the technological choices built into a website, app, device, or digital platform. The term is meant to reflect that a reciprocal feedback loop exists between people, institutions, and technology, while also eschewing the pitfalls of both social and technological determinism. In short, my argument is that the choices built into digital media don't *cause* a certain outcome, but they do make certain outcomes *more likely*.[10]

When looking broadly at networked digital communication technologies, certain sets of affordances become evident. The internet, for example, offers users the potential to circumvent geographical limitations and enables everyday communication between individuals based on similar interests, ideas, or values. Users can easily form communities with people they have never—and likely, will never—meet in person. Similarly, individuals can connect with their offline friends on the go, during their commute, or as they drift off to sleep. An individual can fluidly shift between numerous different web spaces and identities. In the span of only a few seconds, a user can reply to a post on social media, check the news, refresh their work email, and text their partner about that evening's dinner. These digital communications are often multimodal, containing a mix of oral, written, and visual elements. Some are private; many are very visible, often in ways that users neither intend nor expect.

However, "the internet" is not a monolithic space. Different network locations offer users distinct sets of affordances, and legend performances online often emerge differently based on the availability of different sets of affordances. This includes not only the affordances of the internet in general (connection, fluidity, multimodality, etc.) but also more localized sets of affordances enabled by various websites, apps, and digital devices. A smartphone, for example, makes it very easy to document a legend trip via photos or video. The subsequent sharing of that media to one's online community or social network is subject to not only social processes (approval, discussion, sharing, etc.) but also structural properties of the website itself, which may affect how other users see that media (if they even see it at all). A legend may emerge very differently in the chronological post-and-response environment of an old-school discussion board like Something Awful versus on a site like Reddit, where user posts are curated and sorted based on a combination of user feedback ("upvotes") and algorithmic filtering. Hence, even a static "paranormal" image (which, when removed from this social/technological context, appears to be a single, unaltered legend "text") will emerge differently in the various spaces where it is shared due to different social and technological contexts.

The idea that individual legend performances are localized variations based on larger legend cycles is not new, nor is the idea that these localized variations (and the discourse on belief they participate in) express both personal and communal identity. Legends have always presented a challenge for researchers because individual "texts" both inherit from wider practices while also being localizations specific to the group and specific performative context. What *is* new here is the role that modern digital technologies play in this localization process alongside these expressive social and communal dynamics. These localized changes, when considered in aggregate, begin to flow outward, and as a result, these technologies begin to affect the potential for legend performance not only on the local scale but also on a broader cultural level.

The result of this process is that the new possibilities for legend performance and circulation offered by digital media stretch far beyond the boundaries of the internet. The confluence of social and technological factors that extend oral legends in digital spaces ultimately feed back into those same offline behaviors, which suggests that implications of digital media on legend and belief are far-reaching. Just as the internet cannot be considered in a vacuum that excludes embodied performance and other forms of media, digital legend performance reciprocally influences how we understand the potentialities for legend performance in both mass media and everyday life. Therefore, when talking about digital contemporary legends, we are really talking about the evolving nature of legends as a whole in an age defined by networked digital media.

Chapter Summaries

Widely adopted new media technologies—ranging from smartphones to social media—offer vast new potential for extending the traditional and expressive social practices that are commonly regarded as folklore. Far from being relics of a bygone past, folk practices persist and change to suit their contemporary environments. Understanding those changes, I argue, is fundamental to understanding how those same technologies offer new potential for the formation and circulation of belief in the digital age.

The Slender Man is an ideal case for analyzing the changing nature of contemporary legends because its clear origins and widespread circulation provide the opportunity to follow a single legend cycle as it gets adapted across a wide variety of contemporary media contexts. It helps us understand how different sets of affordances—ranging from the discussion board that birthed the legend cycle to the social networks where it found popularity—affect the possibilities for legend performance and circulation. Attempts to capitalize on the legend cycle by institutions ranging from filmmakers to video game designers help us understand how the increased visibility created by digital networks also creates new opportunities for the commercialization of folk practice by media industries. The ostensive practices sparked by the Slender Man legend can help us understand the changing nature of contemporary legend performance offline, and journalistic coverage of the Slender Man in the wake of the Waukesha stabbing demonstrates what happens when the cultural norms of digital media come into contention with the framing power of mass media.

To that end, this book uses the case of the Slender Man to explore the changing relationship between digital legend and belief. By analyzing the specific ways that digital media technologies extend Slender Man legend performance, this book demonstrates how these media create new potential for creation, circulation, commercialization, ostension, and sensationalism. These five facets form the basis of the chapters that follow, which tell the story of the Slender Man chronologically, starting from its creation in 2009 and ending with reflections on the character's impact on digital culture over a decade later.

Chapter 1 looks at how users on Something Awful collaborated in an ongoing process of performance, interpretation, and negotiation that constructed the details, motifs, and shared expectations of the Slender Man legend cycle over a period of several weeks in June 2009. This chapter considers what it means to call a legend performance "emergent" in an age of clearly demarcated user posts and near-perfect copy fidelity and argues that the Slender Man legend cycle combines the generic conventions and emergent qualities of oral and visual performance with the collaborative potential and mixed media modalities of networked digital communication. By applying these traditional and emergent frameworks to the ways in which individuals perform and discuss the Slender Man, this chapter ultimately demonstrates how collective performances in digital communication contexts emerge as co-creations that are influenced not only by factors like prior performative choices, audience feedback, and shared expectations for legend performance, but also by the underlying role of the technology itself.

Chapter 2 follows the Slender Man legend cycle as it began to circulate beyond its origins on Something Awful and analyzes how legend conduits change when performances start to leave a temporally durable trace. Focusing on the popular YouTube series *Marble Hornets*—as well as its reception in different web communities—this chapter argues that digital circulation is marked by a synthesis of social and algorithmic filtering. While much communication on digital media may resemble the decentralized and informal channels typically associated with the transmission of oral folklore, the affordances of digital platforms create new possibilities for acts of social filtering while also introducing new technological filters that further mediate user choices. As content begins to circulate across the web, this intersection of social and algorithmic filtering renders certain nodes in the network more visible than others. The most visible of these nodes function as networked gatekeepers, framing the legend cycle for a larger audience while also facilitating its spread.

Chapter 3 looks at what happened after the Slender Man legend cycle was commercialized in a series of video games. While the games initially met with a lukewarm reception, they went on to garner significant popularity because of the attention they received from professional content creators on social media. I argue that the reason for this disparity lies in the divergent ways that the games and the videos of influential YouTube users playing them constructed a sense of vernacular authority. The Slender Man video games tried and failed to create a folkloric frame, and the resulting sense of contradictory hybridity limited further engagement and variation from users. Conversely, videos that featured YouTube celebrities playing through the games tended to integrate a variety of tactics that cultivated a sense of vernacular authority much more effectively. Ultimately, this chapter argues that while both the games and the videos were forms of commercial media, the latter's skillful use of the vernacular mode invited acts of further engagement from their viewers, which effectively reintegrated the games back into the legend cycle and led to novel forms of variation.

Chapter 4 looks at various ways users enact aspects of the Slender Man legend cycle in their offline lives, a type of behavior called ostension. This chapter argues that the increased visibility provided by digital networks necessitates a reorientation of terms from ostensive action to ostensive practice. Before the internet, these legend-inspired actions tended to be isolated, ephemeral, and limited to small groups. However, digital communication has normalized the documentation and sharing of everyday behaviors across networks, which has resulted in ostension becoming both more mediated and more visible. This increased visibility creates awareness and draws connections between individual actions, consequently encouraging a sense of collaboration. As users collaborate on ostensive practices, they begin to develop hierarchies of performance that privilege certain types of interaction. This creates an atmosphere that facilitates acts of vernacular critique and offers users an opportunity to reflect not only on the nature of legends but also on the nature of the ostensive practices themselves.

Chapter 5 analyzes the abundance of mass media coverage the Slender Man received in the wake of the 2014 Waukesha stabbing as well as how users reacted to that sensational coverage. These mass media reports frequently portrayed the Slender Man as a corruptive force awaiting children on the dark corners of the internet—a folk devil born out of common adult fears regarding internet use among children and adolescents. While this portrayal was reminiscent of earlier folkloric moral panics, like the Satanic Panic of the 1980s, this chapter demonstrates how our current interconnected media environment can quickly amplify and distort a digital legend through the convergent actions of everyday users, mass media gatekeepers, and social media algorithms. Legends that are amplified risk becoming distorted as they circulate, with previously unfamiliar users supplying their own context and interpretations. The resulting moral panic is difficult to counter because it goes beyond questions of fact and enters the realm of interpretation, enabled by widespread, networked belief.

This book's concluding chapter reflects on what we can learn from the case of the Slender Man and returns to our initial conversation about the nature of belief in an age of digital networks. I suggest that the implications of this book are far-reaching because the question of how digital networks mediate belief has increasingly come to the forefront of public discourse in recent years. I argue that advancing our understanding of belief through legend can help us better understand how similar belief genres—like fake news, conspiracy theories, hoaxes, rumors, meme culture, and anti-expert movements—are enabled by the affordances of digital media. This understanding also helps us break down conceptual boundaries between the increasingly intertwined realms of popular, mass, and folk culture and consider what such a collapse might mean for the future of both media and folklore scholarship.

CHAPTER ONE

Creation

At first glance, the Slender Man appears to be a tall, thin humanoid wearing a black suit. A closer examination, however, quickly reveals how very inhuman the creature actually is. The Slender Man is faceless, with only a featureless, white visage where its face should be. Its limbs are uncannily long, giving the creature its slender appearance as well as its name. Wispy black tendrils writhe and slither as they erupt from its back. Its true nature is unknowable, and what appears as a black suit might simply be a way of making sense of a facade that is too eldritch, otherworldly, or Lovecraftian for mere humans to comprehend. Just knowing about its existence begins to chip away at one's sanity and thinking about it only draws the horror closer. If you have read this far, then it is already too late.

But it wasn't always this way, and none of these traits were ever a forgone conclusion. Although the Slender Man has an identifiable individual creator, the majority of the key details of the Slender Man legend cycle were formed not by a single author but by a collaborative, networked process. Through an ongoing series of digital performances, discussions, and negotiation of legend dialectic, the Slender Man emerged not from any singular occult tome or work of mad genius but from somewhere far more terrible and chaotic—an internet comedy forum.

The Slender Man is a crowdsourced monster (Peck 2015b). But to some extent, the same can be said of almost any legend cycle or cryptid. After all, the collaborative, open, and diffuse dynamics that underlie crowdsourcing have also traditionally enabled oral legend performances as well as other forms of predigital folklore (Tolbert 2013). Unlike a static text (e.g., an episode of a television show or a chapter in a book), legends have always been emergent—they come into being in the moment as a result of an ongoing negotiation between performer, audience, and context. What is different about the case of the Slender Man is that digital media not only affect how legends emerge but also challenge how we think about the emergent nature of legend performance. For instance, what does it mean for a performance to be "emergent" in a media environment that offers the potential for asynchronous interaction and fluid group membership? How do users interact with each other to negotiate varied, multimedia performances in digital spaces? What can an understanding of the emergent nature of digital legend performance reveal about the underlying reasons for a legend cycle's initial appeal and long-term success?

The collaborative creation of the Slender Man legend cycle on the Something Awful forums offers an ideal starting point to address these questions because it provides an easily bounded, chronological look at how legends emerge online. What the case of the Slender Man offers, then, is the opportunity to observe this emergent process of digital legend creation and negotiation from its inception.

In this chapter, I examine how the Slender Man developed on Something Awful during June 2009 to show how digital media extend the emergent nature of performance by creating distinct opportunities for connection and interaction compared to face-to-face or mass communication. Digital connections may be more fluid than offline connections, but they also enable an ongoing, iterative process that facilitates collaborative forms of multimedia performance. These digital performances emerge as co-creations that are influenced not only by factors like prior performative choices, audience feedback, and shared expectations for legend performance, but also by the underlying role of the technology itself.

To make this argument, I begin this chapter by explaining what it means to call a performance "emergent"—that it comes into being in the moment as a co-creation between performer and audience. Adopting this emergent framework has presented methodological difficulties for the study of oral legends, as solicited and transcribed versions represent only a single instance of many potential variations. These difficulties are further complicated by the affordances of digital media, which extend many of the contextual factors that influence the emergent nature of legend performance. Although digital media challenge how we think about facets like temporality, orality, and generic expectations in legend performance, I argue that users are continually adapting these changing affordances to create mediated legend performances that are still emergent, just in different ways.

To demonstrate this process, I then turn to the case of the Slender Man. Through an analysis of the character's collaborative development on the Something Awful forums, I suggest that the Slender Man legend cycle combines the generic conventions and emergent qualities of oral and visual performance with the collaborative potential of networked digital communication. Understanding the Slender Man as the ongoing product of emergent digital legend performances reveals that the character's initial and enduring popularity stems from a sense of communal ownership that is uniquely enabled by the affordances of digital media. By applying these traditional and emergent frameworks to the ways in which individuals perform and discuss the Slender Man online, this chapter ultimately demonstrates how collective performances in digital communication contexts may vary from face-to-face performances while also extending these traditional folk practices in new ways.

The Emergent Nature of Performance

Calling a performance "emergent" means that it comes into being in the moment, through reciprocal interaction between performer and audience (R. Bauman 1984; Buccitelli 2012). Both performer and audience bring an array of existing social knowledge to this communication event, meaning that any such social interaction begins by drawing on preexisting social frames (Goffman 1974). These social frames act as a shared resource for communication and performance, giving rise to the generic expectations that "make up the structured system of conventionalized performance for the community" (R. Bauman 1984, 37–38). Performances influence and imagine their audiences, and in turn, audiences participate in the creation of the performance (38). This mutually constitutive interaction between performance and audience creates an ongoing feedback loop, affecting not only what is currently being performed but also the nature of successive performances. Each new performance draws upon prior performances—emphasizing and diminishing different aspects based on both the communal negotiation and the individual performer's experiences and perceptions.

In this way, each performance is, in and of itself, a statement about what makes for good performance.

We often think about the emergent nature of performance in terms of big performative moments—an orator extemporaneously addressing a crowd or a storyteller entertaining an audience—but even our more quotidian performances are still emergent. We are constantly performing as we go about our everyday lives, and the choices we make when swapping stories at a bar, sharing personal experience narratives, or recapping vacation highlights to friends, family, and co-workers all emerge as the product of shared expectations between communicators and various forms of interactive feedback (verbal, nonverbal, social, contextual) (R. Bauman 1984; Goffman 1959; Meyrowitz 1985). These everyday performances may contain the potential for transformation, but they often also do significant work to reinscribe our social realities as well as to uphold a hegemonic sense of self and group identity (Sawin 2002, 45).

Understanding oral performances as emergent creates a set of methodological challenges for legend scholarship. Recording and transcribing a legend only captures one version of a highly variable performance, and it would be a mistake to position that single version as quintessential or definitive. The act of interviewing itself can also lead legend performances to emerge differently than they would in a more organic context. Even writing about legends observed in their natural habitat can be difficult because these emergent performances are multilayered, contextual, and often draw on implicit knowledge of the performer and audience (Prizer 2018, 131). The ethnographic researcher who is interested in accurately capturing the performance of oral legends must seek to convey more than just the plot of a story; a legend performance also includes a wide array of other contextual factors, including intonation, body language, emotions, side conversations, and digressions (Ellis 2001a, 13–25). These context-rich fragments should then be placed into an "intelligible frame" that renders the performative context comprehensible to a cultural outsider (Geertz 1973, 26).

Positioning these communication events as emergent processes reveals that legend telling is about more than just the stories themselves, and it draws our attention to the conditions (social, structural, technological, etc.) that help shape them and help those involved derive meaning from them. This has several significant implications. First, legends are not isolated texts with hidden, static meanings; instead, legends are inherently polysemic and compel their audience to construct their own meanings, often as part of a related discursive process (Dégh and Vázsonyi 1983; Ellis 2001a, 75). Second, that which is left out or left implicit by the performer (or by the conversation) can be as important for understanding the group's conception of cultural reality as that which is directly stated or alluded to (Ellis 2001a, 12). Third, understanding the audience not only in terms of its actuality but also as it is implied or imagined to be by those involved yields insight into a process of meaning-making as well as into ideas of community membership, reflexivity, inclusion, exclusion, and how subject-positions are constituted or reinforced through performance (Berger and Del Negro 2002; Sawin 2002). Finally, a focus on understanding legends through their performative context suggests that the medium of performance plays an important role in both structuring performer-audience interaction and guiding the shared expectations that shape how legend performances emerge.

Emergence and Media

Dominant forms of media exert influence on the emergent nature of performance, even in unmediated, face-to-face contexts. Most overtly, this is because mass media storytelling tropes and structures provide large-scale cultural touchstones that often get integrated into expressive performances. For instance, it is very likely that when parents and children tell the story of Cinderella, they are at least somewhat influenced by the aesthetics or narrative of the Walt Disney film. Alternatively, a group of teenagers may create their own fantasy world for a roleplaying game that is distinctly their own while, at the same time, being inspired by a mélange of popular fantasy media (such as the books of J. R. R. Tolkien), official tabletop gaming manuals, and their own perceptions of authentic folklore (Milspaw and Evans 2010). In other contexts, mass media may also circulate legends, such as when news outlets report on rumors of local satanic cults or poisoned Halloween candy (Ellis 2000; Grider 1984). This reporting, in turn, serves to propagate and legitimize those performances (Laudun 2020; Peck 2020c; see also chapter 5).

But the bigger influence of media on the emergent nature of performance is also much more subtle. The affordances of a medium like writing, when widely adopted, can begin to shift our ideas of expression (Ong 1982). Although writing as a technology has existed for thousands of years,[1] widespread literacy is a fairly recent development enabled by the invention of the printing press around 1440 (Eisenstein 1980).[2] Before this development (and even for some time afterward), Western culture was dominated by auditory processing, and the majority of individuals lived in an oral culture (Ong 1982, 120).

Whereas oral cultures tended to be defined by informally circulating performances that were re-creative, collective, and contextual, print culture enabled new modes of performance that formed the basis for ensuing romantic notions of authorship, such as the singular great work created by an individual artist (Pettitt 2007). The mass production of media texts (starting with the printed word in the fifteenth century and followed more recently by forms of popular mass media like radio, film, and television) facilitated ideas like centralized ownership, professional creativity, and copyright (Lessig 2008). When folklore was translated to media, there became an "original" (the first version to be performed or, in many instances, to be copied down and mass produced) and an author (Lord 1960, 124–25; Thompson 2020). Contrary to the emergent dynamics discussed above, the cultural changes brought about by the printing press first made singular ownership over ideas possible, then dominant (Ong 1982, 131).

The cultural changes brought about by print culture aren't limited to mass-produced, finalized media texts because being socialized in a print culture affects the nature of oral performances as well (Ong 1982, 133).[3] As Walter J. Ong has argued, writing restructures consciousness (78; see also McLuhan 1962). Print cultures tend to be more visually oriented than auralcentric oral cultures. Words, even those in our minds, begin to inescapably take up space and have shapes in print cultures (Ong 1982, 117). Perceptions of temporality change, as interiorized print culture more actively and consistently situates the individual in time, making days, appointments, and birth years all the more mundane to everyday existence (97–98). Cognitive faculties like memory fundamentally change when words are committed to paper and can be referred to and referenced at a later point in time (96–101).

So, if widely adopted media have the capacity to influence performance (whether or not that performance is itself mediated), then how do the affordances of digital communication challenge how we think about the emergent nature of performance? After all, many of the elements that are crucial to understanding the performative context (e.g., intonation, body language) are seemingly absent in some digital communications. Digital media continue to play with our sense of place and time, further complicating ideas like audiences, feedback, and shared expectations for performance. Digital performances maintain elements of oral and written communication, but don't seem to fit comfortably in either category. Users can create variations, but digital networks make it extremely easy to simply circulate existing texts ad infinitum.

In light of all these challenges, what we might expect to find online is a vast world of static texts and an environment of networked individualism—that is, everybody is talking but nobody is listening, sharing, or engaging. If this were true, then it would be easy to dismiss these changes as inferior or less authentic than oral legend performances. But even early digital folklore scholarship repeatedly showed that this was far from the case, whether looking at widely forwarded emails, personal websites and blogs, digital humor, photoshops, or memes (Ellis 2001b, 2002b; Foote 2007; Frank 2004, 2009, 2011; Howard 2005, 2009; Kibby 2005; Kuipers 2005). In actuality, the digital age forefronts many of the communicative dynamics previously associated primarily with oral culture, which suggests that the emergent nature of performance persists online in a way that diverges from—but is not inferior to—oral performance (Blank 2007; Fernback 2003; Foley 2012; Pettitt 2007).

Digital legend performances—like the Slender Man—occur through various media modes that are often impractical for face-to-face performance (Dégh 2001, 298; Buccitelli 2012). Digital technologies allow performances that blend and extend written, oral, and visual communication in novel ways. For example, a digitally shared performance could take the form of a written transcript, an "authentic" oral interview, or a photoshopped image—or it could include elements of all three. Since digital communication often bears the signs of written, spoken, and visual language, it is best viewed as a mixed modality (Baym 2010, 63–64). This modality, as Barbara Kirshenblatt-Gimblett eloquently writes, "is neither speech nor writing as we have known it, but something in between, and, increasingly, with the convergence of technologies, it is multimedia" (1998, 284). Ong provides a similar perspective, writing that "Technology, properly interiorized, does not degrade human life but on the contrary enhances it" (1982, 83). The remainder of this chapter is concerned with the immediate nature of that enhancement—how the affordances of digital media offer new potential for connection and community, which, in turn, affect how contemporary legends emerge online.

Digital Legend Performance

While digital media enable many dynamics reminiscent of oral communication (e.g., recreation, collectivity, etc. [see Pettit 2007]) they also offer new potential for technologically mediated forms of expression, connection, and community. When it comes to the digital performance of folklore, "familiar forms occur in markedly unfamiliar ways" (Buccitelli 2012, 61), and these changes affect how we think about the shared expectations that guide legend performance as well as the collaborative dynamics that create those performances. If legends are "subject to communal composition and performance . . . more than any form of oral discourse" (Ellis 2001a, 9), then the digital performative context includes not only the performances themselves and the discussion and digressions surrounding them but also the underlying role of shared expectations and technological affordances in mediating those performances. Although the specific expectations and affordances may vary between digital groups and spaces, these digital legend performances will always emerge from a synthesis of social and technological factors. The result of these changes is that digital legend performance becomes an iterative process—one in which the aggregation of performative choices, shared expectations, audience feedback, and technological affordances continually feed into each other in mutually constitutive feedback loops.

Digital media extend our ability to connect and maintain groups, which challenges how we think about the shared expectations that guide performances in digital contexts. Unlike face-to-face performances, networked digital communication technologies offer the potential to decouple interpersonal connection from geography and locality (Lee and Lee 2010). Conversely, digital communication also enables users to connect more readily to those they see every day and to the local cultures around them (Blank 2013, 101–2; Buccitelli 2013). Whether local or global, the connections enabled by digital communication are always on and persist even when the user is not actively engaging with them. The resulting connections are more fluid than those of predigital communication, presenting users with many more options for where to engage and how to define themselves. At the same time, users are also more enabled to easily shift between those spaces and identities (Giddens 1991; Z. Bauman 2007).

The fluid nature of digital group membership among individuals means that every network location maintains a unique set of shared expectations derived from the product of ongoing group interaction yet belonging to no specific individual. Digital communities are sustained because individual users continually enact social identities that they perceive to be consistent with group expectations and values (Howard 2008a, 202). These shared expectations are "displayed, reinforced, negotiated, and taught through members' shared behaviors" (Baym 2010, 80) and "any newcomer to an internet chatroom, or a Facebook page, or even a back-and-forth mobile phone texting scenario, will know that there exists a certain shared body of knowledge about how to behave in such settings" (McNeill 2009, 82). The implication of this argument is that a website doesn't have a culture; cultures exist on websites (Massanari 2015). Some cultural elements may be site-wide while others exist only in subsections or in small groups of communicators, "but getting a handle on the latter requires a good understanding of the former" (Massanari 2015, 14).

These shared expectations affect how individual users manage and perform their sense of self, compelling them to do so in ways that are consistent with their perceptions of group identity. The affordances of digital media allow users to edit or more selectively choose how to present their "networked self" (Papacharissi 2010), but it is important to remember that even in their offline lives, individuals are always performing a sense of self to some audience, whether embodied, imagined, or both (Goffman 1959; Marwick and boyd 2011). Most users unintentionally engage in this identity work as a matter of course while going about their daily digital lives, although some websites—especially social networks that are public-facing or career-oriented—can make this identity work a much more deliberate process. Whether on social networks or discussion boards, these public displays of connection are vital to personal identity work in digital spaces (Van Doorn 2010; see also Toma and Hancock 2013, 322), and as Robert

Glenn Howard notes, "If the vernacular process of public self-imagining were to stop, no geographic location would be there to bind the individuals together" (2008a, 202). The duality here is that group membership in the digital age may be more fluid, but users still imagine a static community whenever they communicate online.

These digital performances emerge not only from an individual user's sense of self but also from their sense of audience—that is, who they perceive themself as engaging with during a specific communicative interaction (Buccitelli 2012). As in face-to-face performance, this consideration of audience—while often done unconsciously and in an instant—does not ensure that performances will always be well-received. Miscalculations are always possible, and digital media exacerbate this potential to misunderstand social cues, especially when new users find themselves interacting with established groups. The fluid nature of digital communication means that users must frequently deal with unintended audiences, especially when communicating in highly visible, connective spaces like social networks (Buccitelli 2012, 74). Similarly, digital media make it easier for performances to circulate well beyond their intended audience through the ease of actions like copying, pasting, or sharing. In turn, users engaging in such actions also consider *their* audiences. Even something as simple choosing to share an image always considers factors like the user's sense of self, their imagined audience, and their assumptions of shared expectations—even if the increasingly mundane nature of digital communication often obfuscates those decisions in a split-second mental process.

On the internet this ongoing interaction between performer and audience often occurs asynchronously and remotely, and more confoundingly, it doesn't do so in the same way across digital spaces. Some spaces—like the discussion boards on Something Awful—involve an iterative post-response style that catalogs posts chronologically and organizes them into discrete discussion threads. Social media tend to be more rapid in iteration and idiosyncratic in structure, with conversations more akin to a noisy bar and feeds of user-generated content curated by algorithms tailored to each individual user (Meraz and Papacharissi 2013; Pariser 2012). Other platforms mimic face-to-face performance even more closely, offering users the opportunity to engage in voice chat, video chat, or real-time personal broadcasts. This suggests that the study of digital performances must attend not only to the connective capabilities of digital media in general but also to the affordances at play in the specific digital spaces where performances emerge (Buccitelli 2012, 79–80).

While neither temporal nor spatial gaps preclude the possibility of digital folk culture or legend performance, the ways in which digital communication diverges temporally and spatially from face-to-face communication does require a shift in thinking about the role of feedback in constituting digital performances (Buccitelli 2012, 70–71; Dégh 2001, 298; see also Blank 2009; Foote 2007; Howard and Blank 2013). While digital feedback lacks social and body language cues, digital users have learned to compensate for this with reactions that are more overt than in face-to-face communication, such as posting written feedback or clicking a button that publicly signals "I like this content" to both the performer and other users. Other communicative shorthands involve users actively deploying digital expressions like memes, reaction animations (GIFs), and ideograms (emoticons, emojis) to evoke the intonation, body language, and emotion present in face-to-face performances. Such responses have become so ingrained in users' everyday communicative repertoires that websites frequently integrate collections of easily usable reaction media into their platforms.

Actions like sharing, liking, or commenting constitute prevalent forms of digital feedback that emerge between performers and audiences and guide the potential for further performance. The absence of such actions can similarly be construed as an implicit commentary on the performance's perceived quality (or lack thereof) (Buccitelli 2012, 61). These actions and inactions (as well as their perceived significance and meaning) are both site- and group-specific, and shared expectations develop around these feedback mechanisms, with group-specific cultural knowledge dictating when to "like" or "love" a status, the dominant meaning of a GIF, or the appropriateness of the eggplant emoji.

The spatial and temporal changes enabled by digital communication simply mean that the relationship between performer and audience is reoriented, not eliminated. As I have argued above, a similar reorientation also affects the shared expectations that digital performers and audiences bring to the communication event, the feedback provided during and following digital performances, and the subsequent adjustments to shared expectations for further expression. The result is that digital performances are still emergent, but they are emergent in different ways based on the media that facilitate them. This suggests that observing digital legend performances means viewing them as part of an iterative and ongoing process that is simultaneously social and technological. In the sections that follow, I analyze the emergence of the Slender Man on the Something Awful forums in June 2009 to demonstrate this iterative process of digital legend formation and show how the emergent nature of performance is extended by the affordances of digital media.

Something Awful This Way Comes

On June 8, 2009, user Gerogerigegege created a discussion thread on the Something Awful forums called "Create Paranormal Images."[4] In the thread's initial post, Gerogerigegege expressed a long-held interest in creating paranormal images and invited other users to create and share mundane images that had been manipulated to appear paranormal. The resulting images, Gerogerigegege hoped, could be used to fool or hoax paranormal investigators and discussion boards. Gerogerigegege supplied other users with a few photoshopped examples, links to usable photographs, and some tips on digital editing techniques to create more "authentic" looking images. Gerogerigegege ended the post by inviting other users to join in.

Such acts of coordinated and collaborative play were not uncommon among the users of Something Awful. Founded in late 1999, the website hosts a front page[5] with rotating comedy articles and a robust discussion forum, divided topically, where users congregate. The site's users, who collectively (and self-deprecatingly) call themselves "Goons," were responsible for many of the early internet's most well-known pranks and memes. Most interaction on the site centers on the various forums, including FYAD, GBS, and PYF[6] as well as more interest-oriented forums based on topics like video games, political discussion, and fitness. The threads in these subforums exist in the chronological post-and-response style typical of many Web 1.0 discussion boards. Each "page" of a thread is made up of forty user posts, and it is not unusual for a thread to go on for hundreds of pages over periods of months or years.

Despite maintaining a reputation for irreverence and crude humor (though not entirely unwarranted), the forums have several mechanisms meant to enforce order that separate Something Awful from more "anything goes" digital environments like 4Chan.[7] While the forums have over two hundred thousand registered users, forum content is frequently blocked by a paywall, preventing nonregistered users from viewing it. To register an account and post on the forums, users have to pay ten dollars, which keeps out many younger users and creates a small but effective barrier for potential trolls. Users who disregard forum rules risk losing their ability to post or losing their accounts, and each subforum has a small stable of moderators tasked with enforcing the site's rules. These moderators can issue probations, bans, or permanent bans for users who post inappropriately or break forum rules.

Gerogerigegege's original post, which called for the creation of paranormal images for the purpose of playful hoaxing, set the tone for the thread by effectively keying a performative frame and by drawing on the shared expectations for playful irreverence and mischief in the Goon community. Gerogerigegege's invitation to participate (couched in equal parts mischief and "let's see what happens") demonstrated a working knowledge of Goon culture that made this invitation to play seem eminently sociable. The directions for participation were simple and straightforward, and Gerogerigegege's solicitation (e.g., "So, let's make a shitload?") was actively inclusive of a variety of possible responses. By supplying examples of their[8] own work and creation tips, Gerogerigegege built elements of reciprocity and reflexivity into the foundation of the thread. These qualities emerged from an awareness of the shared expectations for interaction in this digital space and worked in tandem to create a favorable environment for the emergence of compelling forms of digital play (see Ellis 2020). The result was that this post functioned as more than just a simple invitation—it actively sought to create a performative frame by working to constitute the users viewing it into potential co-performers.

The thread proved popular, and soon other users began sharing their own images that seemingly captured ghosts, UFOs, wisps, smoke, shadows, and phantasms on film. Users began writing stories to accompany these images and suggested that the images were real by linking them to personal experience. At the same time, users often discussed the process of creating their images by asking for advice or offering tips on photoshopping. User guandi said of their photoshopped UFO: "It looks strange in the picture thanks to my crappy camera, but it was actually transparent, just reflecting and diffusing the light of the sunset at the edges and in three moving patches on the bottom of the craft," while adding below that the poor picture quality was actually the calculated result of image manipulation.

Like a game with concealed and mutable rules, users learned what made for good posts by observing the content of others. For example, at no point did users agree to start writing contextual blurbs for images (and, indeed, on the first page of the thread, nearly all images lack accompanying text), yet by the end of the second page, nearly all images were accompanied by text. Most images were either black-and-white, blurry, or grainy. Many contained hazy, translucent shapes that, upon examination, revealed themselves as humanoid or monstrous figures. These qualities made the images reminiscent of spirit photographs, cryptozoological images, and other popular traditions of supernatural photography (Wojcik 1996, 2009; Phillips and Milner 2018). In doing so, users drew upon a matrix of lived experience with paranormal images in order to create further paranormal images. Put another way, users engaged in performance by referencing existing frameworks that, in turn, gave rise to further shared expectations. It was in this atmosphere that the Slender Man emerged.

The Creation of the Slender Man

On June 10, 2009, user Victor Surge posted two images to the Create Paranormal Images thread. Both images looked like black-and-white photographs taken a few decades earlier. In the first image, a group of children walked together outside (see figure 1). Due to a shallow depth-of-field, only the face of the lead child was fully in focus. The lead child stared at the camera, looking oddly dire for such a lively scene. To provide context, Victor Surge supplied a few lines of enigmatic text to accompany the image:

> "we didn't want to go, we didn't want to kill them, but its persistent silence and outstretched arms horrified and comforted us at the same time . . ."
>
> 1983, photographer unknown, presumed dead.

In the second image, several young children played outside on a suburban playground (see figure 2). The children in the foreground ran, smiling, near a slide, while the children in the background formed a circle under a large tree. The background children were oddly shadowed for a daytime

Figure 1. The first of two images in the initial performance of the Slender Man legend. Posted by Victor Surge to https://forums.somethingawful.com on June 10, 2009.

photo, appearing almost as silhouettes. This time, Victor Surge's caption more actively drew the viewer's attention toward the anomaly in the image:

> One of two recovered photographs from the Stirling city library blaze. Notable for being taken the day which fourteen children vanished and for what is referred to as "The Slender Man." Deformities cited as film defects by officials. Fire at library occurred one week later. Actual photograph confiscated as evidence.
>
> 1986, photographer: Mary Thomas, missing since June 13th, 1986.

Closer examination of the "film defects" mentioned in the second caption revealed an unmistakably humanoid figure standing in the center of the silhouetted children's circle. The figure had an excess of inhuman appendages, with several wispy tendrils erupting from each limb. Scrolling back to

Figure 2. The second of two images in the initial performance of the Slender Man legend. Posted by Victor Surge to https://forums.somethingawful.com on June 10, 2009.

the first image revealed the same figure in the background—its blurry face had been staring at the viewer the whole time, arms outstretched and beckoning. Although the resolution and black-and-white composition of each photograph obscured any fine details of the creature, it seemed to resemble a tall, slender humanoid with eldritch physiology. This post is the first recorded performance of the Slender Man legend.

Victor Surge's initial performance of the Slender Man legend established only a few details about the creature. The Slender Man was a tall humanlike figure. It was shadowy, blurry, and ominous, with tentacles reminiscent of the otherworldly abominations penned by horror writer H. P. Lovecraft (best known for creating the eldritch entity Cthulhu). Despite—or perhaps because of—this mysteriousness, the Slender Man was an immediate hit, and other users lauded Victor Surge's contribution to the thread:

> BEERDEER: As an amateur paranormal investigator, you'd be surprised how much the Slender Man appeared in pictures in times of disaster during that historical period. (AKA I'd like to see more of those)
>
> ZOMBIESCHOLAR: You are an amazing and terrible bastard, sir. Well played. Now to look over my shoulder every couple seconds for the rest of my day . . .

Part of the reason for this success was that Victor Surge's initial performance created a sense of conspicuous incompleteness, which drew on each audience member to connect the posted information in order to complete the performance. These images thrived on a sense of creeping realization (e.g., "What am I missing here?") that drove users to engage as active participants in completing the legend performance. Leyendecker, one of the first users who responded to Victor Surge, articulated this emergent quality in a different way, "Oh fuck you when i finally saw the guy in the background i lost it this is going to give me nightmares." Consequently, it is immediately apparent that digital legend performances are not only more visual than face-to-face performances, but they also allow users to play with performative linearity in ways that would be impractical for nondigital contexts.

Users were enamored with the Slender Man, and the thread quickly shifted focus to the creature. When asked where the creature had originated (and if it was an original creation), Victor Surge replied:

> The Slender Man as an idea was made-up off the top of my head, although the concept is based on a number of things that scare me. The name I thought up on the fly when I wrote that first bit. The asset I used for a couple of the pictures was the creepy tall guy from Phantasm, which sadly I have not seen, and the others various guys in suits. All of the things that aren't the torso and legs, like the tentacles and Slender Man's face, were painted from scratch however.

As Victor Surge's response demonstrates, even the earliest performances of the Slender Man legend exhibited a sense of hybridity. Like the paranormal images posted before it, the Slender Man drew upon an existing matrix of belief that included mass media representations of paranormal creatures, informally circulated ideas about legends and folk performance, the user's personal experiences and fears, and the influence of previous posts to the discussion thread. In other words, the Slender Man was influenced by a vast network of vernacular and institutional performances that had directly and indirectly preceded it. By mixing a pastiche of mass media–influenced horror tropes and imagery with his own vernacular legend performance, Victor Surge's creation emerged to other users not only as familiar but also as a discrete and mysterious entity accessible for further acts of folk expression.

In the hours that followed, several users asked Victor Surge for more images of the Slender Man. Victor Surge coyly replied, "Maybe I'll do some more research. I've heard there may be a couple more legit 'Slender Man' photographs out there. I'll post them if I find them." True to his word, the next day Victor Surge posted more images of the creature. The first image showed the Slender Man reflected in a mirror, wrapping its tendrils around the unknowing photographer. In this image, the creature's obscured face appears more ghoulish, with empty sockets where its eyes should be. Supplementary text revealed that the photograph had been taken in the early 1990s at the Wilks Estate, where several other paranormal occurrences had been reported before the investigation was abruptly closed without further explanation in June 1993. A few hours later, Victor Surge posted another image of the creature as well as an image of a bloody police report, partially filled out by a survivor. This image was more overt than previous photographs and showed a humanoid torso clad in a black suit using several long spiderlike appendages to stalk outside the window of a potential victim.

But what's remarkable about the case of the Slender Man isn't just that Victor Surge created a mysterious and intriguing character or the skill of his digital performances; instead, it's that less than twenty-four hours later, other users started actively performing their own versions of the Slender Man legend.

The Formation of the Slender Man

On the morning of June 12, 2009, LeechCode5 posted two images of the Slender Man to the Create Paranormal Images thread. LeechCode5 began their post by keying a performative frame that actively built on Victor Surge's performances and their constructed sense of authenticity, writing that "I've been seriously debating sharing these, but after Victor Surge's posts I feel I have to." The first photograph showed a group of teenagers sitting around a campfire at night while a faceless figure peered at them through the darkness beyond the surrounding birch trees. To contextualize this photograph, LeechCode5 recounted a story from their uncle about a police investigation into nine teens who vanished from a campsite six years earlier:

> This first photo was given to me by my uncle, a police officer who was part of the investigation trying to find nine missing teens who had gone camping in the local mountains six years ago. It was developed from a disposable camera found at the campsite. None of the missing teens have ever been found, and all their possessions were still at the campsite. He was pretty drunk and shaken up when he gave me this, and made me promise I'd never show anyone else.

LeechCode5's second photograph featured a sepia-tinged image of a school burning to the ground with the following caption:

> The second photo is of an elementary school fire in 1978. No official cause was ever found. Seven students and a teacher became trapped and died before firefighters could respond. Many of the students and teachers from the time have a history of anxiety disorders and panic attacks, even those who weren't at the school on that day. At least one has since committed suicide, and several others legally changed their names once they reached adulthood and have disappeared.

Careful scrutiny of the image revealed a familiar figure standing amid the thick black smoke billowing out from the collapsed roof of the school.

These two images were some of the earliest Slender Man legend variants, and LeechCode5's performance of the Slender Man legend further developed the shared expectations created by Victor Surge's performances. LeechCode5 carried forward several elements established by Victor Surge's performances. As in the original images, the Slender Man tended to hide in plain sight, partially obscured by the composition of the photograph. The idea that the police had been alerted and were choosing to either cover it up or remain willfully ignorant was preserved, as were the creature's shadowy appendages and association with otherwise unexplained disappearances.

But LeechCode5 also built on these existing performances in novel ways. The first photograph gave the Slender Man a clearer association with wooded areas and nighttime. In the second photograph the Slender Man was implied to be more actively malicious than in prior representations. No longer do individuals experience spontaneous psychosis or just mysteriously disappear; in LeechCode5's telling, the Slender Man was also associated with arson and long-term mental health issues. LeechCode5's performance also diverged in its depiction of the creature, skewing closer to Victor Surge's original images, while ignoring several aspects of Victor Surge's subsequent posts, like the clarity of the window image and the ghoulish face in the mirror photograph. The implication of these acts of fixity and novelty suggest that LeechCode5 had seen all of Victor Surge's previous posts and had chosen to include only the elements from these prior performances that they found particularly effective.

Following LeechCode5's example, other users began performing their own Slender Man legends. The process was slow at first, but as more people began performing their own Slender Man legend variants, participation rose exponentially. Over the next three days, a wide variety of performances emerged, which began to form the character more concretely. User Trench-Maul contributed an image linking the Slender Man to the 1959 Dyatlov Pass incident.[9] Victor Surge supplied another image that placed the Slender Man in the background of a child's birthday party, with accompanying childlike drawings. VR Native American photoshopped the creature into the background of a sermon delivered by Jim Jones. The character was adapted to appear in sixteenth-century German woodcarvings, old newspaper clippings, and märchen-like fairy stories. And, like LeechCode5's initial variants, each performance added and subtracted a bit from how the group imagined the Slender Man.

By performing and discussing these legends, users filled in the fine details of the character through a process of negotiation. What's more, users were generally aware that the Slender Man legend had become a collaborative process:

> DOOM MATHEMATIC: I'm a big fan of the big organic collaborative creative horror thing that's going on in this thread. Reminds me of the SCP series.[10]
>
> TOMBS GRAVE: Think I might hammer out a short story about Slender Man tonight, as words are my area of relative expertise. Should I base it on one of the pictures, or no?
>
> NURSE FANNY: [Replying] Oh! Do your own and try to get somebody to do a picture based off of the story.

As these posts suggest, imagining the creature collaboratively and through a variety of media was highly encouraged. Users would often build on the performances of others or create performative fragments for others to complete. Gerogerigegege, for example, posted an image of a farmhouse that was photoshopped to include the Slender Man. In this post, Gerogerigegege added: "Story tellers, you're more than welcome to write a backstory for this one." A few hours later, BooDoug187 used the photograph as the basis for posting an interview transcript between Ted Henderson, a farmer committed to a mental hospital, and his doctor. Later that day, Leyendecker posted an audio file wherein he and a friend performed a dramatization of BooDoug187's transcript, adding to the previous post that "at the permission of Faye Dauton, the doctor's daughter, the recording of the interview with Mr. Henderson was released." As might be expected, the increase in performances and collaborations also led to a rise in Slender Man legend variants. The rise in variants, consequently, created some strain between individuals who imagined the creature in different ways. It then became necessary for users to negotiate how to deal with these divergent representations.

Faced with a wide variety of performances of the Slender Man legend, users discussed what they liked and disliked about the myriad of circulating variants. Users debated how much backstory the character should have (if any), if the character was a murderer or drove people to madness, what caused the Slender Man to appear, how overt its inhuman characteristics should be, if the creature was more humanlike or spiderlike, and if the character should be the focus of images or just a part of the background. And while some users made relatively simple points, remarking on a performance or two they thought was "best," other users gave more pointed criticism:

> PUMPKIN SPOON: The only flaw is the conflicting images we get occasionally, I don't know that the more spider-like images work for him, same for when he's out in the open. I was thinking of him seeming fairly human at a glance, with the tentacles and facelessness not apparent until you really look. Although the inhuman height and sort of "stretched" look are pretty consistent. Love it!
>
> NURSE FANNY: I think a more modern thing would be best. You know like kids start disappearing in the 50's. More contemporary with less of a back story or explanation. I dunno it seems creepier if he just shows up out of no where.
>
> MOOSEYFATE: The Slender Man should appear in seemingly innocent pictures (bright colors, happy people, etc.) somewhere in the background for realism.

These responses provide an important glimpse into the standards by which users judged the authenticity of performances of the Slender Man. In the moment, shared expectations developed around such basic questions as "Does it appeal to realism?" and "Is it plausible?" The real negotiation here is not whether the legend is literally true; instead, it is over how much it *seems* true—its "plausibility as a representative of the legend genre" (Tolbert 2013, 16). These conversations express an awareness of legend as a performative genre as well as a sense of informal continuity to folk practice more broadly. For instance, when a user like TrenchMaul writes that "I'm not really digging these folklore backstories," they are not dismissing the folkloric qualities of the Slender Man; instead, they are expressing their preference for performances that adhere to the generic conventions of a certain folk genre (contemporary legend) over those belonging to similar genres (e.g., märchen or myth).

These discussions actively worked to keep performances of the Slender Man in the realm of legend dialectic. Despite the knowledge that the creature was fake, users (such as those cited above) tended to prefer performances that were believable, placing the creature in the "real" modern world. This is consistent with the basic social function of legends: they place events in the group's concept of the real world while also challenging the boundaries of that world (Ellis 2001a, 11). Correspondingly, Slender Man legends that seemed more "plausible" tended to receive more praise, while expectations for joking and hoaxing diminished rapidly. In aggregate, these performative and discursive choices functioned to preserve this dialectical tension between the real and the supernatural. This unresolved tension, in turn, offered users space for further acts of conjecture, discussion, and performance.

The more users who performed these legends, the more fleshed-out their shared expectations for the Slender Man became. Although several different aspects of the character emerged from these performances, certain sets and subsets started to become more performed than others. Performances that located themselves in more immediate circumstances remained fairly common, whereas performances that placed the Slender Man in pseudo-märchen, woodcarvings, and hieroglyphs became rarer. Choosing motifs when performing Slender Man legends seemed to privilege those elements with closeness to the group's lived experiences. Performances became rooted in "reality," sharing the results of research, contributing an obscure local news story, or—in true contemporary legend fashion—suggesting personal involvement, whether through firsthand experience or relayed by a friend-of-a-friend:

KITH_GROUPIE: All this talk about a slender man from the forest rang a bell with something that happened to me when I was six or so.

VIET TIMH: I find this tall man stuff Fascinating and wanted to learn more. So I chcked around and found some really cool stuff. This was the scariest cause it occurred so close to where I live[.]

CALCIFER: After getting to the slender man stuff in this thread I went nuts for about an hour rummaging through the boxes in my attic looking for my brother's old stuff. Finally I found his old mountaineering journals, and sure enough my memory wasn't just playing tricks on me.

This shared expectation for plausibility resulted in successive performances playing down some of the more fantastical aspects of the creature. These expectations did not dictate future performances, but they certainly influenced which Slender Man motifs were chosen and how they were performed. Performances began to portray the creature as more humanlike, though still with uncanny limb proportions and a featureless face. Its black tendrils remained but were often hidden. Its shadowed body now consistently resembled a black suit. Performances tended to simply acknowledge its presence, forgoing explanations or backstories. It often lurked in the background, sowing paranoia in those who discovered it and slowly eroding their sanity as they pursued it. If the Slender Man killed, it was often implied, not explicit.

Through an ongoing process of performance, collaboration, and negotiation, users in the Create Paranormal Images thread had created a monster. The Slender Man emerged from a reciprocal feedback loop of digital performance and discussion. Jeffrey Tolbert has called this process "reverse ostension"—the formation of a new overarching narrative through the collaborative correlation and connection of smaller fragmentary narratives (2013). Tolbert correctly notes that this process is fundamentally participatory, but I would go a step further and argue that this process is also quintessentially digital.

The Success of the Slender Man

The internet enables being participatory in new ways, and the affordances of the Something Awful forums gave users a variety of performative options that helped enable the emergent and collaborative performances that formed the Slender Man legend. These digital legend performances were shaped not only by social processes but also by the affordances of the communicative medium. As John Dorst notes in his essay on joke cycles, graffiti, and early digital media, "These social circumstances and technologies are not extraneous to the lore, merely providing new conduits for its circulation. They inform and inhabit the lore from within" (1990, 181). In her book *Memes in Digital Culture*, Limor Shifman expresses a similar view about the role of technology in extending offline folk practices, and like Dorst, she uses the example of street graffiti to illustrate her argument (2014, 24–30).[11]

Whether online or off, practices that persist through diffusion and iteration tend to (1) be easy to reproduce, (2) be available to potential future performers, and (3) lack a definitive or singular meaning (26). As with all affordances, the presence of these qualities doesn't guarantee repetition and variation, but their absence can certainly make sustained iteration more difficult. The Slender Man's initial success on Something Awful—when viewed in light of these three sustaining qualities—suggests just how fundamental digital media were to shaping and propagating these legend performances.

The first sustaining quality is that a performance should be easy to reproduce, but conversely, it must also remain distinctive enough to be recognizable throughout this process of reproduction. A performance that is highly distinct but difficult to reproduce makes variation difficult by requiring significant skill or effort. A performance that is highly reproducible but not distinctive risks getting lost as it circulates, making it difficult for other individuals to recognize it as part of a performative genre or to connect it to other performative fragments as part of an overall picture. Take, for example, a simple shape like an X that has been spray-painted on a wall in a public space. This tag is very easy to reproduce, but—at the same time—it is difficult for the viewer to discern what significance such a mark has (if any). Is it someone's personal tag? A reference to a graffiti tradition? Does it designate the imminent demolition of the wall? Has it simply been reproduced incidentally? So, performances that are widely reproducible have generic conventions that are simple, straightforward, or easy to understand while also allowing ample room for additional depth, variation, personalization.

On a technical level, Victor Surge's initial posts contain several key elements that foster reproducibility while retaining distinctiveness. This is not only because the affordances of digital media make it easy to copy and paste or share Victor Surge's images (though this capacity does certainly increase reproducibility) but also because of how the images themselves are constructed. Obscuring the Slender Man behind objects and in shadows meant that the character lacked the definitive details that might be present in clearer or more close-up photographs, and its viewable attributes changed from image to image. So, while Victor Surge's images and captions contained some general guidelines (tall, humanoid, shadowy, wispy appendages), they also implied that the creature's essential nature was both unknowable and protean. These choices made it easier for other users to reproduce their own Slender Man performances using image-manipulation software like Photoshop. By adding smudges, tendrils, or hints of an elongated human shape to an existing image, users were encouraged to create recognizable Slender Man performances by hinting at the creature rather than by having to reproduce a singular entity in its entirety. By establishing the character's true nature as a mystery, subsequent performances could be recognized, considered, and evaluated as part of the burgeoning legend cycle as long as they connected with some permutation of the shape or name Victor Surge gave the creature.[12]

Much like the evolving shared expectations that developed around Slender Man performances, the affordances at play in this digital space also actively shaped how users imagined the creature. For instance, elements that were easy to reproduce with image-manipulation software (like the Slender Man's facelessness or uncanny long limbs) tended to recur while elements that required more user skill to achieve convincingly (such as the grotesque face present in some of Victor Surge's early performances) tended to not be reproduced as frequently in subsequent performances. Because elements that were easier to reproduce occurred more often across performances, they began to coalesce into the generic expectations for the legend cycle. The resulting expectations reinforced certain distinctive traits for the legend cycle that persisted across performances and favored accessible replication. In other words, the technology that enabled these multimedia performances was an active participant in the emergent feedback loop of performance and negotiation that formed the shared expectations for this legend cycle.

The second sustaining quality is that a performance should be available to potential future performers, but what constitutes availability is contingent on the medium. Oral performances require the audience to be present at a certain time and place, such as sitting around a campfire listening to a storyteller. The affordances of other media alter these temporal and spatial constraints in various ways. Graffiti, for example, is available when it appears in public places where viewers can see it as they walk past. The viewer and the artist don't need to be present at the same time, but once created, graffiti is fixed to a specific location and only available to those in close physical proximity. Graffiti may be more durable over time compared to an oral performance, but these individuated sites (which are frequently off the beaten path) can make it difficult for viewers to understand the connections between them. An individual may stumble across a popular form of graffiti on only a handful of occasions during their lifetime, rendering the breadth and variation present in this artistic expression practically invisible (Shifman 2014, 28–29; see also chapter 4). Digital media make these types of connections more readily visible for users by preserving not only performances but also variation and context.

A discussion thread, like those that comprise the Something Awful forums, centralizes and preserves digital performances. Users do not have to be present when the performance takes place because the website creates an unintentional archive not only of performances but also of the discourse and feedback surrounding them. Whenever a user views the thread, they can easily see the chronological progress of negotiated performances over time. Conversely, the structure of a discussion board also enables nonlinear viewing, allowing users to navigate between nonconsecutive pages, skip performances they find uninteresting, or go backward to revisit prior performances. This unintentional and flexible archive serves as a repository for the shared expectations that have formed around the digital legend over time and enables an uninitiated user to quickly learn the generic expectations for performance without requiring active input or socialization from other users. Because of the fluid nature of digital communication, this means that these digital performances remain perpetually available to both new and nonimmediate audiences (see also chapter 2).

The third sustaining quality is that each performer should feel as if they can make the performance their own. This means that performances that persist tend to be open to further acts of interpretation and personal expression, whereas performances defined by a prescribed meaning or an insistent authorial intent significantly foreclose this possibility. Shifman uses the example of "Kilroy was here" graffiti (popular in the United States during and after World War II) to suggest the importance of active interpretation in sustaining collaborative engagement. She writes:

> That the slogan's "real" meaning was mysterious and open to interpretation was also an advantage, as it allowed each person to endow it with his or her

> own preferred meaning. Moreover, this lack of obvious meaning made the meme hard to contradict and, at the same time, enhanced peoples' engagement with it as they tried to solve the mystery. (2014, 26)

Although Victor Surge created the first Slender Man performance (which remained influential), his role as creator wasn't privileged over the contributions of other users; instead, digital media enabled the generic expectations for performance to emerge organically from the aggregate volition of the digital crowd.

The sense of communal ownership that enabled these acts of personalization is perhaps the most salient element of the emergence of the Slender Man legend cycle because it is the one that users actively fought to preserve. Over time, the Slender Man developed generic expectations for performance based on a mixture of affordances, performances, and feedback that emerged from interactivity among the users who frequented the Create Paranormal Images thread. Nowhere in the thread were these expectations written down. Each user was responsible for discerning these expectations through observation and interaction. When users tried to systematize these expectations by creating unsolicited lists, charts, or facts detailing the essential nature of the creature, they were met with derision.

When 21stCentury posted an image outlining what they believed to be the key points of the Slender Man legend cycle in order to "get facts straight as much as possible," other users were quick to caution against such attempts. BooDoug187 wrote: "[We know] what he does, don't try to reason the whys and hows. Because there will never be an answer that will make you understand or happy . . . or make you sleep again." User creepy old man shared a similar sentiment (while also upholding a performative frame), expressing that the mystery was part of the character: "All we know is that anyone who knows how the Slender Man works or why, has never been allowed to share his secrets."

In this and several other instances, users were resistant toward systematizing the Slender Man legend cycle because these individual assertions of authority disregarded what made the Slender Man so successful. As user moto42 noted, the lack of a defined set of characteristics was precisely what made the character so accessible:

> I'm loving the Slenderman. That's just an awesome name to start with. The minimal backstory to the image was just perfect. Victor, you have a gift for horror it seems.
>
> You posted one image and a tiny backstory. Planting a small seed of an idea into the internet, without even knowing (or planning) for others to run with it, and make it grow.
>
> Then, people saw your idea, and started expanding on it. The Slenderman went from an isolated incident to a full mythos, with woodcuttings, incident reports, coverups and multiple killings to its name in just a few pages of collaborative effort.
>
> . . .
>
> What I'm trying to say with both of these, is that I am continualy [*sic*] amazed with how a single idea on the internet can sprout and grow into something more incredible than you ever expected, simply through a small amount of creative effort on the part of many individuals.[13] I won't be getting to sleep anytime soon thanks to you all.

The view expressed by moto42 echoes many of the points made above and suggests that the ability of users to tap into the ideas of others while also supplying their own helped inspire the collaborative culture that arose surrounding the Slender Man. The individual imposition of a standardized schema would undercut this collaborative and discursive potential, as would privileging the choices of the original media creator as canonical (as is often the case in commercial media; see chapter 3). By resisting a rigid and formally defined set of characteristics for the creature, these users defended their ability to create ongoing and varied legend performances. The repeated rejection of a single dominant interpretation reinforced a sense that the creature belonged to the community and served to perpetuate further collaborative performances by keeping the Slender Man as an ongoing object of legend dialectic (Ellis 2001a; Dégh 2001).

In effect, the success of the Slender Man was that users perceived it as a shared public resource for ongoing acts of expression that were simultaneously individual and communal. This perception fundamentally derived from the intersection of shared expectations for oral legend performance and the affordances of digital media. The result of this convergence between traditional forms of folklore and new forms of media is a mixed modality where elements of oral, visual, and written performance are extended by the new forms of connection and expression enabled by networked digital communication. What the Slender Man represents, then, is a crowdsourced monster that is quintessentially digital in every aspect of its creation, formation, and propagation.

The Emergence of a Legend Cycle in the Digital Age

By the end of those first few weeks on Something Awful, the Slender Man had begun to take a recognizable shape. The resulting legend cycle was formed not through any individual post, performance, or schematized outline, but through the informal aggregation of user volition that emerged via a social process of ongoing performance and negotiation in this digital space. Although the thread would continue for twenty more pages and into 2010,[14] many of the shared expectations for the legend cycle emerged through this process of rapid digital iteration during the latter half of June 2009. Through this process certain details became routine over time, and the resulting creature resembled a tall, thin, humanoid wearing a black suit. It had uncannily long limbs and its face was featureless and white. Its true nature and motivation remained a mystery—interpretable for a variety of performative purposes—but performances consistently demonstrated that the more one learned about the Slender Man, the more of a danger it became. These expectations—including both the settled and actively unsettled elements of the legend—would remain influential for years to come, even when the character transitioned to other digital communities and purposes.

By understanding the formation of the Slender Man as a series of performances that were both digital and emergent, we can begin to understand how legend cycles take shape in the digital age. Much like face-to-face communication, each performance emerges from an ongoing interaction between performer and audience. This process of negotiation draws on existing expectations of performance and genre while also establishing new ones. These negotiated expectations emerge not only from perceptions of self and group identity but also from the nature of networked communication.

Digital media extend many elements of face-to-face performance by creating new opportunities for ongoing acts of serial collaboration and mediated expression. Elements like increased connectivity and fluidity are fairly foundational characteristics of networked digital communication, while other elements—like the potential modes for interaction or providing feedback—tend to be more site-specific. However, despite differences between the available affordances on any given website, folk performances on digital media still emerge through a mediated process of interpersonal interaction. Therefore, understanding contemporary legends on the internet relies on understanding not only the legends themselves but also the underlying social and technological process of negotiation that circulates them, defines them, and makes them meaningful.

But digital media technologies don't just affect emergence—they also affect how legends circulate, and the Slender Man couldn't be contained for long. Following those first few weeks on Something Awful, Slender Man performances began to materialize across the internet in a variety of communicative modes, and references to the character began appearing in blogs, videos, social media posts, and wikis. Having developed an understanding of how digital legends emerge, in the next chapter I analyze what happens when digital legends start to emerge in more varied spaces—with more varied audiences and affordances—as they begin to circulate across digital networks.

CHAPTER TWO

Circulation

In 2006 Alex Kralie abruptly halted production on his student film, *Marble Hornets*. The film was about a young man returning to his rural hometown and had been primarily shot in the woods near Alex's home. Over the course of the three-month shoot, the film crew noticed that Alex was becoming increasingly paranoid and irritable. Near the end of principal photography Alex suddenly shut down the project. His rationale was vague; he simply claimed that conditions on the set had become "unworkable." Alex stashed the tapes in his attic, refused to talk to anyone about the project, and became reclusive, avoiding contact with family and friends.

When a friend came to check on him a few weeks later, Alex was noticeably thinner with a sickly pallor. Before leaving, the friend—a fellow film student named Jay—asked Alex about what he intended to do with all the tapes of footage that remained from his former film project. "With almost no hesitation," Jay would later recall, "[Alex] simply said, 'burn them.'"[1] Curious about the project, Jay asked if he could borrow the tapes. Alex agreed and told Jay he could have them on two conditions: Alex never wanted to see the tapes again or talk about their contents.

Jay took the unfinished *Marble Hornets* footage home. Shaken by the unsettling encounter with Alex as well as his friend's dire warnings, Jay filed the tapes away, intending to watch them later. Not long after, Alex transferred colleges, and the pair lost touch. As time passed, Jay forgot about the tapes gathering dust in the back of his closet, and there the tapes for *Marble Hornets* sat, forgotten, until June 2009.

A little over a week after Victor Surge shared the first Slender Man images on Something Awful, Jay (posting as ce gars)[2] posted a response in the Create Paranormal Images thread. All the talk about the Slender Man had jogged his memory about the tapes. He now intended to watch them, hoping to discover what had driven Alex to paranoia and seclusion. He promised to post updates if he found anything abnormal or unusual in the footage. While the lack of dates, timestamps, and other metadata made it difficult to know where to begin, by June 20 Jay had already watched through one-and-a-half tapes and found an aberration.

Jay posted the short, fifteen-second excerpt from Alex's footage to YouTube and linked the video to users in the Something Awful thread.[3] Unlike other footage, this video wasn't filmed on the *Marble Hornets* set; instead, it was captured at night from inside Alex's house. In the clip, Alex rushes to the window, and the camera shakes from his hurried frenzy. He pushes the camera past the curtain and pans right across the porch. A familiar horror—faceless, dressed in a dark suit—stands in the darkness, and the camera strains to keep the creature in frame before abruptly shutting off. In less than two weeks since emerging on the Something Awful forums, the Slender Man had spread to YouTube.

Marble Hornets, the found-footage YouTube series named for the fictional student film at its center, was one of the most formative conduits for the Slender Man legend cycle as it began to circulate beyond Something Awful and across the web (Tolbert 2013; Chess and Newsom 2015). A decade later, the channel has received over one hundred million views on YouTube, with nearly one hundred entries spanning five years. It spawned related YouTube channels like *totheark* and set the tone for several subsequent web series centered on the Slender Man, including *EverymanHYBRID* and *Tribe Twelve*. The series proved so popular that a tie-in movie, *Always Watching: A Marble Hornets Story*, received a limited theatrical release in 2015. *Marble Hornets*' growing popularity throughout 2009 and into the early 2010s exemplifies not only the growth of the Slender Man legend cycle but also how digital media influence the circulation of legends in new ways.

As the Create Paranormal Images thread gained popularity on Something Awful, more and more users read through the thread and discovered the Slender Man. Much like oral legend transmission, a portion of these users began to perform, share, or discuss the Slender Man legend in other digital spaces. When these performances took hold, the process repeated, leading to a cascade of new performers, audiences, and variants that ultimately became self-sustaining. Although folklorists have been studying this process of wide, diffuse, and informal circulation for well over a century (Georges and Jones 1995, 127–55; see also Cochrane 1987), the affordances of digital communication enable digitally mediated folklore to "move faster and spread farther, reaching an exponentially larger audience in an exponentially shorter time than face-to-face transmission" (McNeill 2013, 181–82). These changes in the volume and velocity of variants raise several questions about the circulation of legends via digital media. For instance, if a rise in participation leads to a proliferation of variants, then what mechanisms allow users to make sense of a legend that has "gone viral?" How do localized performances interact with the shared expectations for legend performance more broadly? Why do certain performative nodes—like *Marble Hornets*—become more popular than others, and how does this increased visibility feed back into the legend cycle?

In this chapter, I argue that the circulation of digital folklore is governed by a synthesis of social and algorithmic filtering. As folk practices begin to circulate and proliferate online, users—especially those who lack prior knowledge of a practice—rely on several mechanisms to sort through and give order to an ever-growing universe of content. Some of these mechanisms are social and resemble traditional forms of folk transmission that take advantage of our digital connections (e.g., sharing a legend on social media). Other mechanisms, like algorithmic filtering, are more computational and form the backbone of content curation on many digital platforms (e.g., the top results of a Google search; YouTube's recommended videos). These algorithmic filters sort content for the platform's users, which, subsequently, influences what does (and does not) get seen. The aggregated result of this ongoing filtering process causes certain performative nodes to become more seen—and, subsequently, more influential—than others.

To make this argument, I begin by showing how digital circulation encourages further acts of variation despite a high level of available copy fidelity. These variations, I suggest, can quickly become too numerous for any individual to sort through and require filtering mechanisms to organize them. Whereas oral transmission is shaped by aggregated acts of social filtering, digital media not only enable social filtering to occur in new ways but also provide structure via algorithmic filtering. Through this process a small subset of legend performances—like *Marble Hornets*—can gain concentrated popularity and begin fulfilling the framing function of a networked gatekeeper. To demonstrate this process, the second half of this chapter traces *Marble Hornets*' influence as it crosses a variety of digital spaces. First, I explain the scope and significance of the series, offering an analysis of how it built on the emerging legend cycle from Something Awful. Next, I look at how other users on Something Awful interacted with *Marble Hornets* as well as with a growing recognition that the Slender Man was beginning to spread more widely. Finally, I turn to an early *Marble Hornets* discussion thread on the Unfiction forums to demonstrate how unfamiliar users tried to make sense of both *Marble Hornets* and the Slender Man. I conclude by suggesting that although these digital filtering mechanisms don't dictate future performances (which remain emergent and expressive), they can have a significant effect on the overarching shared expectations for performance that form the basis for these emerging, localized variations.

Transmission, Distribution, and Circulation

Folklore spreads through interpersonal interaction. In offline contexts, this interpersonal interaction tends to be oral in nature, which imposes certain characteristics on the transmission of face-to-face folklore. The temporal and spatial limitations of the spoken word constrain the possible scale of this interpersonal interaction, making face-to-face folklore more suited for transmission either in small groups or between individuals (Ben-Amos 1971; McNeill 2013, 176). Because the spoken word lacks the permanence of writing or centrality of a singular text, face-to-face folklore is propagated through an informal chain of these one-to-one, one-to-few, or few-to-few communications. This informal transmission process isn't uniform—folklore doesn't simply spread across an area like water; instead, folklore travels through subsets of connected individuals inside larger social networks (Dégh and Vázsonyi 1975; Fine 1979; Von Sydow 1977). The inherently diffuse nature of these informal communicative chains leads to acts of individual variation. Those who participate in folk traditions reproduce them in emergent ways based on factors like personal taste, local norms, or even just imperfect attempts at perfect replication (see chapter 1). While it may seem counterintuitive, such acts of dynamism are essential to sustaining these practices because without this multitude of ongoing small-scale interactions, oral folk practices would not be able to persist over space or across time (Toelken 1996, 37).

The decentralized transmission of oral folklore stands in stark contrast to the more centralized distribution model used by the majority of mass media (Jenkins, Ford, and Green 2013, 1). Whereas folklore is transmitted from person-to-person in highly variable ways, mass media distributes singular texts to wide audiences (McNeill 2013, 176). The widespread adoption of this one-to-many or "broadcast" model is necessitated by limitations inherent in various forms of mass media. Mass media technologies enable a high level of copy fidelity, which makes it easy to distribute a message to a wide audience but also makes it difficult to change or amend that message after it has been widely distributed. As a result, mass media texts tend to be static and unchanging. Additionally, printing five thousand copies of a book or maintaining a broadcast tower are expensive propositions, and the costs associated with distributing a message via mass media mean that most printed or broadcast media are owned by a relatively small number of institutions, which tend to be subject to various levels of either government control or market demand (Benkler 2006). The nature of these costs and singular, definitive texts mean that elements like broadcast time or page space can quickly become limiting factors in mass media. Professionals working for these mass media institutions in various capacities (e.g., editors, producers) are often tasked with performing gatekeeping functions—making choices about what information gets included, the extent of that inclusion, and what gets left out.

While digital communication more closely resembles the decentralized conduits of oral folk transmission rather than the one-to-many distribution model of mass media, the process of digital circulation doesn't fit neatly into either category (Howard 2008a, 192; see also Blank 2013, 2018; Bronner 2009; McNeill 2013). The key difference from orally transmitted forms of folklore stems from how digital media enable folk behaviors to persist over time. The record of informal communication created as a by-product of interaction on many digital platforms functions as a sort of incidental archive for folk behavior. This archival function promotes visibility by sustaining a variety of entry points where unfamiliar users can observe a performance despite temporal distance. This visibility, in turn, inspires further acts of participation and variation, which are similarly preserved on the network, creating even more entry points and visibility—thereby perpetuating the cycle. Therefore, my use of "circulation" is meant to evoke how digital media extends the transmission of folklore by enabling a process of sharing and performance that is constantly and visibly circling back on itself.

Digital Circulation and the Durable Trace

Digital media flows are more diverse than one-to-one, one-to-some, or one-to-many models and often more complex. Unlike oral forms of folklore, digital platforms tend to preserve communications between their users, which leaves a durable trace of their communicative interactions (Buccitelli 2016). In doing so, digital platforms "enable the temporal extension and durability of what in offline spaces might otherwise be much more temporally condensed and ephemeral discursive events" (Buccitelli 2016, 87; see also boyd 2010; Buccitelli 2012).

These temporal changes call for a reorientation in how we think about what is moving (or being moved) when digital folklore circulates. Like mass media, it could be that circulation occurs as legend texts are being moved online. Through actions like copying or sharing, digital users can perfectly replicate existing performances in new digital spaces, which then become the basis for new communication events. Like oral folklore, circulation could occur as the result of people moving (albeit to new digital platforms instead of geographically). Such acts of personal movement across digital spaces are both faster and more fluid than predigital forms of transmission (see chapter 1). A user might observe a legend performance in one digital space (or across multiple spaces) and then carry that knowledge to a different digital space where they attempt to reproduce their own localized version (e.g., Von Sydow 1977). Alternatively, users might move *to* performances. Since digital media extend performances in time, a performance can stay in one place while new (or unintended) audiences move easily to it. If the performance is ongoing or iterative, these users can potentially become part of the interpersonal process that shapes its emergence. The confounding aspect of this plurality of circulation is that these elements are very rarely discrete in digital communication, and a single performance may experience circulation in all the aforementioned senses of the term.

Much like the performances themselves, these interactive choices also leave their own durable traces, which feed back into the legend cycle. As discussed in chapter 1, when this process occurs in a specific web space, like a thread on the Something Awful forums, this record of volition is obvious, bounded, and sequential. But as a digital legend begins to circulate outward from its point of origin the links between these acts become more abstruse. The size and scope of the internet facilitates a wide variety of possible entry points and interpretations, which only multiply as a legend cycle expands across digital spaces. These new performances remain emergent, but the influence of specific prior performances is often less clear. In many ways, this part of the circulation process resembles the widespread transmission of oral folklore. The difference is that when folklore circulates digitally each new act of performance or circulation is also preserved on the network. The result is that as legends circulate across digitally networked spaces, they inadvertently participate in the creation of ever-growing archives that recursively provide structure for the shared expectations of the legend cycle (Kaplan 2013).

Unlike older forms of electronically mediated folklore, digital artifacts don't inherently show signs of circulation (boyd 2010).[4] As Michael J. Preston suggests in his work on folklore transmitted via photocopier (1974) and fax machine (1994), the act of replication via these devices creates a patina—in this instance, resembling dots or visual noise on paper (see also Dundes and Pagter 1975). Each act of copying forwards the existing patina while also adding new visual noise—the more something is replicated, the more obvious the patina. Therefore, the patina is a sign of circulation among the folk—a visual signifier that expresses a sense of continuity in these social processes (Preston 1994, 160). But this doesn't happen with digital artifacts. Digital media enable a high level of copy fidelity, which means that it can be hard for users to tell whether a digital legend performance is an original, a variation, or a copy. Instead, the digital patina emerges from the record of volition created as digital legend performances circulate (e.g., through performances, shares, views, etc.). The durable trace *is* the patina—a very visible trace that expresses vernacular continuity and connects otherwise disconnected fragments as part of a larger social process.

As the digital folk begin to circulate legends beyond a specific web community, the durable trace enabled by many digital platforms incidentally renders these recorded behaviors as *visibly traditional.* "Traditional," in this sense, does not mean old; instead, it refers to a sense of continuity in the sharing of social practices (Blank 2013; Howard 2013; McNeill 2013, 176–77; Peck and Good 2020; Phillips and Milner 2017, 23–25; Preston 1994). This is tradition not in the vertical sense (that which is handed down through generations) but in the horizontal sense (that which is passed, informally, between people) (Blank 2013, 12–13; see also Kaplan 2013, 124–25). Similarly, calling these traditions "visible" is meant to acknowledge "the ways in which digital technologies are increasingly commonly aggregating, multiplying, and layering both practices and performances" (Buccitelli 2016, 91). This digital aggregation of many small-scale interactions results in a widely accessible archive of folk behavior where "it only takes a couple of mouse clicks to see hundreds of versions" (Shifman 2014, 30), allowing previously uninitiated users to quickly learn the informal rules for participation through observation of the myriad variations at play (Kaplan 2013).[5]

The increased visibility and sense of traditionality enabled by the durable trace invite further acts of participation. Choosing to participate in a digital tradition simultaneously draws on and enacts continuity, creating "a chain of shared experience that is meaningful simply because it forms a chain" (McNeill 2013, 184). The visible record of these actions conveys that a behavior is shared, accessible, and adaptable, which encourages further participation as a way for users to demonstrate (or cultivate) social bonds and in-group knowledge (Shifman 2014, 28). The visibly traditional nature conveyed by these incidental archives encourages individual users to continue the circulation process (by liking, sharing, performing, etc.) as a way of expressing both their uniqueness and their connectivity (29–30).

And here the feedback loop—the circulatory nature of this digital process—comes into focus. A legend emerges in a local context and incidentally persists due to the nature of digital media. Some users take the legend with them to new spaces, sharing it or performing their own versions. This, again, leaves a durable trace. Users in these new spaces see these circulatory actions and may become aware of the legend. A portion of *these* users will then repeat the process by sharing, reacting, performing, or seeking out more information. These actions, again, extend the durable trace, increase visibility, and interpolate more potential circulators into the process. This process continues until the legend hits a point of saturation, new performances begin to dwindle, and it enters a period of stasis. But, while a legend is still actively circulating, its durable trace is continually expanding. This persistent record exerts influence on further performative and circulatory choices, but not all influence is equal (Halavais 2009, 57–65).

The Role of Social and Algorithmic Filtering in Digital Circulation

While it isn't necessarily true that digital communication transmits more legends than oral communication, it certainly records more of them. As more and more legend performances emerge across digital spaces, mechanisms become necessary to sort them, order them, and render them comprehensible. Such mechanisms are called "filters," and the internet relies on two interrelated types of filtering: social and algorithmic. Because these filters structure how each user sees the internet, they fundamentally shape the circulation of digital legends.

Filtering mechanisms are a necessary response to an excess of information, and such mechanisms are not unique to digital media. All folklore involves choice, but more than that, "[choice] is the very essence that folklore cannot exist without" (Dégh 2001, 412; see also Dégh and Vázsonyi 1975). Individual choices, ranging from whether or not to share something to how to share it, are fundamental to the transmission and dynamism of oral folklore (Dégh 2001, 420–21). These acts of social filtering—choosing what information to include, omit, highlight, adapt, and so on—are so ubiquitous in everyday communication that people constantly perform this function without even realizing it (Benkler 2006, 169). So, while the internet has greatly expanded the amount of information both recorded and available, social filtering has always been a significant element of the folklore transmission process. What is new here is not that digital media uses filtering mechanisms; instead, it's how the affordances of digital platforms *change* social filtering while also introducing new technological filters that mediate those choices.

The affordances of digital media make social filtering actions more visible, identifiable, and potentially collaborative. Various digital platforms facilitate many different types of social filtering actions, which include liking, sharing, linking, commenting, (hash)tagging, rating, replying, following, moderating, or subscribing. This list is far from exhaustive; instead, it is meant to suggest the many varied ways in which digital platforms encourage users to provide feedback on the perceived quality, relevance, or credibility of content (see also chapter 1). These digital acts of social filtering are "more explicit, formalised and easily accessible" than those in oral communication (Willson 2014, 221). Such actions leave their own durable trace, becoming visible metrics of engagement available to other users inside one's own social network.[6] When considered in aggregate, however, these social filtering choices (liking, sharing, tagging, etc.) also have significant implications that flow well beyond our immediate digital connections.

These acts of social filtering lead to various forms of metadata (e.g., "like" ratios, view counts, hashtags) that help legends jump between indirectly connected nodes in the network, creating legend conduits where they wouldn't otherwise exist. For example, while individual uses of a hashtag may hail attention (Meraz and Papacharissi 2013), align a statement with a broader collective narrative (Thomas 2018), or establish a certain communicative frame (McNeill 2020), when considered in aggregate, these choices participate in the creation of user-generated taxonomies, commonly called "folksonomies" (Bronner 2009; Cocq 2015; Howard 2008a). From this perspective it becomes clear that hashtags not only function as a system of classification but also "contribute to knowledge production and social networking processes that stimulate knowledge-sharing" (Cocq 2015, 275). These forms of user-created metadata that emerge as a by-product of social filtering cluster together content that would otherwise be isolated, drawing discourses together across digital platforms and technologies (Davisson and Leone 2018, 93; Rambukkana 2015, 30). They enable forms of affiliation that are ambient, "in the sense that the users may not have interacted directly and likely do not know each other, and may not interact again" (Zappavigna 2011, 801). So, while oral legend conduits "entail transmission of folklore between interested parties who have the opportunity to interact" (Fine 1979, 87), digital media also allow interested individuals ample opportunities to find interactions beyond their immediate networked connections (Cocq 2015, 282).

The systemization of social filtering actions on these digital platforms isn't an accident; it's a business model. User interactions online are fundamentally hybrid, with vernacular expression taking place on digital platforms created and maintained by institutions (Howard 2008a). Many of the institutions running these platforms have a financial interest in sustaining user engagement. This is because the data produced by users engaging on a platform can be valuable as both a commodity (to be sold to data brokers, marketers, etc.) and as a way to selectively target users with relevant content (ranging from advertisements to search results) (Gillespie 2018, 19; Tufekci 2017, 135–37). To keep users engaged, these sites use algorithms that draw on these social filtering actions and their associated metadata to structure how individual users see content.[7] These algorithms do more than just reflect user preferences, they also "participate in meaning-making, affecting human communication, understanding, and behavior on both small and large scales" (Reyman 2018, 115).

Algorithmic filters increasingly structure our everyday interactions online (Noble 2018; Reyman 2018, 114; Tufekci 2017, 135–38;). Algorithmic filters are abstruse, often invisible sets of instructions that intercede between users and platforms for the purpose of curating content. Different web platforms use different proprietary algorithms, which are often opaque to the site's users (Reyman 2018, 114; Willson 2014, 221). These algorithms are so complex that it would be nearly impossible to predict how a site's algorithm shapes the experience of an individual user (Pariser 2012, 13).[8] This is because the algorithms built into apps, platforms, and search engines evaluate a vast multitude of signals (including geographic location and individual browsing habits) in order to present each user with a specifically tailored view of their network (Pariser 2012). Google, for instance, has been personalizing search results for all users (even those not logged into a Google account) since 2009—the same year the Slender Man was created. The data used by the algorithm is often provided unknowingly by users (Halavais 2009, 47) and structures everything that the user sees, from the content in their social media newsfeed, to the top search results on Google, to recommended videos, trending hashtags, and the latest viral challenges.

As content begins to circulate across the web, the intersection of social and algorithmic filtering makes certain nodes in the network more visible than others. Digital media scholar José van Dijck uses the popular video-sharing website YouTube to describe this relationship between social and algorithmic filtering:

> YouTube users are steered towards a particular video by means of coded mechanisms which heavily rely on promotion and ranking tactics, such as the measuring of downloads and the promotion of popular favourites. The site's users indeed serve as providers and arbiters of content—both unwittingly by means of download counts and consciously by rating and commenting on videos—but rankings and ratings are processed with the help of algorithms, the technical details of which remain undisclosed. (2009, 45)

As Van Dijck observes, algorithmic filtering is fundamentally based on user choice—the agency of both performers and audiences—but at the same time, it actively shapes that agency, drawing attention to certain performances while obscuring others. The result is that a few nodes in the network emerge as dominant, while the majority of performances languish in relative obscurity—a phenomenon known as "the long tail."

Despite appearances to the contrary, the internet on the whole is actually fairly centralized, with the vast majority of web traffic clustered around a few major websites (Hindman 2009; Tufekci 2017). Web traffic tends to follow a power-law distribution, which resembles an inverted exponential curve. This curve demonstrates that a handful of sites receive the majority of digital traffic while the majority of sites are much less visited, splitting the remaining traffic between them (Hindman 2009, 41–45). This forms a "long tail," where nodes in the network get exponentially smaller as they spiral further and further away from the most-trafficked core of the internet (54). While folklorists have traditionally concerned themselves with the more localized, small-scale interactions that make up the long tail, we can't fully understand the circulation of digital legends without also understanding its inherent imbalance. In many ways, the resulting digital model hybridizes elements of mass media distribution and informal folk transmission into something new. The result of these social and algorithmic filtering choices is that certain nodes become more prioritized, more seen, and, subsequently, more influential than others. These visible nodes effectively begin to function as networked gatekeepers.

Gatekeeping is the process of filtering and disseminating information, and like folklore, it is about making choices—what to pass on, what to omit, and how to adapt it (Hindman 2009, 12–13; Shoemaker and Vos 2009, 15). Although the term tends to be used by scholars in fields like political science and journalism to describe how mass media filters information,[9] Karine Barzilai-Nahon offers a more holistic definition. She writes that "[gatekeeping] activities include, among others, selection, addition, withholding, display, channeling, shaping, manipulation, repetition, timing, localization, integration, disregard, and deletion of information" (Barzilai-Nahon 2008, 1496). These actions are reminiscent of the performative choices that—as I have argued above—tradition participants make in deciding when and how to pass on a legend.[10] In other words, tradition participants have always performed a gatekeeping function when it comes to transmitting oral and material forms of folklore. Therefore, what's different about digital media is not that gatekeepers exist; instead, it is how specific nodes *become* gatekeepers.

Because of the role of social and algorithmic filtering on the web, networked gatekeeping diverges from both mass media and folk gatekeeping. Unlike mass media, where gatekeepers typically include professionals like journalists, editors, and publishers, digital networks allow for a broader plurality of gatekeepers (Shoemaker and Vos 2009, 6–7). These networked gatekeepers are crowdsourced into prominence through ongoing and visible forms of interpersonal interaction (Meraz and Papacharissi 2013). Unlike oral folklore, algorithmic filters intercede and interpret these vernacular digital interactions (Tufekci 2017, 162). These computational processes mean that relatively few nodes in the network become prominent while other performances—overlooked or ignored by the algorithm—effectively cease to exist beyond their immediate audiences (Noble 2018, 88). As a result, these prominent nodes have a lot of framing power to shape the legend cycle by conveying a performative touchstone to a large audience. While they do not dictate future performances, they do maintain a sense of continuity as a legend cycle goes viral and exert significant influence over how users begin to understand a legend cycle's shared expectations.

To demonstrate how the conjunction of social and algorithmic filtering shapes the circulation of digital legends, in the sections that follow I analyze *Marble Hornets*' influence on the early circulation of the Slender Man legend cycle and its role as a networked gatekeeper. I begin by discussing the series itself and how it emerged from Slender Man performances on Something Awful. I then track the early spread of the Slender Man legend via *Marble Hornets* in two different web locations. By looking at how in-group and out-group users came to understand the Slender Man legend cycle,

I conclude that while local performances, discussions, and understandings remain highly variable, these filtering mechanisms transcend specific web locations and offer users a series of consistent entry points into the larger legend cycle.

Marble Hornets

The Slender Man was only nine days old when Troy Wagner made his first post in the Create Paranormal Images thread on the Something Awful forums. Wagner, posting with the username ce gars and in-character as "Jay," told the thread about an unsettling interaction he'd had with his friend and fellow film student "Alex" back in 2006. After several months of work, Alex had abruptly stopped production on his student film project—titled *Marble Hornets*—and had grown increasingly withdrawn and paranoid. Jay was now in possession of all the raw footage for *Marble Hornets* and planned to watch it for clues as to what was responsible for the sudden shift in his friend's behavior as well as his subsequent disappearance. Jay promised to update the Create Paranormal Images thread if he found anything out of the ordinary—which, of course, he did.

Two days later—on June 20, 2009—Jay posted a pair of videos to YouTube. The first video was an introduction designed for unfamiliar viewers, which told a similar story and keyed a similar performative frame to what Jay had shared on Something Awful two days prior. The second video—and first official "entry" in the *Marble Hornets* series—was footage from a tape that Jay regarded as an anomaly. In introductory text, Jay explained that he had watched through several tapes already and had found nothing unusual. But, unlike previous tapes, this tape wasn't filmed on the *Marble Hornets* set; instead, it was filmed at night in Alex's house. Near the end of the entry, Alex turned his camera out a window and into the night, where a tall, slender, faceless figure was lurking outside in the darkness. By the next day, a swell of user interest in the YouTube channel led Jay to create a *Marble Hornets* account on the social networking site Twitter to curate and share his findings more broadly. By the end of the week, the first entry had been viewed over five thousand times on YouTube—a number that would continue to grow exponentially over the next several months ("Marble Hornets Radio Interview" 2010, 22:28–22:50).

The first narrative arc (or "season") of *Marble Hornets* would go on to span twenty-six entries over the course of ten months. Although Jay frequently posted updates to the Create Paranormal Images thread, the series outlasted the thread by several months and spawned its own discussion threads on Something Awful (as well as in many other digital spaces). The viral success of the first season led the creators to film an open-ended finale, which left the series open for continuation.[11] A second season was released from late 2010 to late 2011 and the third and final season spanned 2012 to 2014. By the time the series concluded, it had received millions of views on YouTube and inspired a plethora of Slender Man legend performances across both vernacular and commercial media. Although the entire series is noteworthy for its role in spreading the Slender Man legend cycle, this chapter focuses primarily on the first season of *Marble Hornets* in order to demonstrate the initial stages of how digital legends begin to circulate across digital spaces.

The first season of *Marble Hornets* cataloged Jay's attempts to unravel the mystery of what happened to his friend Alex. The series used a nonlinear narrative structure (explained in-universe as the tapes being unmarked) as well as a "found footage" style that resembled movies like *The Blair Witch Project*.[12] Each video was bookended by short contextual notes and explanations from Jay—always in the form of white text on a black background. As the entries progressed, it became clear that Alex was being followed by the Slender Man, which the story only referred to obliquely as "The Operator."[13] Around the halfway point of the first season, Jay started to take a more active role in the story, filming himself as he explored key locations and searched for answers. This pivot from Alex to Jay roughly divided the first season into two halves.

The first half of *Marble Hornets*' first season centered on found footage from Alex's tapes. While much of the raw footage was said to be mundane and unremarkable, Jay quickly began to find peculiarities, which he posted to YouTube as numbered entries. Additionally, in his introduction to Entry #3, Jay noted that a significant portion of the footage on the tapes had nothing to do with Alex's student film and that at some point Alex had inexplicably begun to film himself constantly, even when off-set. Many videos contained audio or video distortion, and some were even missing their audio tracks altogether. A viewer would quickly realize that these aural and visual anomalies heralded the proximity of the Slender Man.

In Entry #7, for example, Alex sits in the driver's seat of his car filming a scene with his lead actor Brian. Brian sits in the passenger seat, framed in a medium close-up shot. Around forty-five seconds into the two-minute entry, the pair are joking and preparing to do another take when a visual tear appears at the bottom of the shot. The visual distortion persists for less than two seconds before disappearing. Nothing else seems amiss and both actor and director are relatively at ease. It's only a minute later, when Brian finishes the take and leans back, that the mood in the car changes. Brian asks if they're going to do another take, but Alex has become agitated and frenzied. Alex immediately ends the shoot, much to Brian's surprise and consternation. On closer scrutiny, the viewer can observe the familiar form of the Slender Man peering out from behind a building in the background that had previously been obscured by Brian during the take. The entry ends with Alex putting his key in the ignition and the engine turning over as the shot cuts to black.

Around the halfway point of *Marble Hornets*' first season, the narrative shifted, and Jay started to actively investigate what happened to Alex. Jay began to film himself constantly, much like Alex had done. At the same time, an account identifying itself as only "totheark" began to harass Jay on social media, posting cryptic videos resembling experimental films and containing hidden messages like "watching you" and "listen." Some of the videos also suggested that Jay was under closer observation than he realized. As part of his investigation, Jay shared the account's eerie videos to his social media followers.

By Entry #16, Jay was fully integrated into the legend performance. His investigation brought him to Brian's house well after nightfall. When several knocks at the door proved fruitless, he moved to the side of the house and found an unlocked patio door. Inside the house only the narrow beam of Jay's flashlight cut through the darkness. Everything was in disarray. As Jay moved from room to room, he slowly illuminated a makeshift sleeping space and a sink covered in dried blood. Jay left with a bottle of pills, a bullet casing, some delirious drawings of The Operator, and more questions than when he started. Although the tense, six-minute exploration revealed the house to be ostensibly empty, totheark would later taunt Jay with a video taken from inside the house during his search. Jay's visit to the house provided a narrative turning point—he was now the one being stalked by paranormal forces and, increasingly, unable to get away.

In considering *Marble Hornets*' role as a networked gatekeeper (i.e., the primary node that many outside of the Something Awful forums would have seen for their first exposure to the Slender Man in 2009 and into 2010), it is important to understand the series as a point of both continuity and divergence from the Create Paranormal Images thread—that is, how it expresses both tradition and variation.

Marble Hornets codified many of the generic expectations for Slender Man legend performance that emerged through informal negotiation in the Create Paranormal Images thread (see chapter 1) for an expanding digital audience. The series strove to maintain the mysterious nature and inscrutable motivations of the Slender Man, and the creators often created more questions than they answered. While the creature was certainly malevolent, its actions were neither violent nor direct—the Slender Man was almost always relegated to the background or hidden in plain sight, with many videos requiring multiple views to find the creature. *Marble Hornets* maintained that knowing about the Slender Man grabbed its attention, and that the creature was always watching those who knew too much. Such proximity created paranoia and began to wear away at one's sanity. Its form was decidedly humanlike—it wore a black suit and had a featureless white face and uncannily long limbs.[14]

Marble Hornets also added several new elements to the legend cycle, many of which were the product of the transition to a new medium (video) and to a new set of digital spaces (social media). The Slender Man's presence now caused audio and visual distortion, making it difficult to clearly capture on film and alerting viewers to its presence even when obscured. Long-term proximity to the Slender Man caused a chronic illness, with Jay repeatedly complaining about high fevers on Twitter and succumbing to coughing fits in his later videos.[15] The series associated a unique symbol with the Slender Man—a blank circle overlaid with a large X—and encroaching paranoia and madness compelled its victims to scrawl frenzied drawings, symbols, and messages across reams of notebook paper (see figure 3). The series even added ideas to the legend cycle that the creators did not intend, like the idea of Slender Man proxies—individuals who work on the creature's behalf.

Figure 3. Entry #8 of *Marble Hornets* shows Alex scribbling barely coherent messages on sheets of notebook paper. The symbol of The Operator (a circle overlaid with an X) can be seen on the topmost page and on a page in the background. *Marble Hornets*, 2009.

But perhaps the most significant variation came in the form of the series' narrative shift during the second half of its first season. When *Marble Hornets* began, it took the form of a friend-of-a-friend style narrative, which resembled many of the performances from the Create Paranormal Images thread. While Jay's early performances displayed paranormal incidents that had happened to his friend Alex several years prior, halfway through the season the narrative shifted to become about Jay's personal experience with the supernatural. These first-person elements resonated with the series viewership. Jay's first-person flashlight search, for example, was not only repeated in subsequent *Marble Hornets* entries but also became the basis for a series of Slender Man video games (see chapter 3). *Marble Hornets*' shift to a first-person narrative structure, "fake out" opening where the creator slowly becomes part of the story, and interactive social media focus,[16] would ultimately become the basis for countless performances across blogs, vlogs, and other forms of social media in the years to come.

In hindsight, *Marble Hornets* seems like the quintessential performance of the Slender Man legend. While many elements of the series—both traditional and variational—would go on to become common motifs in other Slender Man legend performances, it is important to remember that this was not a foregone conclusion when the series began in June 2009 and that *Marble Hornets* actually played a significant role in maintaining the continuity of the legend cycle as it circulated. As one of the first major Slender Man performances to go viral, *Marble Hornets* represents an early and prominent touchstone in the lifecycle of the Slender Man legend, and understanding its influence can illuminate how digital legends circulate as they spiral outward from their point of origin.

Making Sense of Circulation on Something Awful

Jay's initial post to the Create Paranormal Images thread was widely overlooked by other users. It wasn't until a few days later when he posted the first video installment for *Marble Hornets* that he began to capture the thread's attention. The video, which contained brief footage of the Slender Man, met with almost immediate approval from thread regulars like TrenchMaul and Victor Surge and was part of a growing realization among users that the Slender Man was now appearing in other digital spaces. This realization would grow in tandem with the popularity of *Marble Hornets* and often intersected with it. As Goons began to recognize that the Slender Man had circulated beyond Something Awful, various users began to celebrate or bemoan the way the legend was spreading across the network. These varied reactions led to several informal debates over performance and plausibility in other digital spaces, which ultimately culminated in an acknowledgment that viral spread meant that control of the character had been ceded to a broad and nebulous digital crowd.

The transition to social media introduced new concerns into the development of the Slender Man legend cycle that did not exist when it was confined to the Something Awful forums. Referencing Jay's post, user Pr0digal informed the thread that #slenderman was starting to show up on Twitter. Pr0digal went on to encourage other users in the thread to adopt the hashtag in their own social media performances—a suggestion that proved divisive. User BlueDeanie responded to this suggestion by chiding Pr0digal,

"No. FORGET to use #slenderman. You don't know Slender Man by name, or have any idea what he is or why he's bad yet, remember?" While Pr0digal quickly relented, this exchange represented a larger tension that was beginning to emerge between hailing broader user involvement and preserving a sense of control over the character's mysterious nature as it spread across the network. Growing use of a hashtag would work as a framing device, linking together otherwise disparate performances and favoring increased interactivity and visibility. But, at the same time, users worried that discovering the character via these ambient folksonomies would ruin the sense of mystery and plausibility that the thread had worked hard to cultivate over the previous week-and-a-half, reducing the legend's impact by making it an easily identifiable (and Googleable) known quantity.

Similarly, Goons struggled with what comments—if any—to leave on the YouTube entries for *Marble Hornets*. Many users in the Create Paranormal Images thread argued that the YouTube comments on the early *Marble Hornets* entries were having deleterious effects on the perceived authenticity of the legend cycle. "In regards to comments on the videos," user TheRiffie wrote, "can we have less of the 'HE KNOWS ALL, HE IS COMING FOR US, HE WILL KILL US ALL' stuff, it's just a little too over the top and cheesy in my opinion. It kind of ruins any feeling of authenticity the whole thing has and turns it into some sort of attempt at a bad horror movie or something." User KicksYouInHalf responded affirmatively to TheRiffie's suggestion, noting that other comments had already begun to emerge debunking the character as a Something Awful hoax.[17] In light of this, KicksYouInHalf suggested that Jay disable comments entirely: "In fact, it might be even better that way since from a non-SA viewer standpoint, they have no idea who the slender man is and the marble hornets channel never references him as such(yet?). Keep the mystery there and whatnot." YouTube comments were soon disabled on both existing and new *Marble Hornets* entries. This choice, Jay would later acknowledge, was made "because YouTube comments suck" ("Marble Hornets Q&A" 2014, 25:42–27:10).

These arguments over comments and hashtags were essentially debates about the role of social and algorithmic filtering in spreading Slender Man legend performances. While most participants in the Create Paranormal Images thread were interested in seeing the character spread, they initially disagreed on how to make the character seem authentic to outsiders. The general consensus that emerged was to focus on social filtering over algorithmic; in other words, Goons agreed that the Slender Man legend should spread because people were performing it and not because #slenderman was trending on Twitter. Many of these choices were couched in the language of authenticity—with the goal of keeping the creature more mysterious and decentralized—and the thread's idea of authenticity fundamentally derived from the generic expectations for oral forms of legend transmission. These users were effectively advocating for digital transmission via interpersonal legend conduits. But, despite their intentions, the affordances of the medium interceded.

While it had been relatively easy to negotiate and maintain shared expectations for performance in a single web location, broader digital circulation meant that algorithmic filtering had also begun to influence the Slender Man legend cycle. Goons quickly realized that search engines like Google were frustrating their attempts to preserve the creature's sense of mystery. User Nurse Fanny, for example, noted that "googling leads to a Thread that some [overexcited nerd] made,"[18] while other users observed that the Slender Man already had entries on several prominent online databases. For instance, an early entry for the Slender Man on Wikipedia read:

> Slender man is a made up character, presumably by the website https://www.somethingawful.com. On this website's forum, the character is described as a man wearing a costume with white collar and a black tie, stalking persons or groups of people in various places. Slender man is also described as having extra arms that keeps growing longer, depicted by the pictures in the forum. His name being Slender man is apparent on one of the oncoming pictures in the forum.[19]

Because Wikipedia entries often rank highly in related internet search results, entries like the one above had a lot of power to frame and define that which they are curating for a broad digital audience (Westerman 2009; Kaplan 2013). In doing so, such entries provide a definitive interpretation, origin, and synopsis of their subject, which the Create Paranormal Images thread had worked hard to avoid and obfuscate since the character's inception two weeks prior. The result, users like Rambowjo worried, "pretty much debunks all the horror we're starting in here."

Many users in the thread became frustrated as it became clear that the Slender Man legend spiraled beyond their control. Some users suggested a short moratorium on Slender Man legend performances, hoping a temporary cessation would give the internet time to "forget" what it was and where it had originated. Others suggested deleting or archiving the Create Paranormal Images thread and petitioning Wikipedia to remove its page on the creature. But ultimately, the thread recognized that the affordances of digital media made such actions futile. The durable trace of Slender Man legend performances already existed in multiple web locations and could not be easily expunged. Several users argued that—in light of these affordances—the only realistic course of action was to embrace the character's sudden viral success:

> BOZART: Hey, if the cat's out of the bag, why try to put it back in? This whole thing is creepy as hell even as we see it put together piece by piece, by anyone. As much as I hate the whole web 2.0 thing, this has basically become a collaborative ARG and it is awesome.
>
> NEMESIS OF MOLES: I think the slender man idea just snowballed out of control, sure there's been some incredible stuff, the [*Marble Hornets*] videos strike me in particular. But it was pretty dumb to try and make it a 'real' myth.

With the realization that the Slender Man was now beyond their attempts at control and curation, users in the Create Paranormal Images thread began to take stock of how widely the legend cycle was circulating. Goons posted and discussed a growing assortment of Slender Man fan art, videos, and wiki entries they had found in other digital spaces. One Goon even claimed that someone in their offline life with no connection to Something Awful had—without prompting—told them all about the Slender Man. Amid this ongoing conversation, KicksYouInHalf shared a link to the Unfiction forums, an internet community dedicated to Alternate Reality Games that was now following *Marble Hornets*. User Reverend Gnome shared the same link a few days later, the product of their own "independent research to see how far this Slenderman thing had gotten outside of [Something Awful]." The users on Unfiction, Reverend Gnome suggested, were not only trying to figure out the most recent *Marble Hornets* video but also had found a constellation of blogs and other vernacular media that they could scour for clues related to *Marble Hornets* and the Slender Man.

By the end of July 2009, the Create Paranormal Images thread had slowed immensely, with most interaction occurring in the wake of each new *Marble Hornets* entry. In September, a discrete *Marble Hornets* thread was created on the Something Awful forums, and the Create Paranormal Images thread slowly began to dwindle before ultimately being archived in the site's "Comedy Goldmine" section with other notable and infamous pieces of Something Awful history. But, as Reverend Gnome noted in that July 2009 post about Unfiction, "I guess Victor Surge created something that's well beyond his control. Well beyond any of our control, for that matter." Reverend Gnome was right—the Slender Man now belonged to the internet.

Making Sense of Circulation on Unfiction

So far, this chapter has looked at digital circulation from the perspective of the Slender Man's originators. In doing so, I have argued that both social and algorithmic filtering influenced how the Slender Man legend spread and that algorithmic filtering frustrated its creators' intentions. In this section, I flip this perspective by examining digital circulation among a group of initially unfamiliar users. Discussion of *Marble Hornets* on the Unfiction forums, I argue, presents a glimpse into how cultural outsiders in one digital space came to understand and participate in the Slender Man legend cycle. As with the preceding section, an examination of the ways that users made sense of *Marble Hornets* on Unfiction reveals many of the social and algorithmic dynamics that underlie digital legend circulation.

It didn't take long for the Slender Man to spread to the Unfiction forums.[20] Three days after the first *Marble Hornets* video was posted to YouTube, Unfiction user OpenClear created a discussion thread for the series on Unfiction—a web forum dedicated to Alternate Reality Games.[21] OpenClear's initial post included links to the Twitter and YouTube accounts for *Marble Hornets* as well as a brief description that reiterated the contextual information from Jay's introductory video and noted some strange occurrences in the videos "involving a 'tall, slender man.'"[22] OpenClear ended the post by wondering if *Marble Hornets* could be the start of a new Alternate

Reality Game, calling the series promising, and soliciting thoughts and reactions from other users.[23]

OpenClear's post immediately captured the attention of other users on Unfiction, and discussions quickly coalesced around the tall, sinister figure lurking in the videos. Despite OpenClear's subtle reference to a 'tall, slender man' in their initial post, Unfiction users were initially uncertain of what to make of the creature lurking outside Alex's house, and the first page of the thread was filled with appreciation and conjecture. User enaxor, for example, compared it to faceless aliens from the television show *Fringe* and wondered if there might be some connection. This ambiguity lasted for only about a dozen posts until another user, Scarlytte, inadvertently revealed the existence of the Slender Man to the thread.

Scarlytte's post, which mostly expressed interest in the thread, made an offhand reference to a user named Jeph. Scarlytte was excited because Jeph's tweets had been picked up by the account of another Twitter user named Ethan, which brought the Unfiction thread's attention to the latter user's tweets. Ethan had also been interacting with *Marble Hornets*' Twitter account and sharing links to their videos, but more pertinently, for several days he had been appending his tweets with the #slenderman hashtag. Ethan knew about the creature because the account actually belonged to Something Awful user Pr0digal,[24] whose early insistence on hashtag use had sparked an argument in the Create Paranormal Images thread the day before. Just as the users on Something Awful had worried, Ethan's use of a hashtag acted as a framing device, and naming the creature allowed users on Unfiction to quickly discern the durable trace and link otherwise disparate artifacts.

Following Scarlytte's post, users on the Unfiction forums immediately began to identify the creature as the Slender Man, and conversations shifted toward understanding *Marble Hornets* through the lens of the Slender Man legend cycle. Google searches led users to the Slender Man Wikipedia article, which, in turn, revealed the character as a creation of users on Something Awful.[25] Other users who were combing social media for clues quickly realized that one week prior Ethan had named the specific thread on Something Awful where the Slender Man was emerging. The discovery of this durable trace allowed users to find more information on the Slender Man using Google searches and social media metadata, but the exact information gleaned varied from user to user:

NJOKER8: from what I've seen (google) he does not like to be seen. Since I'm a bit of a noob on the subject. Is there anything characteristic about slender man besides not wanting to be seen?

SHININGFIST: Well, through reading the SomethingAwful thread, I can see he prefers children as victims over older subjects. He also occasionally invades the victims dreams prior to their disappearance. He also likes to rip open the chest and impale the victim on a tree or other tall, jagged objects. He also puts their organs in small bags.

As the preceding exchange suggests, while many users were able to find basic details about the Slender Man via Google and Wikipedia, fewer users found the Create Paranormal Images thread, which was usually buried deeper in search results, wiki footnotes, or older tweets. This meant that when new users found the *Marble Hornets* thread on Unfiction, they often brought in understandings of the Slender Man that were not only variable (in the sense of varying interpretations) but also consistent (stemming from a handful of sources and images that Google's search function routinely ranked highly). Veteran users would frequently have to actively socialize these new users into the thread, filling in informational gaps and background on the Slender Man not covered by Google search results.

But even among the portion of Unfiction users who had become aware of Create Paranormal Images, interpretations of the Slender Man legend varied. In the quote above, for example, Shiningfist highlights many elements of the legend cycle that—while present on Something Awful—were fairly minor aspects of the Create Paranormal Images thread. Other users were quick to associate the Slender Man with children or nineteenth-century German folklore. Since these users were all viewing the original thread, these choices are far from being a chain of degradation; instead, they represent choices made by each user (whether consciously or not) based on what material in the original thread appealed most to their own proclivities for what a legend should be (Dégh 2001; Dégh and Vázsonyi 1975). Even other Unfiction users began to recognize this interpretive disparity, with some users going so far as to suggest disregarding the influence of Something Awful and viewing *Marble Hornets* as a discrete performance.[26] To these users, Something Awful represented *a* node in the legend cycle, but it was neither their primary node nor did it intrinsically deserve to be elevated over other content. User DavFlamerock responded to these criticisms by offering a conciliatory reminder about the fundamentally variable nature of legends, "This is and has always been about Slender Man, though as with every addition to myth there WILL be inconsistencies. That's what makes myths so awesome [winking smiley]."

To stem the dual problems of catching up new users and reconciling a plethora of accessible, obfuscated, and dubious information,[27] DavFlamerock created a *Marble Hornets* wiki to collect the information discerned by Unfiction users in a central location. Other users actively asked DavFlamerock to participate in the process, inadvertently helping to shape the series for a broader digital audience. The *Marble Hornets* wiki represents an aggregation of the volition, discussion, and discernment of Unfiction users and frames itself as a resource for the curious who may have discovered the series via "its unfiction forum or maybe even Reddit and the Marble Hornets tags on Tumblr!" The wiki's splash page offers links to the entries for both *Marble Hornets* and totheark as well as links to Jay's YouTube and Twitter accounts. It also concisely explains the context for the series as a product of Something Awful and shares the introduction Jay wrote for the Create Paranormal Images thread with a link to the original text. The work that Unfiction users did to try and understand the Slender Man and *Marble Hornets* fed back into the legend cycle, creating a durable trace that was not only more visible than the Unfiction forums but also outlasted them. The Unfiction forums went dark in 2017, but even in 2020—over a decade after it was created—the *Marble Hornets* wiki still shows up as a top Google search result for "Marble Hornets," along with the series' Wikipedia page, official YouTube channel, and Internet Movie Database page.

When asked to explain why they were drawn to the series, users on Unfiction kept reiterating one central point: *Marble Hornets* had been their first exposure to the Slender Man. "I personally think I was [drawn to *Marble Hornets*] at first (like many others) because MH was the first place I ever saw the Slenderman," user Slendylvr wrote. But Slendylvr was far from the only person to make this case. Users repeatedly remarked on *Marble Hornets*' role as a prominent entry point into the Slender Man legend cycle:

WATSON: Before, you had this interesting but obscure [paranormal] meme from SomethingAwful, and it was fun for thsoe [*sic*] who knew about it

(I was not one of those), but to anyone else it was just like "Wtf? Weird looking picture." Then Marble Hornets showed up on Youtube, and the whole thing kicked into overdrive.

Suddenly you have these blogs and these copy-cat videos, and there's all this discussion about it all over the internet. It has become a phenomenon and . . . the experience has been quite an important one for some people.

As Watson and others suggested, *Marble Hornets* was central to the early circulation of the Slender Man legend cycle and ultimately inspired a vast swath of new discussions and performances. As the first exposure point for many users during the early life of the legend cycle, *Marble Hornets* functioned as a networked gatekeeper—a large node in the network that effectively framed what the Slender Man was (and was not) for a broad digital audience. Whether intentional or not, Jay's performative choices functioned to distill the emergence of the creature on Something Awful into a single set of widely viewed performances, which laid the foundation for subsequent acts of performance and emergence in a variety of digital spaces. But while *Marble Hornets* was often the first Slender Man legend performance users saw, it was seldom the last.

Reflections by users on Unfiction also made it clear that both social and algorithmic filtering played an important role in learning more about the Slender Man legend. *Marble Hornets* often functioned not only as a gatekeeper but also as a gateway, and its purposely mysterious nature drew users to search elsewhere for more information.[28] These users frequently turned to search engines like Google to learn more about the series and the Slender Man:

K-ELIZABETH: I started reading through these forums after i accidentally clicked marble hornets instead of super 8 (the arg i'm currently following) and saw a thread title with slender man in it. Then later i googled it and found a web article about the Slender man legend and found it really interesting, and from there i browsed through some threads and ended up on the [*Marble Hornets* wiki that DavFlamerock created].

ARISON: I actually started watching Marble Hornets before I knew what Slender Man was. They both got mentioned on Halloween in a chat

> with some friends and by chance I ended up looking up Marble Hornets first. . . . Then after a few entries I googled Slender Man himself.[29]

In each of these quoted instances, divergent discoveries ultimately led users along similar paths of investigation. While k-elizabeth discovered the Slender Man because of how threads on the Unfiction forum were organized, Arison's exposure—a recommendation from friends—more closely resembled oral transmission. In both cases, however, exposure to *Marble Hornets* subsequently led both users to seek out more information about the Slender Man legend cycle. To accomplish this, they did what most users do when faced with the new and unfamiliar—they Googled it. The search engine filtered results for these curious users, cutting through the growing corpus of available performances and organizing them.

Although many legend performances were potentially available, user interpretations of the Slender Man legend cycle tended to be formed and framed by the most accessible results. In other words, many users saw the Wikipedia and *Marble Hornets* wiki entries, while fewer followed citations and links to the Create Paranormal Images thread. Therefore, while there was an awareness that the character had been created by users on Something Awful, it was the prominent off-site performances (like *Marble Hornets*), user-driven metadata (like hashtags) and sites of vernacular curation (like wikis) that were most responsible for sustaining the circulation of this digital legend. In these cases, social and algorithmic filtering worked in conjunction to bring users to the legend cycle in personalized yet consistent ways.

These early attempts by Unfiction users to make sense of both *Marble Hornets* and the Slender Man demonstrate how the circulation of a legend cycle is inextricably bound by the affordances of the medium that conveys it. Digital legend circulation maintains some elements of both oral transmission and mass media distribution, but appreciably diverges from both. The synthesis of social and algorithmic filtering prioritizes a comparatively small cluster of performances while others are relegated to the periphery. New performances continue to emerge in local contexts, but their wider visibility and influence decrease exponentially the further they fall from garnering the attention of these aggregation mechanisms. The digital medium doesn't dictate these outcomes, but it does make them far more likely. While local performances, discussions, and understandings remain highly variable (based on both the culture and the affordances at play in various web spaces), these filtering mechanisms transcend specific web locations and offer users a series of consistent entry points into the larger legend cycle.

It is essential to remember, however, that the mesoscale-level filtering[30] enabled by search engines and user habits isn't static—the algorithms continually adjust for new information, and social preferences naturally shift over time. Furthermore, preexisting financial and communicative resources often influence these filtering functions. So, while *Marble Hornets* was a prominent networked gatekeeper in the early circulation of the Slender Man legend cycle, the imitators and variants it encouraged would ultimately go on to supplant it. By 2012 *Marble Hornets* remained popular but had become less quintessential; instead, its centrality had been upended as the Slender Man began to appear in more popular forms of commercial and mass media.

Consequences of the Digital Legend Conduit

By the time *Marble Hornets* concluded its first season in April 2010, it was obvious that the Slender Man could no longer be contained to any specific network location. The social and algorithmic filters that facilitated its early spread from Something Awful to the internet more broadly reveal the constant, asymmetrical give-and-take between local variations and widespread belief. As a digital legend goes viral, users must increasingly rely on these digital filtering mechanisms to give structure to (and make sense of) the existing totality of legend performances. Although digital performances inherently leave a durable trace, when it comes to wider visibility, not all nodes in the network are equal. These highly visible nodes created by the synthesis of social and algorithmic filtering function as networked gatekeepers, framing the legend cycle for a larger audience seeking out more information while also facilitating its spread.

This process of circulation repeated until—in a twist of hybridity—this vernacular creation began to garner the attention of institutional media producers and started making unexpected cameos in a variety of commercial media. In late 2011, monsters called "endermen" were added to the popular video game *Minecraft* as Slender Man homages. A pair of Slender Man video games were released in 2012 and 2013. A 2014 episode of the television show *Supernatural* saw the main characters on the trail of a malevolent photo-lurking entity known as the Thin Man. That same year, the Slender

Man was animated into a background frame of an episode of *My Little Pony: Friendship Is Magic*.[31] The character became the subject of occasional references and one-off cameos in television comedies like *Community* (2015) and *Big Mouth* (2018) and appeared as the supernatural antagonist in horror films like *Always Watching: A Marble Hornets Story* (2015) and *Slender Man* (2018).

A decade later, *Marble Hornets* is absent from the top search results for "Slender Man" on both Google and YouTube; instead, these searches return pages clogged with news stories, encyclopedia entries, video game footage, pranks played by social media celebrities, and movie promotions. Google suggests follow-up searches on such popular topics as "Slender Man song" "Slender Man movie" and "Slender Man Minecraft." Similarly, Create Paranormal Images remains buried deep in Wikipedia citations or seven paragraphs into a *Washington Post* retrospective. The information is there for users who wish to pursue it, but the deeper that information is buried, the less likely it is to be seen (Peck 2020c). *Marble Hornets* remained influential, but over time that influence became less direct. Just as Create Paranormal Images had influenced *Marble Hornets*, *Marble Hornets* would go on to influence some of the most prominent early commercialization of the Slender Man legend cycle.

August 2012 brought a huge surge in Google searches for "Slender Man." It is no coincidence that this was the same month that indie video game developer Parsec Productions released their first Slender Man video game, which quickly became a viral hit. The game—initially titled *Slender*—highly resembled Jay's flashlight search in Entry #16 *Marble Hornets*. The game, its 2013 follow-up, and a bevy of reaction videos by prominent YouTube personalities would go on to become the new central nodes for the legend cycle, expanding the circulation of the Slender Man to new (and often younger) audiences. As the first major examples of commercial Slender Man media, the internet's reaction to these games provides the next major step in understanding the ongoing emergence and circulation of the Slender Man legend cycle.

CHAPTER THREE

Commercialization

Kate was gone by the time Lauren arrived. The sun had begun to set while Lauren hiked along the winding, woodland path to her friend's isolated home. Finding the front door ajar, Lauren entered to find the house in disarray. She grabbed a flashlight from a nearby table and began to methodically search the house for any sign of her friend. Initially, she found only a series of notes, a cut phone line, and a locked door. But the dwindling dusk light soon meant that the search was limited to the visible circle cast by Lauren's flashlight, and while searching a second-floor bedroom, the flashlight's beam caught the metallic glint of a set of keys.

Lauren unlocked the door at the end of the hallway but was unprepared for the disturbing sight inside. The window had been broken and the walls were covered in scribbles and phrases repeated in madness: "WHAT IS IT?" "CAN YOU SEE IT?" "STOP IT." Among the chaos were several frantic drawings of a humanoid figure without a face. Not understanding the significance of the supernatural creature that had been tormenting her friend, Lauren walked toward the shattered windowpane. The silence of the night was abruptly broken by a woman's piercing shriek far off in the woods behind the house. Lauren quickly ran back outside, through an open gate, and into the wilderness beyond. As she began the search for her missing friend in earnest, Lauren was unaware that she was being watched by the same creature that had driven her friend into the woods. On a nearby ridge a tall, dark, and loathsome figure stood silently, watching her and waiting.

This grim prologue was only the first stage of Lauren's macabre journey. All told, the video game *Slender: The Arrival* actually had nine stages, including one level that was a remake of Parsec Productions's previous video game *Slender: The Eight Pages*.[1] To translate Parsec Productions' indie game into a more mainstream commercial product, Blue Isle Studios also hired Troy Wagner, Joseph DeLage, and Tim Sutton—the writers for *Marble Hornets*—to provide creative input for the story for the game. While *The Eight Pages* already contained references to *Marble Hornets* (in the form of scrawled notes and flashlight-lit exploration), *The Arrival* added new elements and story structure that more strongly tied the game to the performative tropes used by the popular web series—a search to unravel the fate of a missing friend, a protagonist being stalked by one of the Slender Man's enthralled proxies, and even a user interface meant to resemble the viewfinder of a video camera. The game represented a commodified, authorial version of the Slender Man legend that offered users a digitally mediated ostensive experience for only $9.99 plus tax.

Slender: The Arrival received a lukewarm reception from both users and critics on its release in 2013.[2] Many users cited issues with the gameplay loop, controls, and graphics as impediments to their enjoyment. Others found the story unsatisfying and suggested that the game was a mere simulacrum of the Slender Man legend. Some bemoaned the sheer act of commercialization as a "selling out" point—the death knell for a legend cycle that had previously succeeded because it was an open resource for expression among a small subset of digital users. In light of these reactions, it's likely the Slender Man video games would have remained obscure or mostly forgotten had it not been for the attention they received from several prominent users on YouTube.

The games quickly became popular examples of the "Let's Play" genre,[3] garnering significant attention from users who wanted to watch their favorite YouTube personality play and react to the game. *Slender: The Arrival*, for example, was played by about 350,000 users on the popular video game platform Steam while just one of the Let's Play videos by popular YouTube user PewDiePie has more than 9 million views (Kjellberg 2013; Orland 2018).[4] This disparity—not only in reaction but also in engagement—raises several questions about the changing relationship between commercial media and folk culture in the digital age. Why did the Slender Man video games feel inauthentic to so many players? Why did the games nevertheless draw the attention of these popular YouTube personalities? What was it about these YouTube videos—themselves a form of commercial media—that made them so much more effective at creating and sustaining user engagement?

The answers to these questions can be found in the very different ways that the games and the videos of people playing them cultivated a sense of vernacular authority. While *Slender: The Arrival* tried to appear vernacular, it was unable to effectively balance authorial intent with the open-ended and shared nature of the Slender Man legend cycle (see chapter 1). The result was that the games created a sense of contradictory hybridity for users, which often limited further engagement. Conversely, the videos about the game created by popular YouTube personalities constructed vernacular authority much more effectively, which led to a proliferation of user engagement with the legend cycle. These videos—while highly produced and often monetized—actively integrated the appearance and tone of backstage interaction. In doing so, they created parasocial experiences—that is, they felt more like hanging out with friends and less like commercial mass media. By effectively using these vernacular tactics, these influential social media users reclaimed the perception of open engagement, which the games themselves lacked. This perception motivated viewers to interact with the games in similarly participatory ways, inspiring a bevy of imitators and variants—especially among the preteens and young adolescents who tended to be key audiences for these YouTube personalities.

To demonstrate how these popular YouTube personalities mediated the Slender Man video games back into the legend cycle, I begin by explaining how the act of mass commercialization tends to change folklore and suggesting that digital media increasingly blur the lines between folk expression and commercialization. To deal with this new ambiguity, I suggest a reorientation that understands commercialized folklore in terms of vernacular/institutional hybridity. I argue that institutions frequently appropriate vernacular speech and aesthetics to cultivate a sense of vernacular authority. By expressing these continuities to existing forms of vernacular expression, institutions invoke a shared sense of traditionality that seeks to garner trust and create affective ties with their audiences. When received favorably these vernacular tactics hail further user engagement; when received poorly they limit that engagement.[5] To illustrate these divergent outcomes, I then contrast *Slender: The Arrival* with videos featuring the game created by professional content creators on YouTube. While the games tried and failed to construct a sense of vernacular authority, the videos succeeded because their creators made the games seem like a social experience, which reframed the interactivity of the commercial artifact and hailed further user engagement. Ultimately, the circuitous route to popularity for *Slender: The Arrival* demonstrates how professional intermediaries who are skilled at seeming vernacular can effectively integrate institutional media and ideas back into everyday expression by encouraging users to take up those ideas as their own.

The Commercialization of Folklore

The commercialization of folklore—and its divisiveness, even among scholars—is not new (Bendix 1997; Buccitelli 2014; Dégh 1994; Foster 2016a, 2016b; Goldstein 2007b). Popular media—ranging from books to films—have been appropriating and selling folk culture for centuries, with the animated films of the Walt Disney Company providing some of the most high-profile examples in contemporary American culture (Koven 2008, 4–5; Noyes 2009, 246; Thompson 2020, 165; Yolen 1988; Zipes 1997, 90). In the mid-twentieth century, such appropriations of folk culture for commercial gain garnered significant cynicism from well-known academic folklorists like Richard Dorson (1950, 1959, 1976).[6] But such a narrowly construed notion of "real" folklore is inherently (and unnecessarily) limiting, placing an overemphasis on origin rather than on what people do with it (Foster 2016a, 56–57; 2016b, 8–9).

When folklorists refer to the act of commercialization, they are often implicitly referring to *mass* commercialization—the institutional appropriation of some element of folk culture (e.g., folk art, belief, or practice) into a widely available commodity, text, or artifact. Such acts are "mass" in the sense of their production, consumption, or both. For instance, a folk artist who sells their folk art at a local outdoor exhibition has commercialized their craft, but not in the same way as a mass-marketed book of fairy tales, a mass-produced cultural tchotchke, or a widely read newspaper article about a local legend. I am not suggesting that mass production and/or consumption inherently creates inferior or inauthentic forms of folklore; instead, I am suggesting that the act of commercialization often *changes* folklore, which subsequently *influences* what people do with it. While the specific nature of these changes often varies based on factors like medium, audience, and intended message (Goldstein 2007b, 174), mass commercialization tends to lead to four interrelated effects: *enhanced circulation*, *structural adaptation*, *codification*, and the emergence of *novel forms of variation*.

Commercialization makes legend cycles more visible, which results in *enhanced circulation* (Dégh 1994). Just as mass production can turn a regional craft into a popular item for tourists—visible at every souvenir stand, such trinkets quickly begin to circulate around the globe and become associated with that region—legend cycles are often integrated into various forms of commercial mass media, which broadcast them widely to new potential audiences (Grider 1984; Laudun 2020; Peck 2020c). When mass media report on a legend cycle, for instance, such coverage almost always serves to spread the cycle regardless of whether the intention had been to validate or debunk it (Brunvand 1981, 153). By the twentieth century, mass media had come to play a dominant role in the dissemination of folklore, and scholars like Linda Dégh worried that despite the unprecedented proliferation that legends had achieved through mass media, such acts had also rendered them more trivial as the products of "professional, consumer-oriented formation" (2001, 34, 112).

As Dégh observed, commercialization fundamentally *restructures* legends through market-based considerations. While the exact nature of this restructuring varies from case to case, commercialization tends to sanitize and narrativize legend cycles. Explicit elements like gore and sex are often toned down as part of the transition to commercial media to avoid offending regulators or key segments of the mass market audience (Fine 1992, 14; see also Zipes 1997, 2001).[7] Such considerations also affect the narrative structure of legends. Commercialization typically stabilizes the form of the legend, merging diffuse fragments and altering existing narratives for dramatic effect (Goldstein 2007b, 195, 200; Bird 1992, 165). This type of restructuring often prunes away ambiguity, potential points of confusion, and narrative dead ends while also conforming to professional standards as well as to the conventions of the specific mass media genre (Goldstein 2007b, 200; see also Gonzalez-Martin 2016, 62).

On its own the act of restructuring is not necessarily significant. After all, most acts of variation done by the folk could be construed as analogous to these acts of restructuring (Bird 1992, 165, 188). Furthermore, it would be difficult to deny that such vernacular acts aren't also influenced by popular narrative forms, familiar media genres, and audience considerations (Dégh 2001, 200–203). The key difference between folk variation and institutional restructuring is the scale at which individual choices can resonate. When commercial restructuring coincides with enhanced circulation via mass distribution, then that restructuring becomes potentially significant as a codifying force for the legend cycle.

When commercialization exposes a wider audience to a legend cycle, the variation built into the mass-mediated text (whether movie, news article, video game, etc.) can become seen as quintessential, thereby *codifying* the artifact's consumer-oriented formation in the minds of that audience (Dégh 1994, 23). This selective legend telling "enhances certain aspects of culture and removes other less desirable elements. The act of consuming culture itself is a culture-creating and culture-altering force. New meanings emerge that often conflict with the meanings once ascribed by the local community" (Goldstein 2007b, 194). Salient choices made by the creator(s) (e.g., what was left in, what was added, what was cut) seem natural to the otherwise uninitiated. As with the discussion of gatekeepers in chapter 2, these mass media texts serve as both entry point and framing device. The more popular this text becomes, the more potential impact it can have on forming subsequent vernacular interactions with the legend cycle—especially if its popularity greatly overshadows the scope of the existing legend conduit.

I want to be careful, however, to not overemphasize institutional media's capacity for influence or overestimate the directness (or universality) of its effects; instead, the relationship between commercial media and vernacular expression is best viewed as an ongoing give-and-take.[8] Worries about the triviality of commercialized folklore are often overstated (Goldstein 2007, 173). Media texts, after all, are inherently polysemic and develop different interpretations in different communities (Busse and Gray 2011; Koven 2003). Similarly, commercialized folklore texts both draw on and enter into existing folk contexts, "[They] don't arise intact into a vacuum and stay in a vacuum; they are integrated into pre-existing belief systems where they thrive or die out" (Goldstein 2007b, 205). Although the integration of folkloric content into a commodified mass media touchstone may seem overly centralizing or constraining, commercialized folklore is perpetually in conversation with ongoing vernacular practice.

When mass media appropriates vernacular expression, it also plays a significant role in disseminating and shaping that expression for a wider audience (Dégh 1994, 25; 2001, 34). This increased publicity subsequently forms the basis for *novel acts of variation* among the folk (Bird 1992, 163; Dégh 1994, 25, 30; Grider 1984; Foster 2016a, 59). Restructuring may stabilize the form of a legend, but it only does so temporarily. As discussed in chapter 1, adopting a legend-telling frame encourages variation, and variation draws on known generic forms. These forms may derive from folk expression or mass media, but in a culture saturated with both, the resulting performances likely emerge in various degrees of hybridity (Howard 2008a). This means that a fundamental part of such hybrid performances involves the act of translating select fragments from commercial media texts back into the more ambivalent and unsettled form of legend. We can see this hybridity at play in the earliest performances of the Slender Man legend cycle—Victor Surge created the character based on a mélange of legend tropes and horror movie imagery that he found particularly frightening (Peck 2015b).

Alan Dundes recognized this reciprocity decades ago, writing in 1963 that "the mass media also provide the basis for the formation of new folklore" (143, quoted in Buccitelli 2014, 239). Similarly, Dégh suggested that integration into commercial mass media tends to multiply legends and that this process "produces many variants" while also influencing popular understandings of what folklore *is* (1994, 24, 30; Foster 2016b, 16–18). It would seem that Dégh's incisive observation about contemporary folklore bears repeating, "It is not enough to recognize that mass media play a role in folklore transmission. It is closer to the truth to admit that the media have become a part of folklore" (1994, 25).

On social media, however, the boundaries between folk and commercial expression are often not well-defined, which leads the familiar characteristics of commercialized folklore to emerge in potentially unexpected ways (Milner 2016, 207; Willsey 2020, 157). Videos of a popular YouTube personality participating in the newest digital trend may appear to offer an unfiltered (and highly imitable) look at their creator's everyday life while actually being monetized, industry-sponsored, or including paid product placement. User-created memes may reproduce commercial slogans and imagery, get appropriated by institutional social media accounts, or come from institutional agents who are posing as vernacular users (Milner 2016, 202–8; Peck 2020b, 2020c). Unlike mass media commercialization, digital media often obscure institutional roots and intentionality, whether it be in specific content or in the commercial basis for the platforms themselves (Howard 2008a; Peck 2020a; Willsey 2020). This blurring means that any comprehensive understanding of the commercial appropriation of folklore in the digital age requires moving beyond the commercial/folk dichotomy and thinking more in terms of vernacular/institutional hybridity (Blank 2018; Howard 2008a).

The Value of the Vernacular

The distinction between vernacular and institutional expression grows increasingly blurry in digital communication (Howard 2010, 2013; see also Phillips and Milner 2020). This leads to two related implications for commercialized folklore online. First, it is more productive to view vernacularity and institutionality not as absolutes but as qualities that emerge in hybridity through discourse (Howard 2008a).[9] Viewing vernacularity as a discursive mode suggests that commercialized folklore may be less about the specific characters or motifs that are appropriated and more about cultivating a sense among an audience that something feels "folkloric." Second, positioning vernacularity as fundamentally discursive draws our attention to what such a perception *does* and *how* it might be cultivated. Such a perspective underscores the role of reception and mediation as key to understanding how the vernacular choices encoded in a commercial media object only become meaningful through user engagement (Howard 2017). My argument is that effectively cultivating a perception of vernacularity can spark further engagement from other users, which has significant implications for the ways in which a commercial text is (or is not) integrated into preexisting belief systems.

Vernacularity is not an essentialized quality (i.e., it is not something that someone does or does not have); it is a communicative mode defined by institutional alterity (Howard 2010).[10] This vernacular mode emerges whenever a communication asserts difference from institutional norms or authority. This alterity might be linguistic in nature, such as when an individual invokes the knowledge of their local community over that of licensed experts. Alternatively, vernacularity could just as easily emerge through format, aesthetic, or practice-based choices (Howard 2017; Peck 2014). The use of informal, local, or vulgar language is a common vernacular tactic, as is communicating through a format like a meme, a blog post, or a video filmed in an obviously lived-in space (Blank 2018; Howard 2010; Peck 2020a; Peck and Good 2020). The vernacular mode is both a perception and a construction—maintained and invoked through a vast array of ongoing discursive interactions.

Since the vernacular must define itself as different from the institutional mode that enables it, the two are never truly separate and exist in varying degrees of hybridity (Howard 2008a). Understanding vernacularity as fundamentally hybrid not only illuminates how vernacular interactions are often influenced by institutional choices but also reminds us that institutions frequently appropriate vernacular expression for their own ends (Hess 2010, 110). A political campaign, for instance, may use blogging as a way to seem more "everyday" or "authentic" to their base, while a corporation may appropriate memetic practices to brand themselves as irreverent or transgressive to their followers on social media (Howard 2010; Peck 2020a). Conversely, an everyday user may use the vernacular mode to support hegemonic or institutional ideas. Vernacular expression can support or oppose institutions, but it often does a little of both (Howard 2008a, 205). Therefore, calling something vernacular acknowledges how a communication or practice works; it is not a value judgment.

Deploying the vernacular mode for persuasive ends is appealing to both users and institutions because such tactics facilitate the construction of vernacular authority. This form of authority represents "a central way tradition functions discursively" (Howard 2013, 76). As discussed in chapter 2, tradition is used here in both its horizontal and vertical sense, suggesting that the imagined totality of these informal interactions is potentially empowering because "it seeks to garner trust from an audience by appealing to the aggregate volition of other individuals across space and through time" (80). By expressing these spatial or temporal continuities, vernacular communication seeks to cultivate authority by appealing to a sense of social trust that is positioned as existing outside of formal institutions. In other words, when expressions build on shared, informal practices to create appeals based on shared, informal (and often constructed) knowledge, those expressions are locating their authority in the persuasive power of the vernacular (81; see also Gencarella 2009).

Commercialized folklore seeks to benefit from vernacular authority by integrating these same perceived continuities. The specific element of folk culture that is appropriated for commercial media is frequently inessential to the actual message of the text; instead, what matters is what the inclusion of folkloric qualities *does* for the commercial text that integrates them (Dégh 1994, 47). Such a text might be considered folkloresque,[11] drawing on an association with folklore "to sell itself, both literally and figuratively, within a commercial venue" (Foster 2016a, 42). By creating a perception that a commercial text derives from folk traditions, these popular culture artifacts are constructed to draw on the power of vernacular expression by conveying a sense of continuity to existing vernacular practices (Foster 2016b, 5; Tolbert 2016, 39).[12] It then becomes apparent that appearing folkloric is a communicative tactic within the vernacular mode and that the reason "certain popular culture forms succeed because they act like folklore" is because they are appealing to vernacular authority (Bird 2006, 346; see also Foster 2016b; Koven 2008, 7).

By integrating elements that seem folkloric, commercial media texts seek to garner trust from their audiences by appealing to the aggregate volition of other individuals across space and through time. For this reason, many commercial appropriations of vernacular practice traffic heavily in allusion and reference (Dégh 1994, 44–45; Foster 2016a). To understand them, the viewer must access their personal cultural inventory (Blank 2013; 2018, 4–5). This serves as part of the communication's appeal and encourages the formation of an affective tie between the commercial media text and its audience. By asking the audience to tap into their personal vernacular or folk knowledge in order to gain understanding, a moment of identification occurs (Burke 1950). In this moment, the institution reaches out to the consumer and conveys the idea of a shared sense of tradition (Howard 2013, 81). By drawing on the knowledge represented by these shared vernacular practices (González-Martin 2016), it is as if the institution is hailing its audience by saying, "Hey, look, we're just like you!"

Effectively cultivating this sense of vernacular authority is appealing to institutions because doing so can lower a consumer's message scrutiny as well as obscure institutional intent and positionality. In her work on folklore and advertising, Dégh suggests that the cavalcade of märchen-like helpers integrated into television commercials are welcomed much more readily into the living room than the "traveling salesperson" (1994, 43). By appropriating these folkloric helpers, Dégh argues that advertisements hide their commercial intentions behind a trusted, authentic, familiar, and affective face. We can see similar phenomena when looking at commercial expression via the vernacular mode online—for instance, when a brand's social media account develops a reputation for being irreverent and posting memes (Peck 2020a) or when Twitter accounts use vernacular speech to push the political agendas of institutional agents (Peck 2020c; Phillips and Milner 2020). Like Dégh's televised advertisements, these commercial deployments of the vernacular mode obscure institutional intentionality behind constructed feelings of familiarity and authenticity, thereby lowering message scrutiny by making the appeal seem more relatable.

When taken up uncritically, this constructed appearance of vernacularity can help spread ideas across digital networks. In previous chapters, I demonstrated how a shared perception of traditionality hails subsequent acts of both creativity and circulation among the digital folk. Elsewhere, I have suggested that adopting a vernacular mode allows institutional agents to interject in this process by encouraging users to engage in certain types of vernacular communication that suit the institution's desired ends, ranging from creating publicity to smearing a political rival (Peck 2020a, 2020c). In taking up ideas that are presented as vernacular (or that come from seemingly vernacular agents), other users enthusiastically circulate those ideas across the network. When done widely enough, this can become a self-fulfilling prophecy, creating a feedback loop that obscures origin and mediates institutional intentions back into aggregate volition (Peck 2020c). This suggests that the vernacular is an appealing communicative mode for institutions because the ambiguity and diffusion[13] enabled by digital media offer the potential to constitute users as willing agents who will continue to circulate and spread ideas as part of what they perceive to be a wider engagement with vernacular practice.

The problem for institutions is that commercial engagements with the vernacular mode are rarely taken up uncritically by their audiences, especially in the highly visible world of digital communication. The goals of folklore and commercial media are frequently at odds with one another, and media that exert too much institutional authority or control inhibit the subsequent potential for user-driven engagement (Peck 2020a; Willsey 2020). Regarding the commercialization of a digital ghost story that had gone viral, Kristiana Willsey writes, "To frame the story as believable and true, it has to be open-ended and debatable—yet to control and eventually market the story [the creator] also has to be the sole arbiter of its ending and meaning. Folklore online must reconcile the tension between the audience involvement that makes a story marketable and the individual authorship that markets require" (2020, 153). The result of this tension is that commercial appropriations of folklore often risk creating a sense of contradictory hybridity, where the text is seen as inauthentic because the vernacular and institutional elements are in direct contention, rendering it uncanny to viewers (Peck 2020a). These perceptions of contradiction and appropriation hail their own user responses that frequently diverge from what the creator intended in unexpected—or even oppositional—ways (Peck 2020a; Tolbert 2016, 37).

While certain elements added to a commercial media text might make it more or less likely to succeed via the vernacular mode, the perception of vernacular authority emerges extrinsically to the text itself, deriving instead from how it is taken up by certain actors in the network (Howard 2017). An influential social media user, for example, may participate in the creation of vernacular authority for a commercial media text through their interaction with it. When these users—whose digital personae are often calculated to appeal to the vernacular mode by forming seemingly backstage, parasocial, and authentic relationships with their fans—interact with a media object in certain ways, they can extend their own vernacular authority to the commercial media text (Marwick and boyd 2011). This interaction often reimagines the text, turning it into something new and influencing subsequent user engagement.

Thus far, I have suggested that understanding the ways in which commercialized folklore is (or is not) integrated back into vernacular practice necessitates an understanding of the vernacular mode that is fundamentally discursive and hybrid. Such an understanding considers not only the elements built into a specific media text but also how that text spirals outward, gaining new meanings (whether intended or not) through subsequent user interaction. But as I argued in chapter 2, this user interaction is not a level playing field, and certain users have a disproportionate say in this process. To demonstrate how *Slender: The Arrival* was mediated back into digital folk culture, the following sections contrast the hybridity present in the game itself with its popular representations on YouTube. I argue that while the former created a sense of contradictory hybridity (which ultimately resulted in its mixed reception), the vernacular tactics used by a bevy of popular YouTube personalities fundamentally recontextualized the game from a ludic experience to a parasocial one. Through these acts of translation, the games developed a sense of vernacular authority (especially among younger users), which ultimately expanded engagement with the legend cycle.

Slender: The Arrival

The first time a player loads *Slender: The Arrival*, they are greeted with a message from the game's developers urging players to approach the game as a form of legend performance. White text on a black background asks the player to "Approach this game with an open mind. Make use of your own personal relatable experiences and memories of desolation in the wild. You're on your own, and your survival is up to you."[14] This plea shows an immediate awareness on the part of the developers about the potential dangers of commercializing a popular folk practice. If this attempt were to come off as overly prescriptive or appropriative, then it would likely draw significant backlash from digital users (Peck 2020a). So, from the very first moments of the game, the developers seek to stem these potentially negative reactions by encouraging users to approach the game differently than a typical commercial media object. By encouraging users to adopt a legend-based frame that draws on their "personal relatable experiences" with relevant forms of folk practice (like legend performances or legend trips), the developers are linking the experience of playing the game with common, informal continuities of folk practice. Before the player's avatar has even taken a single step in the game world, *Slender: The Arrival* has already begun to actively cultivate a sense of vernacular authority.

Many other aspects of the game are similarly designed to appeal to vernacular authority by drawing on informal continuities of practice associated with both legend cycles and the Slender Man. The game is played in a first-person view, and the game's protagonist—Lauren—generally functions as an unobtrusive point-of-view character, letting the player readily project themselves into the experience. Like *Marble Hornets*, the entire game takes place in the viewfinder of Lauren's video camera, which functions as the game's heads-up display and projects static onto the player's screen whenever the Slender Man is in close proximity. The narrative setup—the search for a missing friend who disappeared after drawing the attention of the Slender Man—should also be familiar to any user who has seen *Marble Hornets* (see chapter 2). Many of the game's levels place the player in typical legend-trip locations (e.g., dark forests, empty houses, and abandoned buildings) that are—not coincidentally—also associated with the Slender Man legend cycle. The gameplay is simple and generally involves walking through these varied locales while solving puzzles, collecting items, and evading capture by the Slender Man and its proxies. As these aspects demonstrate, the game is constructed to feel familiar and to encourage users to see themselves as active participants in the unfolding narrative.

However, despite the developers' attempts to cultivate this sense of vernacular authority, *Slender: The Arrival* initially received mixed reviews from both users and critics.[15] For some users, the game succeeded—it felt like playing through a digital legend trip or an interactive season of *Marble Hornets*. Others dismissed the game outright and suggested that the act of commercialization marked the "death" of the Slender Man legend cycle, a common reaction to institutional appropriations of vernacular culture (Peck 2020a). Still others expressed frustration at how various ludic or narrative choices undercut the game's attempt at feeling folkloric and immersive.

These ludic and narrative criticisms begin to expose the contradictions and cracks in the game's construction of vernacular authority. While players generally agreed that the game's introductory section (detailed in the opening paragraphs of this chapter) was especially effective, they diverged regarding the parts of the game that followed this brief prologue. One user on Reddit argued that the prologue was the only worthwhile section of the game, because "it actually feels planned and designed to BE a game, and it builds up tension nicely without actually pitting you against the Slender-Man."[16] Many other users shared this sentiment, arguing that what made the Slender Man an effective form of horror was the creature's scarcity and that the bulk of the game relied too heavily on chase sequences, jump scares, and adrenaline.

In other words, the game's frequent and overt use of the Slender Man violated users' generic expectations for Slender Man legend performance.

To these users, the creature was meant to be used judiciously, and the threat of supernatural observation provided a stronger link to the legend cycle than any jump scare. One user review suggested that while the game was creepy for the first ten minutes, "Then it starts to get frustrating when you see slenderman all the time."[17] Another user expressed confusion about the game's appeal, "I don't understand the Slender games. It's way to [*sic*] easy to catch the Slender man. He doesn't even hide."[18] Thomas Grip, a blogger and developer for Frictional Games, suggested in his review that the developers overused the Slender Man and that the increasing frequency of encounters made the game less scary, "It was spooky at first, but could not compare with the terror felt during the prologue. The encounters became increasingly frequent and the effect was lost" (2013).

The frequency of these supernatural attacks drew players' attention away from experiencing the game through their own "personal relatable experiences" and redirected them to think about the game more in terms of its ludic systems. When these gameplay choices began to frustrate players' attempts to advance the game's narrative, they interceded and reframed how the player experienced the commercial media object. As one user wrote:

> I started to focus more and more on the mechanical systems behind the game with every death to the point of thinking the balance was completely arbitrary/unfair. All immersion was lost for me after my 2nd death in the forest.
>
> [. . .]
>
> I found myself not really caring about any of the narrative elements after the opening level because there was a constant pressure on me to run and collect the next note/item/whatever. In games like Silent Hill and Amnesia, I felt that I was rewarded for taking time to explore every inch of the landscape and yet. [*sic*] Far from removing me from the horror, I felt like I was becoming more immersed in the game world. With Slender I knew that once I picked up that 1st item I'd have to run around the environment in a haphazard fashion to collect the rest.[19]

As this anonymous user suggests, these gameplay choices made *Slender: The Arrival* feel frustrating, rushed, and repetitive, which resulted in an experience that felt less like an interactive legend performance and more like a commercial video game. This sort of challenge and repetition isn't inherently bad (after all, many video games are played *because* they are challenging), but these constraints certainly make it difficult for the player to adhere to the developer's intended folkloric frame.

What we begin to see here is a set of vernacular/institutional contradictions that players must mentally navigate. The Slender Man in *Slender: The Arrival* is much more of a horror movie monster than an elusive cryptid. The game asks players to draw on their own legend tripping experiences, but real-life legend trips are more comfortable with supernatural ambiguity and moments of pause than *Slender: The Arrival* (see chapter 4). Legend performances rarely involve a sense of imminent and conspicuous danger comparable to the climax of a slasher film. Many of the aforementioned user criticisms highlight these contradictions. In doing so, they demonstrate a perceived disconnect between the vernacular practices that are being appropriated by the game's developers and the actual experience of playing the game. This sense of contradictory hybridity highlights a common tension between commercial and folk expression—the game rhetorically solicits its audience to imagine themselves as active participants in an emerging legend performance while ultimately undermining that vernacular appeal through a variety of overly constraining authorial choices.

Such criticisms—that playing the game felt like a simulacrum of a legend experience—were also common from informal conversations with my students the year the game was released. But while many students in 2013 expressed that they felt that the legend cycle had run its course, I began to notice an odd shift in the years that followed. Over time, my students began to view the game more favorably. The reason for this shift wasn't because the game had changed; instead, it was because these students had been younger when the game was released. For many of these students—who had been in middle school or high school in 2013—the *Slender* games had been their first exposure to the Slender Man (see also Koven 2018, 117). As I talked more with this younger generation of students, it quickly became apparent that they had learned about and experienced the games in a fundamentally different way than many of their older counterparts.

Most of my students who expressed an affinity for the game had initially experienced it vicariously through social media. These students often told me that they preferred to watch videos of other users playing and reacting to the game on YouTube rather than playing the game themselves. And this sentiment wasn't just limited to my students—as one user on Reddit explained, "Its on[e] of those games I find more fun to watch instead of play. One of my favorite playthroughs was '12 Drunk Guys Play Slender.'"[20] To many users, such digital interactions felt eminently social, with YouTube personalities sharing the legend in role that felt tonally similar to an older sibling or a close friend.

These videos then formed the basis for further engagement. Students who viewed the game favorably tended to speak less about the game itself and more about the social experiences that these videos had inspired. Students often shared memories about how these popular YouTube videos had inspired them to play the game in similar ways with their own group of friends—for instance, turning off the lights and daring somebody to play while others watched in a ritual oddly reminiscent of other slumber-party games like Bloody Mary. Other students talked about surreptitiously watching a favorite YouTube user play because they "weren't allowed" and then proceeding to discuss what they had seen with their friends on the playground or in the lunchroom. As I argue in the next sections of this chapter, the ways in which these popular YouTube users created a sense of vernacular authority enabled the proliferation of these types of social interactions (whether imagined or embodied). By effectively adopting vernacular expression, these videos encouraged these subsequent forms of engagement, which translated the commercial media object back into the legend cycle.

Parasocial Fear on YouTube

The game starts differently this time. At *Slender: The Arrival*'s title screen, the viewer is greeted by an affable twenty-something who speaks English with a slight Swedish accent. His video feed overlays the top-left corner of the screen, and a display below him shows his current heart rate. His surroundings look like a typical home office, which belies the fact that his wildly popular YouTube channel has recently crested 5 million subscribers (Drehs 2015).[21] With a cackling laugh, he asks his audience "How's it going bros?" and proceeds to introduce himself with an over-the-top falsetto. After this brief introduction, the game begins. The player's avatar once again walks through the forest on her way to Kate's house, but the somber and ominous tone of the single-player experience is replaced with observational humor, player commentary, and a fake-out jump scare meant to play with the video's audience. As the sun goes down and the player begins to search Kate's abandoned house, his tone nimbly shifts back-and-forth between moments of fear and levity. A fleeting glimpse of the Slender Man through a second-floor window is met with shocked yelling one moment and a joking threat to "call the cops" on the creature the next. These videos—posted in four parts totaling about an hour—maintain this tonal duality for the duration of the playthrough.[22] The result feels a lot like goofing around with friends while watching a scary movie at a sleepover.

Watching YouTuber Felix Kjellberg—better known as PewDiePie—play *Slender: The Arrival* is a fundamentally different experience than playing the game alone. PewDiePie was the driving force behind the popularity of the first *Slender* game, which went viral after he played it on his YouTube Channel in July 2012 (Kjellberg 2014). This viral popularity—as well as the widespread reaction videos and Let's Plays it inspired—paved the way for a commercial sequel nine months later that was hotly anticipated by both streamers and users (Blank and McNeill 2018a, 5–6). Within twenty-four hours of the *Slender: The Arrival*'s release, several other major YouTube personalities had also published their own videos playing and reacting to the game, reaching millions of their own subscribers.[23] While PewDiePie may have been the most high-profile of these users, many of the videos posted by these channels contained similar dynamics and aesthetics to the PewDiePie video described above. That is, they almost universally appeared to be vernacular engagements with an institutionally produced commercial media object.

While the tone, language, and aesthetics of these videos initially appear to be vernacular, they are actually complex examples of the vernacular/institutional hybridity enabled by social media. The reason for this hybridity is not just because these users are interacting with an institutionally produced media object or because they are using a major social media platform (although both are certainly factors); instead, it is because being an influential social media personality is a multibillion-dollar industry (Garcia 2017; Schomer 2019). In 2013—the year *Slender: The Arrival* was released—PewDiePie made approximately $4 million playing video games publicly on YouTube (Grundberg and Hansegard 2014). And PewDiePie isn't alone—many of the most famous social media celebrities make millions of dollars a year and far more than that make a living or meaningfully supplement their income by streaming themselves playing video games (Taylor 2018). Even for fledgling users, the possibility of future commercial success can be a powerful incentive and lead them to favor exposure and networking strategies in the short-term as a way of keeping their commercial aspirations alive in the long-term (although the vast majority fade away before ever seeing any financial success [Chen 2016; Marwick and boyd 2011, 155; Morris 2014]). Whether these users have already attained or simply aspire to renown, this suggests that commercial concerns—ranging from attracting new viewers and soliciting positive feedback to encouraging acts of circulation—intercede into the choices that guide the production and promotion of their videos.

Communicating in the vernacular mode is a crucial way that digital content creators navigate these commercial concerns while also maintaining and expanding their audience. Unlike the more polished and formal "frontstage" behaviors associated with institutional communication, these Let's Plays are constructed to resemble authentic "backstage" behaviors (Goffman 1959). In doing so, these users publicly adopt a vernacular mode, which obscures their institutional and financial influences. This type of self-presentational work is common in cases where "the performer may be engaged in a profitable form of activity that is concealed from his audience and is incompatible with the view of his activity which he hopes they will obtain" (Goffman 1959, 43).[24] These videos may seem informal and conversational, like playing the game alongside a friend in their basement, but that's not an accident—it's the point. Through the selective inclusion of backstage behaviors, these users strategically deploy the vernacular mode to develop an ongoing sense of connection with their audience based on the perceived similarity to a shared, informal experience (Fägersten 2017, 9; Marwick and boyd 2011, 156).

The PewDiePie video described above—a fairly representative example of this genre—evinces how many of these choices foster a sense of connection with viewers. PewDiePie starts by greeting his fans as one would greet a friend, and he often speaks to them directly throughout the video. His style seems conversational and extemporaneous, which masks the professional production values of the video—ranging from high-quality video and audio fidelity to subtle edits that skip past segments where the player gets stuck or frustrated. His frequent use of vernacular language (e.g., swearing) replicates a sense of "the intimacy and informality of face-to-face communication among friends" and "actively reduces social distance, creates the illusion of intimacy, and contributes to his unprecedented success on YouTube" (Fägersten 2017, 1, 9). Even a seemingly innocuous choice—like the decision to record in a lived-in space—is significant to how these videos construct vernacular authority because the materiality of such a space has affective and relational qualities that convey a relatable and communal atmosphere to viewers (Taylor 2018, 100).

By strategically deploying these backstage behaviors, these users are constructing a sense of vernacular authority. This calculated backstage framing is a common tactic among influential social media users because these tactics help them grow and maintain a following. By cultivating the appearance of interactivity, affiliation, intimacy, authenticity, and sincerity, these influential users deploy backstage behaviors in ways that build affective ties and create a sense of connection between them and their fans (Marwick and boyd 2011). But despite this backstage tone, these are not truly candid or uncensored views of the user's life; instead, they are calculated deployments of vernacularity that maintain a delicate balance between sharing and privacy (Taylor 2018, 99). When these calculated deployments of noninstitutional expression (i.e., vernacular tone, language, aesthetics) connect with audiences, they do so because they draw on informal continuities of practice, specifically those related to user experiences with embodied interpersonal relationships.

This effect is especially pronounced on younger users, who not only tend to have less-developed media literacy skills but also happen to be major viewers of this genre. For example, approximately 40 percent of PewDiePie's audience is under age twenty-six and 11 percent are younger than eighteen (Genova 2018; Moran 2019).[25] These numbers represent the most significant chunk of PewDiePie's viewer base and indicate that his *Slender: The Arrival* video series has been watched by over 1 million users who are under eighteen years old.

Although we often assume that contemporary young people know how to use the internet because they were born into a world defined by it, media literacy is not inherent. Because of these "digital native" assumptions, many teens and tweens lack a formal education in digital literacy, instead learning about the web through an informal process of trial-and-error. This informal process often leads to misconceptions and inaccurate assumptions, especially regarding the credibility of information, the circulation of content, and the commercial influences at play (boyd 2014, 176–98).[26] This disparity helps explain the odd generational disconnect regarding the game's reception that I noticed in my research. Digital content that "looks real," "feels authentic," or engages in any of the other vernacular tactics discussed above has a higher chance of appealing to younger users due to their still-developing digital literacy skills. This lack of scrutiny allows the vernacular mode to obscure the commercial influences at play more effectively while also reinforcing the perception of an unmediated social experience.

The result is that these videos frequently create a social experience or, at least, the feeling of one. This perception is similar to a phenomenon called a "parasocial relationship,"[27] but social media has blurred many of the traditional boundaries between social and parasocial behavior. Whereas parasocial relationships formed via mass media are typically one-sided, the internet enables affiliative reciprocation through visible acts of interactivity, communicative intimacy, and acknowledgement (Marwick and boyd 2011; see also Chung and Cho 2017). By facilitating this direct and ongoing engagement between media personalities and their fans, social media "de-pathologizes the parasocial and recontextualizes it within a medium that the follower may use to talk to real-life acquaintances" (Marwick and boyd 2011, 148). These vernacular tactics—when embraced by other users—create the perception of camaraderie and hail users to engage with the content under an interactive and collaborative frame (Tucker 2018a, 152).

The point here is not whether these perceptions are real; it is what the shared perception of a social experience *does*. As discussed in chapters 1 and 2, the appearance of widespread vernacular expression hails further user engagement. In the wake of *Slender: The Eight Pages* and *Slender: The Arrival*'s viral success on YouTube, this engagement took a variety of forms. For some, it meant discursively engaging with a social media personality or with other users who were fans of their content. Others imitated, creating their own variations inspired by their favorite YouTubers.[28] Still others engaged on a smaller, less public scale, such as sharing videos with friends or purchasing the game to create their own shared experiences.

As these variations spiraled outward, more novel forms of legend performance became increasingly common. These forms ranged from Slender Man prank videos and Halloween costumes to photobombing and real-life Slender Man legend trips (Peck 2015a, 2017, 2018; Tucker 2018a; see also chapter 4). While the games themselves were constrained by authorial choices, these YouTube videos—and the subsequent behaviors they inspired—circumvented those constraints by mediating the games back into a seemingly vernacular, collaborative experience.

The Neighbor across the Screen

The frequent deployment of the vernacular mode among influential YouTube content creators circuitously reintegrated *Slender: The Eight Pages* and *Slender: The Arrival* back into the legend cycle by inspiring subsequent acts of collaboration and expression. But because of this circuitous route toward reintegration, *Slender: The Eight Pages* and *Slender: The Arrival* maintain an odd position in the legend cycle. Unlike the film adaptations of the character,[29] the games have become generally well-remembered and well-regarded nearly a decade after their release. However, when compared to other performances that helped popularize and codify the legend cycle (like *Marble Hornets*), the video games are more well-known, but they also have a less distinct imprint. Most of the motifs and imagery unique to the games don't appear frequently in subsequent Slender Man legend performances (Chess and Newsom 2015, 35). This is because mass mediated legends tend to be too narratively complex to lend themselves directly to retellings and are instead "more influential in the creation and maintenance of the ideology of the legend—the setting of a system of belief on which legends can thrive—than they are on the formulation of types" (Dégh 2001, 202). While these games directly inspired only limited engagement, the ways in which popular YouTube personalities adapted them hugely expanded the legend's popularity, which led to new forms of engagement and exposed the legend cycle to a new, wider audience.

However, this uptake wasn't completely coincidental. The games lent themselves well to tension and jump scares, and horror games were in vogue in the Let's Play genre in the early 2010s. Their plots were slight—allowing streamers to casually talk over the gameplay without confounding viewers. But most importantly, by including the Slender Man the games drew on a vernacular practice that was already popular among a certain subset of digital users but had not yet gone mainstream. As I have argued, appropriating vernacular practices is appealing to institutions because it helps them cultivate a sense of vernacular authority. Since commercial success on social media often involves an ongoing engagement with the vernacular mode, it makes sense that these YouTube personalities would want to engage with these practices (as well as with media inspired by them) as part of an overall effort to manage their public self-image and connect with fans.

This helps explain not only why PewDiePie chose to play the Slender Man video games on his YouTube channel but also why so many other users quickly followed suit. After all, the mediation of the games on YouTube were themselves a form of commercial expression, designed to connect with digital audiences and sustain viewership. As I have suggested in this chapter, the commercialization of folklore on social media is often more subtle and indirect than mass media commercialization, even when they work in tandem or achieve similar ends. The most effective digital commercialization attempts hide their institutionality behind a veil of vernacular aesthetics and alterity, which enable them to intervene in ongoing vernacular practice (Peck 2020a). By adopting a vernacular mode for commercial purposes, these YouTube personalities were able to draw on existing vernacular practices and perceptions of interpersonal relationships, which created a sense of vernacular authority. While these tactics inspired further engagement from other users, it is important to remember that this engagement was merely a welcome side effect and that the goal for these social media personalities was to maintain their own popularity via the ongoing construction of vernacular authority.

To be clear, I am not suggesting that any media that includes vernacular aspects will get picked up by networked gatekeepers. Similarly, I am not suggesting that all media picked up by networked gatekeepers will appear authentically vernacular and, subsequently, be reintegrated back into digital folk culture. Many such efforts miss the mark for a variety of reasons—the commercial media object may seem too prescriptive or the ensuing social media interactions may come off as too inauthentic or forced (perhaps because institutions are increasingly paying influential social media users for these acts of promotion or product placement). What I *am* suggesting here is that there is a variable constellation of textual qualities and vernacular tactics that make such translations more or less likely, thereby inspiring or foreclosing the ways in which commercialized folklore might be reintegrated back into informal systems of practice.

For users who weren't already familiar with the Slender Man, the videos created by these popular YouTube personalities served as an introduction to the legend cycle from a friendly voice communicating in a familiar and recognizable mode, which hailed further engagement. An offline corollary might be hearing a legend fragment or rumor from a trusted friend or neighbor who had read about it in the local newspaper—after all, we place a similar level of implicit trust in our social media connections (see Grider 1984; McNeill 2018). This suggests that the trusted neighbor who once lived across the street now resides in the social media accounts that we follow. The difference is that while the medium has preserved the power of a friendly voice it has also made it increasingly difficult to separate the neighbor from the salesperson.

Selling Out and Going Mainstream

The commercialization of the Slender Man brought new attention to the legend cycle. This increased visibility—presented in a vernacular mode—became self-reinforcing as it spiraled outward from the commercial media object. Understanding this process requires moving beyond a strict understanding that labels these communications as either "folk" or "commercial," because the clarity of these categories is often frustrated by the affordances of digital media. Instead, regarding these communication events as inherently expressing vernacular/institutional hybridity illuminates not only how and why certain media appear folkloric but also how the construction and maintenance of vernacular authority can both hail further engagement and translate media objects back into vernacular practice. This perspective demonstrates how the commercialization of the Slender Man fundamentally changed the legend cycle, even if that change occurred as the media was diffused outward through networks.

The creature's newfound popularity led to new audiences and consequently to new forms of legend performance (see figure 4; see also chapter 4). But for some users, this increase in mainstream digital popularity marked a turning point in the lifespan of the legend cycle (see Tolbert 2018a, 40–43). Digital trends like these struggle against their own popularity. Users

Figure 4. Homemade Slender Man Halloween costumes proved popular in 2013, the year *Slender: The Arrival* was released. Some individuals also reported engaging in ostensive behaviors, such as purposely sneaking into the background of photos taken by strangers to simulate the media they had seen online. Photograph by Nicky Kurtzweil.

must constantly perform the legend cycle, or else it goes into a period of dormancy. But continued performance also makes the legend cycle more visible, threatening the cultural niche that made it appealing to users in the first place. After all, an inside joke is no longer special when everybody is in on it. For some users who were already familiar with the legend cycle, this new popularity created their own Eternal September[30]—a rapid influx of new users who quickly overwhelmed existing generic expectations. The result is that this act of commercialization not only expanded the audience for the legend cycle but also shifted it.

The Slender Man video games mark 2012 and 2013 as a sort of transitional period for the legend cycle. The legend cycle's subcultural popularity led to the commercialization of the character, which—when effectively mediated through the vernacular mode—transitioned the legend cycle to a much wider digital audience. While the character was still relatively unknown offline, the legend cycle's rise in popularity following the viral success of *Slender: The Eight Pages* and *Slender: The Arrival* exposed many teenage and early adolescent internet users to the Slender Man legend for the first time. In the next chapter, I explore the implications of this transition and consider what happens when the Slender Man legend cycle starts to influence a variety of offline behaviors in children, adolescents, and young adults.

CHAPTER FOUR

Ostension

Armed with a small, portable video camera and a lot of courage, nine-year-old "Javier"[1] was searching for the Slender Man. He spoke to his viewers with breathless enthusiasm, promising them a thorough, three-day search of his backyard. He assured them that if the creature was real, then he would find it. "If he's not here," Javier reasoned, "that means he's not real because he gotta be stalkin' me because I believe in him."

But when a quick, thirty-second walk across the yard revealed little in the way of the paranormal, Javier decided to widen his search. He passed the family dog and headed toward the garage. Although the backyard search had wrapped up faster than anticipated, Javier was undeterred. Not one to shrink from a little darkness or clutter, Javier left the safety of a sunny midspring day for the shadowy confines of the garage.

Sun beams dappled the floor, but Javier immediately noted how much darker it was inside. He loudly decided to be quiet, lest he prematurely alert the creature. He stepped over bicycles and sidled around parked cars. He moved methodically toward the back of the garage, tripping only several times. Finally, he moved past the last sunbeam and toward the blackness at the far end of the garage.

"I used to see a piece of paper here," he mused, perhaps referencing the handwritten notes so often seen or scrawled by victims of the Slender Man. "Well, I guess it's not here anymore," he added as he hurried back toward the lighted entrance.

After a brief moment to catch his breath, Javier returned to his search with renewed vigor. Javier made several more forays into the garage, but they ultimately failed to provide any conclusive evidence for the existence of the Slender Man. Javier understood that if he really wanted to pursue the creature, then he had to take a bigger risk and search somewhere far more terrifying.

It took four installments for Javier to work up the courage to descend the stairs into the basement. "Today I'm going in my b . . . basement," he said nervously, before quietly adding, "to see if he's in here." He passed through the entryway, soldiered on through the laundry room, and whispered, "kinda spooky," as he made his way past the derelict home gym. Several seconds passed as Javier searched for a light switch. Suddenly, the silence was broken by a ghastly clanging. The din reverberated across the basement's sheer walls, but the sound was coming from behind Javier. He moved further into the darkness, taking refuge behind some boxes. Yet, the noise persisted.

"That was not me," Javier told the camera as he turned around.

The room was now illuminated, and a tall figure stood on the far side. The figure was just out of frame when it began to address Javier directly. It asked for his help to reset the exercise equipment. Javier moved to help his father and resolved to continue his search later.

Javier posted a total of five videos documenting his search for the Slender Man to YouTube in 2013. The videos were short, averaging only around two and a half minutes each. Javier often spoke incomprehensibly rapidly and told viewers whatever was on his mind. The smartphone he used to film shook violently as he moved, frequently making it impossible to discern what was actually going on. In the decade since they were uploaded, each video has only been viewed a few dozen times. Suffice it to say, Javier's legend trip through his backyard was a far cry from the viral popularity of *Marble Hornets* or *Slender: The Arrival.* But there is something going on here that's more significant than production values or view count.

Javier was engaging in ostension. That is, the actions he was taking were inspired by the legend cycle, and he enacted the legend cycle through those actions. As an analytic concept, ostension is a way of thinking about how legends are performed in ways that go beyond verbal performance. It is doing rather than telling or "presentation as contrasted to representation" (Dégh and Vázsonyi 1983, 6). A variety of legend-inspired actions might be considered ostension, including traveling to a local landmark that is rumored to be haunted or hunting a cryptid in its natural habitat—even if that habitat just happens to be in one's own backyard (McNeill and Tucker 2018a). Ostensive actions like these have a long, predigital history and have been studied by folklorists for several decades, usually in terms of ephemeral, small-group behavior (e.g., Dégh and Vázsonyi 1983; Ellis 1989, 1996). However, the proliferation of new technologies that are both more mobile and connected create new possibilities for ostensive action by allowing those actions to be documented, shared, and responded to much more easily. In other words, Javier's legend trip is significant because it begins to demonstrate how these new affordances are changing how ostension is practiced in the digital age.

In this chapter, I argue that understanding ostension in the digital age requires reframing ostensive action as ostensive practice. While "action" suggests an individual expression of volition that is ephemeral and shared on a personal scale, "practice" refers to the collection of many actions and acknowledges the connectivity, aggregated volition, and self-awareness enabled by the affordances of networked digital communication. The move from action to practice is essential to understanding how digital documentation and networked sharing raise widespread awareness of ostension in the digital age as well as how this awareness subsequently encourages new dynamics of collaboration and critique among users.

To make this argument, I begin by demonstrating how predigital examples of ostensive action tended to emerge in relative isolation. I then observe how the affordances of digital communication often encourage users to document and share their everyday behaviors, like ostension, across networks. The result of this shift, I argue, is that in an age of smartphones and social media, individual acts of ostension have become both more mediated and more visible (Kinsella 2011; Koven 1999, 2007, 2008; Tolbert 2013). This increased visibility creates awareness and draws connections between individual actions. Consequently, this increased awareness and connectivity encourages a sense of collaboration among users. As these users collaborate on ostensive practices, they begin to develop hierarchies of performance that privilege certain types of interaction, creating an atmosphere that facilitates vernacular critique and the emergence of a "meta-discourse" (Tolbert 2013). This meta-discourse offers the opportunity for users to reflect not only on the nature of legends but also on the nature of the ostensive practices themselves.

Ostensive Action

Ostensive actions are actions that are inspired by legends. In "Does the Word 'Dog' Bite? Ostensive Action: A Means of Legend Telling," Linda Dégh and Andrew Vázsonyi argued that certain actions *show* legends rather than verbally *tell* them. Borrowing from work in semiotics,[2] they introduced the term "ostension" (from the Latin *ostendere*, "to show") into legend scholarship as a way of describing the real-life enactment of legend narratives (1983, 7–8; McNeill and Tucker 2018a, 11). In doing so, they also proposed three variants of ostension:

- Pseudo-ostension: creating the appearance or illusion of ostension. This term is most often used to refer to legend-inspired hoaxes or pranks.
- Proto-ostension: translating a fabulate into a memorate, such as when a performer tells a legend in the first-person as if it actually happened to them.
- Quasi-ostension: misattributing a natural or ordinary phenomenon to a legend. An "error of observation," such as mistaking a mysterious light in the woods for a will-o'-the-wisp. (Dégh and Vázsonyi 1983, 19–21)

As these variants suggest, ostensive actions range from playful to serious and include both intentional and unintentional forms of legend enactment (Dégh and Vázsonyi 1983, 25; Ellis 2000, 204; Tucker 2005). Furthermore, ostension and its variants often function synergistically, and multiple types may exist simultaneously surrounding a specific event (Ellis 1989, 209; 2001a, 163). As such, it may be more productive to view these variants not as discrete categories but instead as diverse ways of understanding the potential motivations and meanings behind ostensive actions (McNeill and Tucker 2018a, 11).

While acting out a legend in its entirety does occur, it is far more common that an ostensive action *suggests* a legend rather than fully enacting it (Ellis 2001a, 162; Goldstein 2004, 121). This means that ostensive actions could be as simple as wearing a vampire costume on Halloween or as direct as reciting "Bloody Mary" three times into a mirror at a slumber party. Alternatively, ostension might involve adopting a legend-inspired habit, like avoiding a fried chicken restaurant for fear of accidentally being served a deep-fried rat[3] or checking the backseat of one's car before driving alone at night to make certain there are no murderers waiting in ambush.[4] Ostension could also take the form of a legend trip, which might involve traveling to a haunted location or hunting in the woods for a supernatural creature. In the rarest and most extreme circumstances, legends can even inspire ostensive acts of violence and murder (Dégh and Vázsonyi 1983; Ellis 1989; see also chapter 5).

These legend-based actions coexist symbiotically with the narratives that inspire them (Dégh and Vázsonyi 1983, 5–7). Expressive behaviors frequently transition back-and-forth between action and narrative with each domain strengthening the other (27, 29). As enacted legend performances, ostensive actions not only enact the narratives that inspire them but also exert influence on future legend performances (see chapter 1). Legend cycles may form the basis for ostensive actions, but ostensive actions can also lead to oral retellings or even serve as forms of evidence for the legend cycle (27–29). Therefore, action and narrative are best viewed as deeply imbricated—two sides of the same coin, which both emerge from the same cultural imperative (Goldstein 2004, 123).

As an analytical tool, the concept of ostension highlights the reciprocal relationship between legend and action (Ellis 1989, 202–3; Goldstein 2004, 30). Legends are maps for action: they not only describe events in the past tense but also serve as a way to make sense of the present and offer options for the future (Ellis 1989, 202; see also Fine 1991, 181). In doing so, these narratives provide "an encoded cultural script for decision making and action" (Goldstein 2004, 121). Hence the study of ostension is the study of how "fact can become narrative and narrative can become fact" (Dégh and Vázsonyi 1983, 29). It is concerned with identifying patterns of legend-inspired behavior as well as examining their potential meaning and significance (Ellis 1996; McNeill and Tucker 2018a, 11–12).

These legend-inspired behaviors are relatively common, but before participatory forms of social media became the norm, they often lacked a direct awareness of each other. In 1991, for example, Bill Ellis observed that ostensive actions like legend tripping were widely practiced among adolescents (1996, 169; see also Lindahl 2005; Tucker 2018a, 146–47). Yet, at the same time, he called this tradition "silent" because the everyday behavior of teenagers wasn't open to adults and researchers unless they sought it out (Ellis 1996, 182). And even then, teenagers might be apprehensive about sharing their liminal, boundary-testing behaviors with those outside their trusted friend group. After all, peers may judge, and parents might punish. The result is that these predigital ostensive actions tended to be transmitted informally between folk groups through decentralized, interpersonal legend conduits (see chapter 2).

It is here that a set of contradictions seems to emerge around predigital ostensive actions—they are everywhere yet nowhere, common yet invisible, unique yet shared. And these contradictions are not unique to adolescents or legend trips. The tendency in the era of mass media was that "only famous copycat activities are noted, whereas everyday copycats escape observation" (Dégh and Vázsonyi 1983, 14). In other words, ostension only made the news when something abhorrent appeared to have happened, as was the case with localized rumors of satanic mutilations and legend-inspired violence in the 1980s and 1990s (Ellis 1989, 1996, 2000; see also chapter 5). The more common forms of ostensive action lacked such visibility because they remained predominantly in the diffuse and ephemeral realm of oral communication. They existed in the moment but left little in the way of a durable trace (see chapter 2).[5] Without this visibility, it would have been difficult for those engaging in more quotidian forms of ostensive action to understand the commonality of those actions and to connect their own experiences to broader social practice.

To illustrate this point, consider a hypothetical version of a predigital legend trip.[6] It is 1985, and Alice and Beth are two bored teenagers hanging out on a Saturday evening. After watching a scary movie on TV, Alice asks Beth if she has heard of a local stretch of road that is rumored to be haunted. Beth replies in the negative and Alice responds by recounting a local variant of "the vanishing hitchhiker."[7] Alice then suggests they go check out the stretch of road to see if the legend is true. Beth is skeptical, so Alice improvises a story about a friend who had a close encounter with the phantom while driving along that road. Beth's curiosity is piqued. She offers to drive while Alice navigates using an old highway map stashed in the car's glove compartment. As the pair gets closer, Beth turns off the car's radio and the girls start swapping scary stories to set the mood. After forty-five minutes, the girls arrive.

The highway is dark and unfamiliar. Thick trees line both sides of the road, allowing only rivulets of moonlight to seep through. After ten minutes of driving, Beth spots an eerie fog on the side of the road.

"I see it too!" Alice exclaims, "Let's check it out!"

Beth parks the car in a small clearing and slings her camera around her neck; Alice grabs a flashlight from the glove compartment and turns it on. The pair exit the car and head cautiously through the woods to where they saw the fog. Beth takes a picture, but she won't see what she captured until the film is developed several weeks later.

As they walk, Alice decides to play a trick on Beth. Beth begins to hear an eerie moan coming from the woods and quickly realizes she is alone.

"Alice! Cut it out! This isn't funny!" Beth pleads.

Suddenly the woods are deathly quiet. Without a flashlight, Beth uses her camera's flash to illuminate her surroundings, but she doesn't see any sign of Alice. The moaning begins again, more intense this time and from a different direction. Beth finally gives up and runs back toward the road in fright. When she reaches the car, a hand grabs her shoulder and a voice yells "Got you!" Beth screams while Alice laughs and reignites her flashlight. Beth punches Alice in the shoulder and begins laughing out of sheer relief.

The two girls get back in the car and drive home. They talk about what they saw, how scared they were, and what else might have been out there. Alice swears she stopped pretending to be the phantom when Beth cried out and that the second set of ghastly noises hadn't come from her. Beth doesn't believe Alice until her film is developed several weeks later, and she swears she sees the ethereal outline of a third girl in one of her photos. This excursion lives in that photo—stashed in a shoebox where Beth keeps various curios and reminders of high school—as well as in the occasional oral retelling whenever Beth or Alice wants to reminiscence or share their unexplained paranormal encounter with others.

This example demonstrates the temporally concise and ephemeral nature of most forms of predigital ostension (Buccitelli 2016; see also chapter 2). Legend tripping to this site may be fairly common, but the records of those trips lack persistence and visibility beyond the scale of interpersonal communication. These limitations draw our attention to the new possibilities for capturing and sharing ostensive action enabled by digital media. What happens, for instance, when those engaging in ostensive action routinely carry handheld devices that can record and share various forms of media? What about when those media are uploaded and become part of the durable trace? How does the ephemeral nature of ostension change when there are innumerable examples available at the click of a button? The answer to these questions requires an examination of how digital media enable and encourage new forms of connection and visibility as well as the broader implications of those new affordances.

Ostensive Practice

Digital media allow users to more easily capture and widely share their everyday behaviors, including their ostensive actions. Because of the increased visibility this creates, individual users can begin to see more readily the connections between their own ostensive actions and those of others. In this section, I explore the implications of this burgeoning awareness and argue that by rendering an existing process visible and spreadable, the affordances of digital communication extend and aggregate individual actions on a large scale, which enables users to recognize bodies of practice. I wish to be clear, however, and acknowledge that ostension has always been a practice. It is not that digital communication turns ostensive action into practice; instead, it is that digital communication *foregrounds* practice. Hence a reorientation in terms from ostensive action to ostensive practice represents a small but significant shift toward understanding how ostension is extended by digital networks.

A practice-driven framework[8] stresses the ongoing and reciprocal relationship between structure and individual agency (Berger and del Negro 2016, 148; Giddens 1984). Structure (in the *structuration* sense) refers to the rules and resources that enable and constrain individual agency (Giddens 1984, xxxi, 25). Such rules might be formalized (as is often the case with institutions) or circulated informally (as is often the case with aggregate volition and vernacular authority), but these structures are constituted by the practices of agents (Berger and del Negro 2016; Schmitt 2016). What is critical here is not strictly defining the nature of structure; instead, it is understanding that structure and individual agency exist in a mutually constitutive feedback loop, wherein each is constantly producing—and emerging in light of—the other (Berger and del Negro 2016, 149–50; Giddens 1984). Individual actions emerge not only in light of past practices but also in anticipation of future ones. In doing so, those actions circuitously reproduce the same structures that produced them (Berger and del Negro 2016, 150).

To illustrate what the digital practice of ostension looks like, let us reimagine our "vanishing hitchhiker" legend trip in an era of smartphones and social media.[9] After streaming a scary movie online, Alice asks Beth if she has heard of a local stretch of road that is rumored to be haunted. Beth replies in the negative and Alice responds by recounting a local variant of "the vanishing hitchhiker." Alice then suggests they go check out the stretch of road to see if the legend is true. Beth is skeptical, so Alice shows her a YouTube video of other adolescents who recorded and shared a video of their own close encounter with the phantom while driving along that road. Beth's curiosity is piqued. She offers to drive and uses her phone for directions to the allegedly haunted location. As the pair gets closer, Beth turns off her phone's map app and the girls start swapping scary stories to set the mood. Beth recalls her stories from memory while Alice uses her phone's internet connection to find stories others have posted about encounters at the site. After forty-five minutes, the girls arrive.

The highway is dark and looks eerily similar to the encounter videos they saw on YouTube. Thick trees line both sides of the road, allowing only rivulets of moonlight to seep through. After ten minutes of driving, Beth spots an eerie fog on the side of the road.

"I see it too!" Alice exclaims, "Let's check it out!"

Beth parks the car in a small clearing and both girls grab their phones, which function as both flashlights and recording devices. The pair exit the car and head cautiously through the woods to where they saw the fog. Beth films every step while Alice opens an app on her phone that dubiously promises to show the user nearby paranormal energy signatures.

As they walk, the app on Alice's phone displays a large orb of energy near Beth, which gives Alice the idea for a prank. Beth begins to hear an eerie moan coming from the woods and quickly realizes she is alone.

"Alice! Cut it out! This isn't funny!" Beth pleads.

Suddenly the woods are deathly quiet. Beth turns her phone in every direction to illuminate her surroundings, but she doesn't see any sign of Alice. The moaning begins again, more intense this time and from a different direction. Beth finally gives up and runs back toward the road in fright. Now alone in the woods, Alice stops filming her prank and takes a selfie, mockingly pretending to be the phantom from the legend. She posts both to social media and tags Beth (as well as several mutual friends). Beth reaches the car just as her phone buzzes with a new notification. Beth sees the photo, realizes it was a prank, and begins laughing out of sheer relief.

The two girls get back in the car and drive home. Beth posts her legend-trip video to social media and tags Alice as well as their mutual friends. The girls talk about what they saw, how scared they were, and what else might have been out there. Alice swears she stopped pretending to be the phantom when Beth cried out and that the second set of ghastly noises hadn't come from her. Beth doesn't believe Alice, until she gets another notification. A friend has commented on the video asking who the third girl is and calling her creepy. The pair rewatch the video and see what appears to be an ethereal figure moving through the trees around a minute in. Alice divulges what she saw on her ghost hunting app, which the girls see as further proof of a supernatural encounter. Beth includes these details in her reply, and more friends start "liking" the video and commenting on how creepy it is—one friend even shares it to her own social media feed. Beth is shaken, but Alice plans to repost the video on YouTube when she gets home. The excursion persists in that video, which remains publicly available and shareable on social media long after the event itself has ended. Thus, it feeds back into the same corpus of visual evidence that catalyzed Alice and Beth's legend trip in the first place.

This example demonstrates how digital networks turn formerly isolated actions into something more visible and connected. While it is certainly true that only some ostensive actions are digitally documented (and that only some of those are shared on the internet), the actions that are both documented and shared are the ones that gain visibility, which reciprocally normalizes the act of documenting and sharing. Supplementing our everyday digital communication with images, videos, and photographs has become thoroughly ordinary (Hand 2012, 11). The mundanity of visually capturing and sharing everyday experiences on the internet is significant because it echoes something that Dégh and Vázsonyi argued about ostension forty years ago—that banality encourages further action and that the perception of frequency "is a green traffic light" (1983, 14). While Dégh and Vázsonyi were concerned with representations of ostensive action in the mass media (which they argued disproportionately focused on violent ostensive acts), digital media provide a multimedia outlet for more quotidian forms of ostensive action. This shift makes it apparent that the increased visibility enabled by digital media encourages not only further action but also the documentation and sharing of that action.

The visibility provided by digital networks also allows users to more readily see the connections between individual actions, which creates an awareness that these actions exist as part of a larger body of practice. To understand the significance of this shift, we can observe a similar transition from predigital memes to a practice-based digital meme culture. Like predigital ostensive actions, predigital memes tended to be ephemeral, and variation was often invisible to participants because they only encountered a limited number of manifestations in their lifetime (Shifman 2014, 28–30). By providing users with a vast and public catalog of memetic variants, the internet transformed these previously isolated and ephemeral events into more ongoing and self-aware digital practices (Milner 2016; Peck and Good 2020). This transition made users more aware of prior actions, more focused on sharing present experiences, and more concerned with potential future interactions (Shifman 2014, 28–30). The implication is that by allowing users to easily see the connections and continuities between individual actions, the affordances of digital media encourage users to perceive themselves as active participants in a widely shared practice.

By constituting users as active participants, the increased visibility and awareness provided by digital networks create a sense of collaboration among those users. This sense of collaboration is twofold. In the first sense, these collaborative practices are past-oriented, building on what has come before and expressing connections to existing structures. There is a tendency for digital platforms to "enable the temporal extension and durability of what in offline spaces might otherwise be much more temporally condensed and ephemeral discursive events" (Buccitelli 2016, 87). As discussed in chapter 2, this durable trace serves not only as a record but also as a pattern that guides future performances. By extending individual actions over space and time, digital networks make "the previously ephemeral expressiveness of the everyday" more widely visible and accessible (92). The implication of this shift is that individual expressive actions potentially become more keyed to these durable and accessible antecedents (92).

In the second sense, these collaborative practices are future-facing. The visibility of those antecedents often leads ostensive actions to emerge in anticipation of future interactions, thereby reproducing the same underlying structures. Smartphones may be standard equipment for contemporary legend trips and ghost hunts, but the role of these digital devices goes beyond just recording the event. Writing about a group of ghost-hunting college students, Elizabeth Tucker explains:

> They planned to upload their video to YouTube and did so immediately after their ghost hunt ended. Because of this plan, they were aware of performing for an audience throughout their search for ghosts. Their video might have 'gone viral' and reached many viewers; most YouTube videos do not become that famous, but one never knows which way the fickle finger of fame will point. (2018b, 206)

While not everyone's intention is to go viral, our contemporary media environment emphasizes the documenting and sharing of these sorts of everyday actions online (Peck 2017). These individuals are performing not only for each other but also for a presumed audience that is not spatially or temporally present. In doing so, these individuals situate themselves in a continuity of practice—inheriting from prior actions while also anticipating (and potentially influencing) future ones.

As ostensive practices circulate across digital networks and hail these forms of collaboration, they also begin to inspire competition and critique. This occurs because more collaboration further increases both visibility and variation, which leads users to develop ways of categorizing some performances as better (or more authentic) than others. As Whitney Phillips explains in her study of 4Chan, when internet memes started becoming popular in other web locations, 4Chan users were incensed. Despite meme culture becoming more widely accessible, users on 4Chan were livid about "the increasing number of 'bad' memes . . . that deviated significantly from the established subcultural format" being shared on more mainstream websites like Facebook (Phillips 2015, 144). As Phillips demonstrates, when a vernacular practice begins to circulate widely there is a rise in the amount of possible variation displayed by users. To respond to this, users engage in acts of vernacular critique that construct and reinforce their own sense of vernacular authority over the practice.

These ongoing acts of collaboration and critique facilitate the creation of hierarchies through which users not only judge vernacular expression but also engage in ongoing acts of vernacular discourse on the nature of the practices themselves. This function represents a "meta-discourse"—a mode of deliberation surrounding a vernacular practice through which users deliberate on the function, meaning, and significance of that practice (Tolbert 2013). By considering how vernacular practice comments on vernacular practice, scholars can better understand the underlying assumptions of the folk—the forms specific genres should take, the informal rules for participation, and the maintenance and contestation of vernacular authority (123).

So far, I have argued that the most significant change in the shift from ostensive action to ostensive practice comes from the increased visibility brought by digital communication, which subsequently increases user awareness of ostension as a practice. This awareness, in turn, encourages new dynamics of collaboration and critique surrounding the practice of ostension. In the next section, I demonstrate this shift by examining both mediated and unmediated acts of ostension related to the Slender Man legend cycle. Ultimately, I argue that the frequently mediated nature of modern ostension is pulling this online/offline dichotomy together, with the former increasingly influencing the latter.

The Online and Offline Practice of Slender Man Ostension

The popular video-sharing website YouTube plays host to thousands of user-produced Slender Man videos. As this sheer volume suggests, a wide range of content is represented, ranging from the seemingly authentic to the obviously playful.[10] A bevy of amateur films and videos purport to have captured the creature in action, sporting eye-catching titles like "[REAL] MAN GET KILLED BY SLENDERMAN 2015!!!," "HIKER KILLED BY THE SLENDER MAN!!!!! MUST WATCH!!!," AND "SLENDER MAN CAUGHT ON TAPE (PLEASE HELP FIND THEM)." Some of these videos strive for authenticity by playing their subject completely straight while others reveal their fictional nature through metadata or by unexpectedly revealing themselves as parodies in their final moments.[11] Video documentation of legend trips and Slender Man hunts are common, as are do-it-yourself costume-making guides, hidden camera pranks, and truth-uncovering hoax videos. The creators range in age from preteens to adults.

These user-created videos frequently blur the lines between ostension, pseudo-ostension, quasi-ostension, and what Mikel J. Koven has called "cinematic ostension." As Koven argues, a mediated legend text may be construed as ostension "particularly when we are *shown* the narrative through actions rather than having the story retold to us in narration. . . . [Then such] ostension implicitly recognizes an audience by encouraging some form of post-presentation debate regarding the veracity of legends presented" (2008, 139). This debate is dual-layered, encompassing the ostensive artifact itself as well as the belief represented by that artifact. In this sense, *Marble Hornets* and the Slender Man video games (as well as the interactions surrounding them) could be considered forms of ostension (Tolbert 2013; see also chapters 2 and 3). Similarly, it is not difficult to extend these ideas to YouTube videos or to photos shared on Reddit in order to see how the digital mediation of various forms of ostensive action hails other users to participate in (and extend) the ostensive experience.

A video titled "Scariest Real Slender Man Attack Caught on Tape Disturbing NSFW!"[12] posted by user The Slender Man provides a typical example not only of this genre of video but also of the collaborative dynamics of digital ostensive practice. The video begins with a simple title card that serves as a warning; white text on a black background informs the viewer that "the more you know about him, the closer he gets." After five full seconds of silence, the video begins with a close-up of a young woman's hands nervously crumpling and tearing a tissue. Her face is never seen, perpetually out of frame. The room is dimly lit, but a beam of natural light falls on her hands. Between sobs, she informs the viewer that her son died several months ago, and that it was only recently that she was able to overcome her depression and sort through his belongings. She made this video, she tells the viewer, because she needs help:

> I took his phone out and . . . and, I was looking through his phone and I don't know what this thing is and . . . and, I don't know where to turn, and so I'm making this video so that maybe somebody will see the images and help me and let me know maybe what you think this is.

The video then cuts to a photograph of a young man with curly hair and a bad teenage mustache. He is standing in a brightly lit yard. After a few moments, the image zooms in on a shadowy figure lurking near the rear of the yard. Several minutes of phone-shot footage follow, documenting the Slender Man consistently lurking on the periphery of this young man's life over a period of years. The final entry is a video from the night of his death. The young man sits in the dark, addled and paranoid. He sees something that we do not. As he collapses and convulses, the video goes dark. Another title card appears, pleading with the viewer, "Please check your photos and videos for sightings of the slender man," followed by a final card, "This is a warning" (The Slender Man 2013).

The video demonstrates collaboration in both senses of the term. In the past-oriented sense, many elements of this video are constructed to demonstrate a working knowledge of how existing ostensive practices surrounding the Slender Man are typically represented. Like *Marble Hornets*, it uses white-on-black title cards to provide context and mask transitions. It employs a handheld, shaky-camera aesthetic that gives the footage a sense of first-person presence. As in many other Slender Man stories and videos, the character causes the individual it is stalking to be saddled with nightmares and paranoia.[13] Through choices like these—both stylistic and referential—this user demonstrates an awareness of a visible constellation of prior ostensive artifacts. This awareness is the heart of the collaborative nature of ostensive practice; it structures how users engage in their own acts of ostension, how they document them, where they share them online, and how those shared artifacts feed back into the larger body of ostensive practice. As a result, through this demonstration of vernacular knowledge, this video is asserting what this user feels makes for a good ostensive artifact that is worthy of sharing on social media.

In the future-facing sense, this video overtly hails further interaction from other users. It begins with a sincere call for help, a mother who is distraught over the loss of her son and wants answers. It also serves as a warning—promoting awareness of the Slender Man while, at the same time, encouraging other users to check their own photos and videos for the Slender Man. The implication here is that this user is encouraging others to engage in similar acts of ostension, documentation, and digital sharing.

Several users responded to the video by sharing their own experiences and trying to interactively extend the ostensive frame. For example, when user Shadow Flame commented, "Guys this is real!! I looked at my photos and

I saw him! Please believe me!!!" several other users replied with skepticism, asking to see the photos. Shadow Flame then offered to show the photos if anyone wanted to chat on an app and proceeded to explain how she saw the Slender Man after school on the playground.[14] While some users called Shadow Flame out as a fake, many others began to engage with her, saying they believed her and offering possible solutions, such as a Bible or Ouija board. While other users began to share their own similar stories, Shadow Flame stopped posting. Roughly a month later, user That Handsome Dude commented on what seemed like an eerily appropriate conclusion to the discussion: "omg what happened to him? is this real or troll? im so worried about him cause after he said that i shall kill myself . . . Im very worried."

This comment thread—which was several dozen posts long—demonstrates how a single mediated ostensive action can hail subsequent engagement with ostensive practice. Shadow Flame took the invitation for collaboration provided by the video and used it to share her own story of ostensive action. She got other users to believe her story of being stalked by the Slender Man, but more than that, she got others to engage in her story with her, interpolating them into her ongoing act of ostension by asking them for help and discussing possible solutions. This then hailed other users to share their own similar stories, just as the video had gotten Shadow Flame to share hers. In this rippling set of interactions, we can see how these ostensive actions are situated as moments in a much larger stream of digital practice.

But these collaborative affordances go beyond the ability for users to post content and comments; several design choices built into the website itself also support seeing ostension less as an isolated act and more as a piece of a larger practice. For example, YouTube is invested in keeping users viewing the site. This means that the more effectively it can suggest content a user might be interested in, the more likely it will retain eyeballs for more advertising revenue. As a result, the institution incentivizes exposing users to related content. When a video ends, a list of related videos is displayed. After a few seconds another related video plays automatically. A user's sidebar quickly fills up with recommendations based on their viewing history. As discussed in chapter 2, all of these small choices add up to hybridized form of social/algorithmic curation, wherein new users may find themselves exposed to a vast network of existing variants after only a few clicks (Kaplan 2013, 133–34). So what we find here is that the collaborative dynamics that underlie the transition from ostensive action to ostensive practice exist at multiple levels of this process—artifact, discussion, website. The issue then becomes how those dynamics might extend *beyond* those boundaries and continue to affect ostensive actions even in primarily offline contexts.

To observe offline expressions of Slender Man ostension, on November 1, 2014, I attended a massive public Halloween celebration in Madison, Wisconsin. Known as "Freakfest," the event attracts tens of thousands of college-aged individuals into the State Street area of the city, encompassing a half-dozen city blocks between the University of Wisconsin and the State Capitol. I was surprised by how many appearances of the Slender Man I was able to record (see figure 5).

While walking near the Langdon Street neighborhood,[15] I passed a college-aged couple on their way to a party. The young man wore a black business suit with a red tie; white gloves hid his hands and a white mask covered and obscured the features of his face (see figure 6 [*left*]). He was flattered when I stopped to ask him if he was the Slender Man. In briefly talking to the couple, it became apparent that he had donned the costume because the young woman he was with had shown him several examples of the Slender Man legend, including *Marble Hornets*, *Slender: The Arrival*, and various costumes other users had shared. They were well versed in many of these specific variants. Putting together the costume was easy, they assured me, and just involved combining a mask and gloves with an existing suit and tie combo. The couple reveled in being recognized and photographed, and they told me that few people had been able to identify the Slender Man costume. Despite this, the costume had been freaking out several of the other pedestrians they had encountered, even those unfamiliar with the legend cycle. Although they were not actively documenting the occasion, they hoped the costume would be picked up in the background of photos and videos taken by others. As they left, the young man reached in his suit and pulled out a folded scrap of paper, one of many in his breast pocket. They suggested I was neither the first nor last to receive such a gift that evening. This crumpled note serves as a memento of our encounter (see figure 6 [*right*]).

Figure 5. Slender Man costumes from Halloween weekend 2014, Madison, Wisconsin. Photographs by Andrew Peck, Nicky Kurtzweil, and Emily Sauter.

Figure 6. Meeting the Slender Man on Langdon Street in Madison, Wisconsin (*left*), and a memento from the encounter on Halloween 2014 (*right*). This note is a close imitation of one of the notes in the Slender Man video games. Photographs by Emily Sauter.

From our short interview, it became evident that this couple saw themselves as engaging with a larger networked practice beyond their immediate surroundings. Digital communication enables practices to emerge from users who are more keenly aware of their permutations. These variants are not just the realm of rumor or word-of-mouth, they can be directly seen and interacted with. As a result, new ostensive actions emerge in more direct conversation with the myriad variants that preceded them, as exemplified by the litany of Slender Man artifacts this couple acknowledged as their inspiration. This suggests that even a singular ostensive act in the digital age has many collaborative facets influenced by the existence of a large ostensive practice. This young couple, for instance, not only collaborated with each other and all the existing variants they had both viewed but also hailed others in their immediate vicinity to engage in the ostensive act—via lurking, jump scares, dropping notes, or even their very presence. They also hoped the ostensive act would be captured on film and recirculated by others, feeding back into the pool of digital variants that had influenced them. Hence, at every level of this process, this couple was co-creating an ostensive experience in dialog with the constellation of existing online documents that inspired them. This suggests a blurred boundary between online and offline ostension—they are not discrete and instead exist in a continuous, mutually constitutive feedback loop wherein one is always considering the other.

Because of this increase in user awareness and shift in collaborative potential, users are also more enabled to engage in the vernacular critique of ostensive practices. As a practice expands to encompass more individuals, those individuals begin to form competing notions about the practice. Although generic conventions may formalize fairly quickly, many users still hold different views as to the most effective way to perform an ostensive act. In contrast to the Halloween example mentioned above, one of my respondents—Ethan, a male in his mid-twenties and frequent viewer of the Slender Man on Reddit, Imgur, and YouTube—had a different take on creating an effective Slender Man costume:

> ETHAN: I've seen plenty of Slender Man costumes online. The best one I ever saw, the guy wore sheet-rocking stilts so he was actually like 10 feet tall. Then he did the blanked out face, and held onto some poles with hands on the end, and I think he had the tendrils coming off of him as well. And he extended the arms and legs on a suit to cover everything.
>
> ANDREW PECK: That sounds pretty elaborate.
>
> E: Well, if you don't go all out, it's a pretty vague costume.
>
> AP: Just a person in a suit and mask?
>
> E: Pretty much. (Jensen 2014)

This exchange elucidates a tricky tension brought about by the visibility of ostensive practice in the digital age. On one hand, this visibility hails more individuals to view and participate in ostensive practices, but on the other, users can casually sort through so many variations that they begin to create hierarchies of performance. In Ethan's view—based on, as he admits, the many variants he has seen online—a Slender Man costume is something anyone can do because the barrier to entry is so low. Doing it well, then, requires more than mere reference, it requires showing commitment and knowledge of the fine details of the character.

E: Depends on how well they are playing the part. If they are drinking and laughing and partying and stuff, then I would actually think it's kind of a lame costume. But if they are really into it, I'd probably feel compelled to talk to them, just to be sure.

AP: How would one "play the part" well?

E: Keep quiet, stay to the back if you are with a group, while alone keep to the shadows. Watch others.

Many of the qualities that my respondents suggested made for a good Slender Man costume—lurking, sneaking into photos, being homemade, and crafting an otherworldly appearance—were elements that made for a more convincing pseudo-ostensive experience. Although individuals differed in their exact preferences, everyone I spoke with had a clear opinion on the matter with only minimal hesitation. The fact motifs exist and users have different expectations is unsurprising. What is new here is that this critical element emerges naturally in vernacular discourse in a variety of web locations.

This vernacular negotiation and critique is evident in the two very different discussions that emerged surrounding a pair of Slender Man costume threads posted on Reddit in the fall of 2012. The first thread, which was received poorly, began with an image instructing other users on how to create the "best halloween costume!"[16] The instructional image was simple and meme-like. It used small stock photos arranged in a square and recycled language from a well-known credit card ad: "White morph suit—$35. Suit and tie $200. The look on people's faces when they see you in the woods at night—priceless." To make the intended reference clear, the final quadrant of the image contained a low-resolution screenshot from one of the Slender Man video games.

Amid collaborative suggestions by many users about how to engage in ostensive action while wearing such a costume, several users pushed back against the original post, suggesting this costume lacked effort and authenticity. User Bazofwaz, for example, balked at the terrible quality of the costume and suggested that the original poster should consider ways to add more authentic extras, like using stilts for long legs or adding tendrils made from cloth to "do it right." Many other users shared this sentiment, suggesting that the perceived ease of making a Slender Man costume (and the implied lack of effort) depreciated the character's value through overexposure and a lack of originality. As user Poseidon-SS noted, "If you go to a Halloween party with this, there will be at least five other people with the same costume" to which user Kinomi added "and none of them will be able to drink. DEFINITELY a well thought out costume." This exchange underlines that the frustration shared by many users was about not only the perceived lack of originality, but also—echoing Ethan's comments—a lack of commitment to the character. As Kinomi's comment reveals, the idea of the Slender Man having fun and drinking at a party lies in direct contrast to the expectations held for ostensive practice by many users—and such ostensive *in*action represents the waste of a costume and potential.

Another Slender Man costume discussion thread posted around the same time demonstrates how criticism may emerge differently if the engagement with ostensive practice is received positively.[17] In posting a thread to Reddit titled "I know you guys aren't digging Slender costumes, but I think my buddy was able to pull it off better than the rest," user The_Bhuda_Palm acknowledges the myriad of low-effort variants and rhetorically positions this thread as containing something different and worthwhile.[18] Unlike the "best halloween costume!" thread, this user's original post shares several pictures that document The_Bhuda_Palm's friend getting into an elaborate homemade Slender Man costume and wearing it while skulking around a dark suburb. The costume used stilts and wooden planks to provide the illusion of elongated, unnatural limbs. Many users expressed their appreciation for this play toward authenticity, with user Drewboy64 commenting that "the pants are a bit baggy, but finally, someone actually acknowledging the fact that the slenderman is supposed to be slender." Furthermore, the criticism in this post (regarding the baggy pant legs) provided a moment for collaboration, with many users offering suggestions to refine the costume to make it even more authentic:

> NO_EGRETS: They have to fit around his feet. Would have worked a little better if he'd managed to engineer the stilts so his feet were more vertical (a bit like high heels), to allow for slimmer pants.
>
> CORBZOR: Or engineer the stilts so the feet can look like knibby knees and have tighter pants the [*sic*] widen only at the knee and slim back down. Do the same at the wrists for knobby elbows, I think that would be more creepy if done right.

As shown by these comments (and others like them in the thread), even well-received instances of ostensive practice offer the space for vernacular critique. These critiques differ from those in the poorly regarded "best halloween costume!" thread by offering constructive feedback to help refine the costume. In such instances, a reciprocal relationship between collaboration and criticism emerges. In this well-received example of ostensive practice, the vernacular dynamics of collaboration and critique enabled by the affordances of the digital age constitute two parts of a singular whole—collaboration enables critique while critique facilitates collaboration.

The stakes for these exchanges are social clout, what many of my respondents called a type of internet prestige or nerd credibility, further underlining the shared nature of ostension in the digital age. As Rob, a twenty-seven-year-old male, put it:

> I think 'Internet prestige' is a good word for it. You know, it's something that you could, if you're looking for karma or points or whatever your current forum uses for currency, it would be a safe bet to create content based on the Slender Man if you were, you know, really good at it. And put something out there if it was kinda creepy and people would eat it up. (Finlayson 2014)

When pressed on why this might be the case, Rob suggested that the often-insular nature of web communities that engage in these ostensive practices exerted great force on the potential for engagement. As discussed in chapter 3, the Slender Man legend cycle relies on the paradox of simultaneously being known while also being niche. If it strides too far toward either direction, it loses appeal to users, becoming too overdone or too obscure. The dynamics of collaboration and critique enabled by the digital age work to both propagate and police widespread engagement. Hence by engaging in acts of collaboration and critique in the pursuit of asserting "nerd cred," these users are self-regulating their own ostensive practices.

Everyday Acts of Ostensive Practice

Nine-year-old Javier was on the third and final day of his search for the Slender Man. He had returned to his basement and assured his audience that if the Slender Man couldn't be found that day, then it must not be real. He passed a mirror and paused, sensing an opportunity. "This is your chance," he taunted, "say 'Bloody Mary' three times." When neither the creature nor the apparition appeared, however, Javier seemed to have found his answer. Heading back upstairs, he concluded that the Slender Man must be "a myth."[19]

Then he stopped.

"Daddy?" he called out, running back down the stairs, "What do you think? Is Slender Man real or not?"

Javier's father had no idea what he was talking about. Javier described the character in a burst of adjectives—tall, faceless, monstrous—to which his father bemusedly replied, "I don't know who that is."

"Oh well," Javier replied. As he walked away, he continued talking to no one in particular, "Bye guys! This is my final episode, and I'll see you guys later."

Production values notwithstanding, what Javier documented and shared in these videos is not so different from the grieving mother on YouTube, the young couple on the streets of Madison, or the costume-makers on Reddit. They are all acts of individual agency within a larger trajectory of ostensive practice. They express an awareness of structure (i.e., precedent, previous action, informal rules) as well as an anticipation of future interactions. Javier was recording on a hand-held camera and talking to his implied digital audience because that is what he has seen others do when practicing ostension. At the same time, his mediated actions reproduced that structure for others. Understanding Javier's ostensive actions as situated in a larger digital practice makes it clear that his choices stemmed from the connective affordances made available by digital networks and elucidates why Javier chose to not only document this experience but also share it with others.

As digital media are increasingly integrated into everyday life, everyday life becomes increasingly mediated. The affordances of digital networks mean that this media is preserved, offering a durable trace to other users who were not temporally or spatially present. In the case of ostension, this visibility serves as an inducement toward further acts of documentation and sharing while also creating an awareness of the connections between individual ostensive actions. The result is that these actions coalesce into visible bodies of practice and maintain an ongoing sense of collaboration. Therefore, ostensive practice is not just about sharing; it is about taking part in a *culture of sharing*—one that encourages ongoing interaction, discussion, documentation, commentary, critique, circulation, escalation, homage, and play—enabled by the affordances of networked digital communication.

My goal in this chapter has not been to advocate for a new subtype of ostension. To simply place "digital ostension" on a list alongside "quasi-ostension" and "pseudo-ostension" would miss the point of what I have argued here. Instead, I have been concerned with how digital networks extend ostensive actions in general, even when those actions are not themselves mediated. What I have observed here is a larger shift in both technology and social norms that has made ostension more visible, connected, and mundane—especially among children, adolescents, and young adults.

The appeal of the Slender Man to these younger audiences is unsurprising. Adolescents and preadolescents often engage in legend performances, acts of ostension, and other forms of macabre play (Ellis 2001a; Tucker 2005, 2014, 2020). Tucker, observing the proliferation of Slender Man prank videos posted by adolescents in 2012 and 2013, writes that "Kids who use YouTube are skilled at portraying Slender man's threatening behavior and discussing its meaning in the context of their everyday lives" (2018a, 153). These acts are appealing because they seem thrilling, subversive, or potentially dangerous (143–44). But far from an assault on youthful innocence, they serve as a way for young people to practice autonomy and navigate the liminal space they occupy between childhood and adulthood (Tucker 2008).

As I have shown in this chapter, the overwhelming majority of these youthful engagements with the Slender Man legend cycle were routine and harmless—a normal part of growing up. But as I explore in the next chapter, it was the mundane and widespread nature of these quotidian practices that made the events of May 31, 2014—and the international headlines they spawned—all the more shocking.

CHAPTER FIVE

Sensation

On the last day of May 2014, two twelve-year-old girls stabbed a friend and classmate nineteen times before leaving her to die alone in the woods of Waukesha, Wisconsin. Their victim crawled, half-alive, until she reached the edge of the forest. Lying in a drainage ditch, bleeding badly, and barely conscious, she was found by a passing cyclist and rushed to a nearby hospital. Of the nineteen stab wounds, two had penetrated major organs and one was less than a millimeter away from severing a major artery. Six hours in surgery was only the beginning of a long physical and emotional recovery, but Payton Leutner ultimately survived her encounter with two very real monsters lurking in the woods.

Her assailants—Morgan Geyser and Anissa Weier—were quickly apprehended by local authorities. Geyser had a knife in her backpack and both girls had blood on their clothes. When questioned about their actions, the girls claimed they committed the crime to win the favor of the Slender Man, who they had learned about online (Effron and Robinson 2014). They told investigators that the Slender Man lived in the woods of northern Wisconsin and presented an imminent danger to their families if they didn't go through with their homicidal plan. The pair explained that they had been in the process of running away when they were apprehended and that their intention had been to join the creature and live in its mansion, which they believed was located deep in the Nicolet National Forest (Gabler 2014).

Of all the gruesome details surrounding the stabbing in Waukesha, the involvement of the Slender Man resonated most in subsequent news coverage. While the legend had become popular online throughout 2012 and

2013—especially among early adolescents—it was still relatively unknown offline. The legend cycle's relative obscurity and decontextualized association with the events in Waukesha served to kindle a moral panic in the weeks and months that followed. Headlines and sound bites focused on the dangers of unsupervised tween media use and the corrupting allure of the dark corners of the internet. By the end of the summer, national news outlets had linked nearly a half-dozen cases of violence to the Slender Man. In Florida, a teen "obsessed" with the Slender Man set fire to her family's home (Mauney 2014). A man accused of killing two police officers in Las Vegas "often dressed up in costume as Slender Man," according to one of his neighbors (Murray 2014a). After her daughter donned a white mask and attacked her with a knife, a mother in Ohio attributed the violence to the influence of the Slender Man (Evans 2014).

During an interview with ABC News in the days following the Waukesha stabbing, I was asked about the Las Vegas case—if it was unusual that someone would be photographed dressing up as the Slender Man. I explained to the reporter that it was not unusual and merely represented a type of behavior that folklorists call ostension—enacting an aspect of a legend cycle in real-life (Manning 2018; see also chapter 4). She proceeded to ask me if attempted murders based on urban legends were common. I explained they were not (see Ellis 1996, 182; Grider 1984; Lindahl 2005, 181n2). Hoping to deter the burgeoning moral panic, I offered the reporter a few images from my archive that captured everyday people engaging in various forms of Slender Man legend performance, ranging from Halloween costumes to practical jokes. ABC News ran several pictures from my archive under the headline "Slender Man Now Linked to 3 Violent Acts" (Murray 2014a).

The Waukesha stabbing—and the ensuing news coverage it received—diverged significantly from how digital users had previously understood and performed the Slender Man legend cycle. Those who were familiar with the legend cycle reacted to this coverage with a mix of dissociation and disbelief. Yet fears of this new digital bogeyman continued to resonate across the country throughout the summer of 2014. This disparity between legend, incident, coverage, and reaction raises several questions about the relationship between news and legends in the digital age. For instance, why did the involvement of the Slender Man get amplified into the most important element of this story? How was the Slender Man legend distorted through these acts of amplification? In what ways did this amplification and distortion ultimately impact the legend cycle?

The answer to these questions lies in understanding the interrelationship between social filtering (chapters 1 and 2), algorithmic filtering (chapter 2), and media gatekeepers (chapters 2 and 3) on digital media. In this chapter, I argue that digital networks have enabled a complex social and technological system that has normalized the amplification of isolated events into seemingly pervasive issues. Through this process, communications that would have previously been one-offs, small-scale events, or local stories more frequently become framed as major news stories, common occurrences, or issues of public concern. Such events routinely get sensationalized and decontextualized as they are amplified, leading to distortion. This distortion encourages users to make assumptions about what is going on and fill in the contextual gaps themselves, turning amplified news back into rumor and positioning small-scale events as indicative of larger cultural trends. This amplification and distortion resulted in the Slender Man entering public consciousness as a synecdoche for wider worries about the intersection of youth behavior, legend performance, and digital media technologies.

To make this argument I begin by explaining how the widespread reaction to the Waukesha stabbing represented a rumor panic—a type of moral panic triggered by legends and ostension. I then suggest that digital networks challenge how we understand rumor panics because of digital media's capacity to amplify both legend and rumor. This amplification, I argue, emerges from a technological system where choices made by everyday users, algorithmic filters, and mass media gatekeepers continually reinforce each other. The resulting media ecosystem feeds, distorts, and sustains rumor panics, potentially turning localized trigger events into widespread, self-sustaining discourses. By analyzing the media coverage and social media interaction that emerged in the wake of the Waukesha stabbing, I not only demonstrate this process of amplification and distortion but also argue that this process encourages the emergence of rumor. These rumors feed back into news coverage as part of the amplification process, circuitously reinforcing and seemingly legitimizing that which is being amplified. Ultimately, I conclude that the reason the Slender Man became the central figure in this story was because of the same interpretative plasticity that had made the creature a popular resource for legend performance.

Rumor Panics and the Mass Media

What emerged in the wake of the Waukesha stabbing was a type of legend-inspired panic facilitated by both mass and digital media. A "panic" describes how certain events, persons, or ideas become constituted as deviant—often by the mass media—and are consequently framed as posing a larger, more generalized threat to societal values (Cohen 2011, xxxiii, 1). Expanding on Stanley Cohen's foundational work, Stuart Hall et al. argue that these moral panics emerge as the product of a system that relies on mass media's ongoing complicity with institutional agents:

> When the official reaction to a person, groups of persons, or series of events is *out of all proportion* to the actual threat offered, when "experts," in the form of police chiefs, the judiciary, politicians and editors *perceive* the threat in all but identical terms, and appear to talk "with one voice" of rates, diagnoses, prognosis and solutions, when the media representations universally stress "sudden and dramatic" increases (in numbers involved or events) and "novelty," above and beyond that which a sober, realistic appraisal could sustain, then we believe it is appropriate to speak of the beginnings of a *moral panic*. (1978, 16)

But while Cohen and Hall et al. focus on the role of institutions, there is often a folk culture element at play in this system as well, which serves to influence how these institutional agents understand the events that have transpired (Grider 1984; see also Best 1991). Persistent legend cycles, fragments, and rumors provide maps not only for action but also for interpretation and blame (Ellis 1989). This relationship tends to be cyclical, with the various parts of this system—institutional, mass media, and folk—reinforcing one another over time in mutually constitutive ways. The communicative capabilities of digital media technologies complicate this system even further by introducing new connective and algorithmic affordances into these relationships (Ingraham and Reeves 2016).

Previous scholarship has suggested that media coverage of the Waukesha stabbing sparked a moral panic that centered on the potential dangers of unsupervised internet use among young people (Chess and Newsom 2015; Koven 2018, 125; Maddox 2016, 244–45; Tolbert 2018b, 97). Of these scholars, it is Tolbert who specifically notes the centrality of legend and belief in facilitating this panic. He argues that this is a panic *about* belief—the widespread fear "that stories of this being could incite belief (and hence action) in the most vulnerable members of society, its children" (2018b, 97). In the half-decade since it originated on Something Awful, the legend cycle had cultivated a sense of traditionality as it persisted over time and spread across digital spaces. By 2014, a child who encountered Slender Man content online would almost certainly have been unsure of its specific origin. This problem would have been exacerbated by the conventions of legend performance, which blur the boundaries between real and unreal. On these points, I agree with Tolbert, but I do wish to suggest that the role of legend in this case goes beyond adult anxieties that children might blur reality and fiction.

My argument is that the association of legend with specific triggering events leads to rumor-based panics (Campion-Vincent 1989; Ellis 1990). While threatening books can be banned and inappropriate websites can be blocked, legends are more fragmented—they represent something closer to a pattern of behavior rather than a text (Ellis 2001a, 10; see also chapter 1). What is important here is not that the media or our respondents directly identify something as a legend (indeed, they rarely do); instead, it is how the quality of being legendary—diffuse, fragmented, behavioral, unsettled—encourages rumor as a social response to purported social threats. Media coverage of legend-inspired action presents itself as a factual account of events, but it is inherently incomplete because there is always an implied and nebulous "more out there" beyond what can be currently identified. This sense of conspicuous incompleteness leads to further acts of speculation and rumor as a way of dealing with the broader social trends hinted at by these actions and in these reports.

What I am suggesting here is that to fully understand the role of legend and belief in this case, we need to view what emerged in the wake of the Waukesha stabbing as a form of rumor panic that was aided and abetted by both mass and digital media (as rumor panics often are). A rumor panic is "a collective stress reaction in response to a belief in stories about immediately threatening circumstances" (Victor 1993, 59).[1] They tend to occur when circulating legends "build momentum and metamorphose into realities in the popular media," where they begin to serve as shorthands for larger political and social issues (Gunn 2005, 94). The result of this process is that rumor panics "are a primary means of moving contemporary mythologies out of the specialized conduits that generate them and into mass culture" (Ellis 2000, 204).

In the last half century, several high-profile rumor panics have emerged around topics like poisoned Halloween candy (Best 1993; Best and Horiuchi 1985; Grider 1984), Western fears of being kidnapped abroad (Drake 1989), organ theft (Campion-Vincent 1997, 2002, 2005), violent gang rituals (Burger 2009; Soltero 2016), and clandestine activity by satanic cults (Ellis 1989, 1990, 2000, 2001a; Gunn 2005; Victor 1989, 1993, 1998). In many of these instances, diffuse and persistent social anxieties coalesced into panics following some triggering event that dramatized existing unrest, created a sense of urgency, and encouraged a collective response (Campion-Vincent 1989; Ellis 1990, 2002a; Victor 1990). The purported role of legends in such events (and the interpretive plasticity that they provide) makes them highly appealing to journalists and other members of the mass media (Victor 1993, 21–23; see also chapter 3). The subsequent media coverage those events received invariably served to connect and structure existing rumors (even if only tangentially related) while also spreading and seemingly validating them.

Compared to legends, rumors tend to be shorter, nonnarrative expressions of belief (Turner 1994, 5). While rumor and legend are not completely synonymous, the age of mass media has narrowed the gap between rumor and legend, which tend to differ "only in the degree of completeness" (Dégh 2001, 127–28). The distinction between legend and rumor is further blurred because the two often reinforce each other (Drake 1989, 275; Fine 1992, 2–3; Fine and Ellis 2010, 4–5; Turner 1994, 3–5).[2] Some rumors may solidify into legends; conversely, legends may birth new rumors or give name and coherence to existing ones (Mullen 1972, 97–98). So, while a rumor panic is not *necessarily* legend-inspired or mass-mediated, the involvement of both is frequently the case (Victor 1998, 543). Therefore, rumor panics should be regarded as deeply contingent upon both contemporary legends and media.

While murders linked to contemporary legends are exceedingly rare, the Waukesha stabbing has several odd similarities to a legend-inspired crime from forty years prior, which gives us a starting point to understand how rumor panics emerge in concert with the circulating legends and prevailing media of the day. In 1974, Ronald Clark O'Bryan murdered his eight-year-old son with a piece of poisoned Halloween candy. Like the Waukesha stabbing, this case built on an existing legend cycle, and the technology of the time amplified it into national news (Grider 1984; see also Dégh and Vázsonyi 1983).

Writing about the O'Bryan case, Sylvia Ann Grider traces legends of tainted, tampered, and poisoned Halloween candy back to at least the 1940s and uses the phrase "Razor Blades in the Apples Syndrome" to refer to this diffuse collection of annual warnings aimed at children and their parents (1984, 133). These warnings routinely come not only from oral tradition but also from the media, experts, and local authorities, all of whom are influenced by those traditions (133).[3] However, despite the persistence of these legends, there are effectively no recorded cases of anonymous sadists widely distributing dangerous candy to neighborhood children (Best and Horiuchi 1985, 490–91). And yet, "every day immediately after Halloween the press reports unconfirmed cases of children who have received contaminated treats. These reports, in turn, pass quickly into oral tradition and thus reinforce the syndrome" (Grider 1984, 133).

In deciding to poison his own son, Ronald Clark O'Bryan was inspired by these legends, which he then used as a smokescreen to deflect blame from himself and onto the machinations of an anonymous sadist living somewhere in his neighborhood (135). O'Bryan initially cooperated with the police investigation until it became apparent that he had recently taken out sizable life insurance policies on his children. Following this discovery, O'Bryan was arrested and subsequently charged with his son's murder.

The story was picked up by news wire services and immediately became a national news item. Coverage of the O'Bryan case maintained a sort of circular logic: "The folklore component of this syndrome was never recognised by either the media or the law enforcement agencies; rather, the media took all previous reports of tainted treats and warnings as empirical truth and therefore linked all that had gone before with the O'Bryan murder. The legend was validated by the murder" (136). Like the Waukesha stabbing, the concept of legend remained mostly absent from this media coverage; yet, in its wake, the legendary nature of the syndrome produced and validated worries that this could happen anywhere.

Following this mass media coverage, dubious rumors of copycat crimes started to emerge. These copycat crimes were allegedly perpetrated by anonymous sadists and adhered much more closely to the legend cycle than to the facts of the O'Bryan case (136). Mass media coverage of the O'Bryan murder served as a lightning rod for these further acts of interpretation and (alleged) imitation because "rumors tend to build on each other. Once a plausible start is made, it is supported through a variety of other material. Reports about other matters thought to be relevant are often treated as though they constituted evidence in support of the developing interpretation" (Shibutani 1966, 68–69). So, even though the veracity of these copycat incidents was highly suspect, the news coverage they received served to further validate both the legend and its newsworthiness in a cyclical fashion. This synthesis between oral tradition and mass media framing demonstrates how rumor panics can become self-fulfilling and self-sustaining, presenting interpretative frames through which new events are filtered, connected, and ostensibly legitimated (Cohen 2011, 199–200).

Both the O'Bryan case and the Waukesha stabbing were inspired by legends and drew media coverage that tied them back to those legends—despite both crimes differing significantly from the legends that inspired them. While media coverage of the O'Bryan case connected and legitimated a bevy of diffuse rumors about Halloween, coverage of the Waukesha stabbing did the same for widespread anxieties about the corruptive dangers of new technology (Koven 2018, 123). Societal anxieties about new technologies serving as a corrupting influence on young people go back millennia and tend to recur whenever a new technology becomes widely adopted (boyd 2014, 14; Marwick 2008).[4] Like contemporary legends of poisoned Halloween candy, worries about technology use among young people remain omnipresent yet diffuse until specific events name them, connect them, and give them a sense of urgency.

While national rumor panics over poisoned Halloween candy or satanic cults were remarkable anomalies facilitated by the mass media, the internet more readily allows small-scale events to receive national or global attention, which normalizes rumor panics. Tucker has noted the increasing frequency of digital rumors and ostensive behaviors related to viral challenges in recent years and argued that their amalgamation "helps us realize how much impact rumors and legends can have through rapid dissemination online" (2020, 221). The interplay between mass media and social media can easily create legend cascades from local happenings by amplifying ideas as they bounce between domains (Laudun 2020). Fully understanding this shift requires recognizing how the affordances of digital media restructure both social and mass media practices, thereby facilitating the amplification of legend and rumor.

Rumor Panics and Digital Networks

Digital networks have an unprecedented capacity to amplify and distort rumors and, in doing so, spread and legitimate them. While Cohen focuses on the role of mass media in creating amplification spirals, rumor panic scholarship has tended to focus more on how informal communication practices amplify rumors into matters of local concern. However, the affordances of digital media make these spheres of activity less discrete while also mediating visibility and structuring interaction in new ways (Ingraham and Reeves 2016, 456). The result of this shift is that networked amplification occurs through ongoing interaction between three interrelated factors: (1) the communication habits of everyday users, (2) the choices made by algorithmic filters, and (3) the coverage and framing decisions made by mass media gatekeepers. These factors continually reinforce each other, potentially amplifying both rumor and panic through a reciprocal feedback loop. Demonstrating this interrelationship reveals not only why the Slender Man became a national fixation in the wake of the Waukesha stabbing but also how our contemporary media ecosystem feeds and sustains rumor panics.

Amplified rumors exist on a continuum. They may or may not have a basis in fact,[5] and they demonstrate varying levels of decontextualization, assumption, sensationalism, exaggeration, and hyperbole as they circulate across the network. The affordances of digital media may make vernacular expression more visible, but they aren't necessarily better at conveying deeper cultural context or meanings to an outside observer (Peck 2015a). As information circulates across networks, it finds new, unintentional audiences made up of users who are unfamiliar with the creator's intention or individual circumstances. Because rumor often functions as a discursive process of meaning-making that emerges in the absence of definitive answers, this process frequently results in users adding new framings or context to content as it spreads, often positioning it as indicative of larger, well-known cultural trends (Fine and Ellis 2010; Shibutani 1966). The result is that amplification often functions like a game of telephone, leading to varying degrees of distortion (via decontextualization or sensationalism) as content circulates between users and across media domains (Cohen 2011, 26–34).

As discussed in chapter 2, algorithmic filters increasingly intercede in this circulation process, giving structure to our everyday interactions online. These algorithms are a necessary response to an overabundance of information, effectively sorting through hundreds of posts or millions of search results in seconds, and their curatorial role is most crucial when content is either rapidly changing or unimaginably vast, such as on content-aggregation sites, search engines, or social media. However, algorithmic filtering becomes problematic when the algorithms are coded to privilege commercial incentives over ethical and accurate representation (Noble 2018; Pariser 2012). While social networks like Facebook claim their algorithms are coded to provide users with convenience and connection,[6] it would be more realistic to say that they are meant to increase user engagement for the purpose of generating ad revenue and financially valuable user data. These commercial concerns exert institutional influence on users' communications by determining what content gets seen and what gets filtered out, which then guides and delimits the possibilities for social interaction. Consequently, algorithmic filters have tremendous potential to affect visibility (Noble 2018), foster belief through repetition (Pennycook, Cannon, and Rand 2018), create ideological echo chambers or hyperfragmented publics (McNeill 2018, 498; Pariser 2012), and change how users perceive both their section of the network as well as the overall network.

The framing power of algorithmic filtering affects not only user-to-user relationships but also how professional journalists and networked gatekeepers observe, interpret, and use the network. On one hand, this means that digital communication's agenda-setting effect is fundamentally mediated by a synthesis of social and algorithmic filtering (see chapter 2). News increasingly takes cues from content that is trending on social media, and these algorithms can affect how journalists come to understand an emergent rumor or trend. So, while it may be true that a hashtag is trending, or that some people disagree about an issue, or that warnings are circulating about a dangerous new viral video challenge, these metrics can be easily gamed and fail to tell the whole story. The hashtag may be trending because several users have taken it up ironically, the controversy may be the result of a few users with extremist opinions gaining disproportionate attention, and the warnings may be based on a video that never actually existed. In this way, coverage of digital trends often fails to account for the exact scope or cultural context of the rumors or controversies being covered. But the tacit implication of this "someone did something" reporting is that when a phenomenon gets attention from a news outlet, it is precisely because it is widespread and, accordingly, newsworthy. Therefore, receiving coverage from a mass media gatekeeper serves to both legitimate and spread small-scale discourse, potentially turning niche sets of networked communication into mainstream issues (Turner 2018, 424).

On the other hand, content produced by commercial news media organizations is also subject to algorithmic filtering, which pressures journalists to adjust and frame their coverage in ways designed to promote user sharing and engagement (Noble 2018, 154). As discussed in chapter 3, engaging with vernacular expression can be highly appealing to commercial media organizations as a way of facilitating a sense of connection and hailing interactivity. The effects of this can be seen in the bevy of digital tabloids, content aggregators, and interest-oriented blogs that routinely jump on emergent trends and rumors in the hope of going viral themselves (Wallsten 2010). The content they publish encourages further user action (whether tacitly or overtly), which often takes the form of liking, commenting, or sharing—subsequently creating more signals that tell the algorithms that the content is potentially relevant to other users (see chapter 2). These pressures create a rush to report, even among reputable news organizations, which further increases the risk of sensationalism, exaggeration, and decontextualization (Ellis 2018, 401; Lowthorp 2018, 489). To adapt an old adage of journalism to the present case: "If it bleeds, it news feeds."

The pressure exerted by these filters is significant because even in an age increasingly defined by the centrality of social media, news coverage from mass media sources still has a lot of power to frame stories and define salient issues for a wide audience (Hindman 2009; Nelson and Taneja 2018; Pennington and Birthisel 2016). The web may facilitate the spread of rumors, but networked social processes alone are insufficient to amplify them into mainstream issues; instead, this process requires garnering the attention of partisan elites, established news organizations, or other commercial mass media gatekeepers (Rojecki and Meraz 2016, 37–39). However, when these gatekeepers cover or acknowledge the existence of rumors, they often become active agents in the rumor-circulation process (Mullen 1972, 101). When a rumor appears in writing or is conveyed by an official or trusted source it creates an air of credibility beyond that which exists in purely oral communication (Renard 1991).[7] This coverage frequently becomes a self-fulfilling prophecy, where reports of emerging trends, incidents, or controversies actually serve to propagate the rumors that are being reported on (Best and Bogle 2014).

Even if coverage does take steps to provide extensive context or analysis, it might not make a significant difference to the ensuing vernacular discourse. The act of reading news functions not only as a way to obtain information but also as a way of reinforcing an individual's preexisting worldview (Carey 1989, 18–21; Renard 1991, 16; see also Zelizer 2010, 17–18). Engagement with news on social media is often superficial and performative, and users do not often engage with a news story beyond its headline before forming an opinion or deciding to share it. A 2014 survey conducted by the American Press Institute, for instance, suggested that only four in ten Americans read news beyond the headlines in any given week. Research by Maksym Gabielkov et al. about the circulation of news on Twitter came to a similar conclusion, offering that "59% of the shared URLs are never clicked" (2016, 185). It is no surprise then that headlines often become the basis for rumors, serving as the "kernels for implied stories" (McNeill 2018, 496). This reinforces the notion that any coverage—even the debunking or analytical kind—may actually serve to spread misinformation and amplify rumors.

As the results of these choices made by algorithms and media gatekeepers feed back into the network, they again become subject to social processes and aggregate volition. Once a singular communication is released onto the network, it begins to become folkloric (McNeill 2018; Mould 2018b; see also chapter 1). In the absence of news that provides definitive context or analysis, users begin to engage in acts of conjecture—filling in the holes and gaps with acts of interpretation (Shibutani 1966, 62). This dialectical dynamic creates a feedback loop, where conspicuous incompleteness serves as an invitation for further engagement (Dégh 1971, 62; see also Fine 1992, 126). The internet is particularly well-suited to sustaining such forms of engagement and facilitates myriad spaces for the emergence of ongoing acts of vernacular discourse through which news may be translated back into the realm of rumor and legend (Ellis 2018; Kitta 2018a; McNeill 2018; Mould 2018a, 413). In short, once news is released back onto the network, news sparks rumor and rumor becomes self-sustaining.

The framing choices made by gatekeepers and algorithms never truly recede as information moves back into nonprofessional social contexts on the network (Frank 2015, 317; McNeill 2018, 496); instead, all three elements (social processes, algorithmic filtering, and media gatekeepers) continue to exert force on each other, forming a mutually constitutive, reciprocal feedback loop that continues to amplify rumor in perceived scope and importance.

But even when amplified, the widespread circulation of a rumor doesn't necessarily herald a panic; instead, a triggering event is required that reframes the legend as an imminent threat (Ellis 2001a, 202–4). The triggering event for a rumor panic is almost always a rumor or report of ostensive action—the allegation that a contemporary legend has caused somebody to do something dangerous. In writing about the Blue Whale Suicide Challenge, Tucker notes that a rumor panic started when English-language websites began reporting that playing an online game had led to over 130 deaths in Russia. Further coverage continued to amplify both the rumor and the panic, and several new incidents of teen suicide were linked to the game by grieving parents. But despite becoming a global rumor panic, no definitive proof linking the game to any of these suicides ever emerged (Tucker 2020, 212–14). Conversely, in the case of the Waukesha stabbing, these reports were direct and verifiable. They were based on real events that implicated an existing legend cycle and subsequently inspired further rumors about the imminent dangers of "dark and wicked things" lurking online. Yet, despite their contrasting origins, these two cases are more similar than different.

In both cases specific examples of ostensive action (whether rumored or real) were amplified by the affordances of digital networks. As each spread outward across the network, contextual gaps began to emerge as users who lacked direct experience learned about the phenomenon for the first time. These contextual gaps created uncertainty, which invited further rumor. Users came to understand these events in terms of their existing worldview, applying familiar narrative or journalistic frames to these incidents while also positioning them as representative of larger social or cultural anxieties. New events became seen through the lens of the rumor panic, retroactively validating it while also sustaining it with new content and connections. While those who were already familiar with digital culture or online legend cycles were dismissive, for many others the result was a self-reinforcing feedback loop through which the threat began to seem more widespread and imminent than it actually was. Significant amplification encourages widespread belief, which begins masquerading as truth and becomes incredibly hard to dislodge from the communal consciousness.

Understanding digital media's capacity for amplification and distortion illuminates both how and why seemingly odd folk behaviors get translated into major trends and panics. We can see a similar pattern in the Momo Challenge, involving a disquieting creature named Momo that allegedly appeared on apps and in YouTube videos, where it induced children to kill themselves. Momo never actually existed—it was a hoax—but that didn't stop this rumor panic from emerging in 2018 nor resurging in 2019 (Lorenz 2019; Radford 2019). Similarly, rumors of young people eating Tide Laundry Detergent Pods were perpetuated by news stations, social media users, and trending algorithms for several weeks in 2018, despite apparently snowballing from a joke taken out of context (Sleight-Price, Ahlstone, and Jones 2018). We might say the same about the abundance of creepy clown sightings that allegedly occurred across the United States in 2016 or about the widespread warnings of THC-laced edibles being given out as Halloween candy in 2019[8]—that regardless of their specific triggering events, each became amplified into a far-reaching rumor panic as a result of this interrelated media ecosystem (Laudun 2020; Peck 2020b).

So far, I have argued that contemporary rumor panics can easily be amplified into matters of national concern through a synthesis of social filtering, algorithmic filtering, and the actions of media gatekeepers. As content becomes amplified, it also begins to suffer from decontextualization and distortion, which creates a sense of conspicuous incompleteness that encourages rumor as a social response. In the sections that follow, I return to the Waukesha stabbing and examine the rumor panic that emerged in its wake. While it might seem absurd that anyone could believe the reports and rumors that warned of the dangers of a verifiably fictional cryptid, we should be careful to "resist assuming that the moral was the same for everyone at the same time" (Ellis 1990, 48).

The Waukesha Stabbing

Morgan Geyser and Anissa Weier planned to kill Payton Leutner for nearly six months.[9] Leutner had befriended Geyser two years earlier, when they were in the fourth grade, after seeing that Geyser didn't have any friends of her own. Weier was a newer addition to the group. She had moved schools that year and found a kindred spirit in Geyser. In an interview with *20/20*, Leutner recalled that she was never really friends with Weier and that Weier was often cruel to her. Leutner attributed this cruelty to Weier's jealousy over having to share Geyser with another friend. Yet despite her cruelty, Weier recalled that it was Geyser who originally suggested murdering Leutner.

During her interview with Waukesha police, Weier couldn't remember exactly when Geyser first suggested murder, placing it around December 2013 or January 2014. Over time, the pair developed code words, shared in whispers, to refer to the attack—*cracker* meant "knife" or "killing" and *camping trip* referred to the forest they would flee to after the murder. By February 2014, Geyser and Weier had a plan: they would invite Leutner to a sleepover on May 30, 2014, for Geyser's birthday and murder her while she slept. All three girls were in the sixth grade.

On the night of May 30, the trio went skating at a local roller rink and returned to Geyser's house for the sleepover. The plan had been for Geyser and Weier to wake up in secret at 2 a.m., cover Leutner's mouth with duct tape, and slit her throat while she slept. They would then cover the body to make it look as if Leutner was sleeping and flee to the woods of northern Wisconsin. However, the skating excursion had exhausted both girls, who decided to temporarily call off the plan. Of this limited reprieve, Geyser would later state, "I wanted to give [her] one more day."

All three girls awoke before 6 a.m. the next morning—Saturday, May 31, 2014. While Leutner played dress-up in the bathroom, Geyser and Weier continued to whisper. "'We're going to do it today at the park,' that's what Morgan said,'" Weier recalled during her police interview. Leutner also remembered that going to the park was Geyser's idea, adding that Geyser normally wasn't allowed to go to the park without a parental chaperone; however, since it was her birthday, Geyser's mother made an exception to this long-standing rule. As the trio walked to the park, Geyser lifted her coat to show Weier the knife with a five-inch blade she had surreptitiously tucked in her waistband.

The three girls arrived at David's Park not long after. Geyser and Weier had decided to ambush Leutner in the park bathroom, as they believed the drains would help hide any spilled blood while they made their escape. Entering a bathroom stall before Leutner, the pair passed the knife back and forth. Weier then hit Leutner, trying to knock her out by banging her head against a nearby concrete wall. It was their hope that Leutner would be easier to kill if she were unconscious. It's unclear how Leutner reacted to being struck, but after the initial hit the pair lost their nerve again. The three girls left the bathroom, moved through the park, and—at Weier's suggestion—began to walk toward a nearby wooded area.

Geyser and Weier again began to conspire. Weier pointed out the foliage to Geyser and told her, "We can take her in there and do the deed." The pair tricked Leutner into entering the woods by telling her they were going bird-watching. "People who trust you become very gullible," Geyser later bragged to her police interviewer, "And it was sort of sad." Leutner, for her part, was simply trying to appease her friends by going on a walk.

When they got deeper into the woods, Geyser and Weier suggested the trio play a game of hide-and-seek. Geyser told Weier and Leutner that they should go and hide. Weier then told Leutner to "hide" by lying on the ground and covering herself with leaves and sticks. When Leutner refused, Weier became violent. Weier later told investigators she pushed and sat on Leutner but ceased when Leutner began to yell, out of fear it might attract unwanted attention. Weier then returned the knife to Geyser, telling her, "You do it. Go ballistic." Geyser agreed but told Weier she'd only "go ballistic" on her command. Weier started to walk away and after about five feet told Geyser, "Now!"

Geyser tackled Leutner and began to stab her repeatedly. When investigators later asked Geyser if she knew how many times she stabbed Leutner, Geyser claimed not to know, saying, "All I heard was screaming."[10] Whether she knew it or not, Geyser stabbed Leutner nineteen times, and to this day, Leutner isn't sure what made Geyser stop.

The two girls stared blankly at their victim. Leutner tried to get up but told the others she couldn't see, walk, or breathe. Geyser and Weier encouraged her to lie back down so she would lose blood more slowly and assured her they were going to go get help. Geyser and Weier backed away and then fled, leaving Leutner alone. Weier later told investigators they had never intended to get help—they intended for Leutner to die by bleeding out in the woods.

Payton Leutner was badly injured, bleeding, and alone. Out of sheer determination, she got up and, clinging to trees for support, walked until she reached a patch of grass where she could lie down. Around 9:50 a.m., she was found by a passing bicyclist, who called 911. Leutner was rushed to the hospital. She had multiple stab wounds on her chest, abdomen, arms, and legs. Her blood pressure was dangerously low and one of the lacerations was a hair's breadth away from piercing a major artery. Had the wound been any deeper, Leutner would have likely bled out in less than two minutes. Before she entered surgery local police were able to confirm several key details of the incident with Leutner, including the involvement of Geyser and the presence of another girl.

Finding Geyser and Weier took less than six hours. They were apprehended around 2:30 that afternoon,[11] sitting on the side of the I-94 freeway on the north side of Waukesha. Stories of the missing—and later found—girls ran on local news stations. By the end of the day, the primary suspects in the Waukesha stabbing had been apprehended, providing what must have seemed like a semblance of closure for this tragic and horrifying ordeal. And this likely would have been the end of the story—save for localized trial reporting and community-based rumors—had it not been for an odd set of details that emerged during the girls' police interviews and went on to eclipse nearly everything I have written about the case thus far.

In the Wake of Waukesha

The rest of the weekend was relatively quiet—at least compared to what was coming. The incident had shaken the local community, but there was little coverage of the event outside of Milwaukee and its surrounding suburbs. Geyser and Weier's motivation was yet unknown, and the crime had none of the popular associations that it would garner in the coming days. This all began to change rapidly on the afternoon of Monday, June 2.

Around 1 p.m. local time, the Waukesha police held a press conference to discuss the incident. Police Chief Russell P. Jack briefed local journalists on the most recent details of the case: a twelve-year-old girl had been stabbed, she was currently in stable condition, and two suspects known to the victim were in police custody and would be charged later that afternoon. On these points, Jack offered concrete information, giving journalists exact dates, times, and locations. But when it came to the suspects' motivation, Jack was tantalizingly vague. "Both suspects had a fascination with a fictitious character that often posted to a website that is a collection of small stories about death and horror," Jack told local reporters. Jack ended his prepared remarks with a warning directed at parents:

> Keeping children safe is more challenging than in years past. The internet has changed the way we live. It is full of information and wonderful sites that teach and entertain. The internet can also be full of dark and wicked things. It is also providing an opportunity for potential child predators to reach children like never before.
>
> Unmonitored and unrestricted access to the internet by children is a growing and alarming problem.
>
> This should be a wake-up call for all parents. Parents are strongly encouraged to restrict and monitor their children's internet usage. We must also remember that "online" is much more than spending time on the computer. Now smart phones and even video games are completely connected to the outside world.
>
> Parents, please talk to your kids about the dangers that exist online.

While Tolbert has suggested that this statement "leaves no doubt as to the source of the problem" (2018b, 95), I would argue the opposite. As an institutional authority, Jack's remarks left a lot of conspicuous incompleteness. They were frustratingly ambiguous—never mentioning specific names but instead alluding to a widespread digital threat that was implied to be both imminent and systemic. The remarks were themselves a sort of rumor, a short expression of speculative belief in the power of "dark and wicked things" that lurked on the internet and ostensibly served as a corruptive force on young people who journeyed too far into the digital woods without supervision. The problem was what exactly these dangers *were* went undefined, which left ample space for acts of assumption and conjecture.

This sense of conspicuous incompleteness was evident from the follow-up questions asked by those in attendance once Jack had finished his prepared statement: What website? What character? Was it a fictional character? Was the website passive or was somebody actively manipulating young girls online? Jack declined to answer many of these questions—citing a need to protect the integrity of the investigation—and noted only that the character was fictional and existed on many websites "that are similar in nature." But in doing so, Jack inadvertently escalated the sense of risk and uncertainty surrounding the case, which led to the following frustrated exchange with a journalist:

JOURNALIST: Well, just, as a parent, I mean . . . can you mention [who this fictional character is]? Just, because we . . . I mean, you're trying to warn parents, but is it something that parents should be concerned about that "my kids are on this site and . . ."

JACK: No, again, it's not one specific site that this character accesses or communicates with children on. [. . .] I hesitate to put the one character out there because that's all parents will look for. [. . .] So I don't think it's beneficial for parents just to watch for "hey, this one specific character on this one specific website." No, it's more than that. We need to protect our children on all websites, twenty-four hours a day, seven days a week, every day of the year. (City of Waukesha Police Department 2014)

In responding to this journalist, Jack again suggested that this was a systemic problem that went beyond any individual character. Yet, at the same time, Jack also gave that character volition. *It* was accessing websites; *it* was communicating with children; *it* required constant vigilance; *it* was parental anxiety personified—and no one in the audience was allowed to know what *it* was. Whether intentionally or not, Jack had cultivated a gnawing sense of curiosity among the journalists present surrounding the possible motivation for this abhorrent incident. And despite his best intentions, parents being warned to avoid "this one specific character" was *exactly* where this was all headed.

At no point during this press conference did Jack mention the Slender Man by name, but when journalists balked at the lack of concrete information surrounding the girls' motivation, Jack directed them toward the criminal complaint, which was due to be filed in court that afternoon.[12] Although scholars like Tolbert (2018b) have suggested the press conference was responsible for the case's association with the Slender Man, it was actually the criminal complaint that contained the first direct association between the Slender Man and the Waukesha stabbing. So while the press conference may have piqued journalistic interest, it was the content of the criminal complaint that began to shift and expand coverage of the case.

The criminal complaint included not only the recommended charges against Geyser and Weier but also a summary of each girl's interview with detectives from the Waukesha police department. According to the complaint, Weier opened up about the attack and the girls' rationale almost immediately:

> Weier explained [that the Creepypasta wiki] was an internet site that talked about horror stories and nightmare stories. People can create and write their own stories and in these stories Weier learned about a man named Slenderman. Weier indicated that Slenderman is the leader of the Creepypasta. Slenderman is at the top of the triangle. Just below Slenderman is the killer and below the killer is the proxy. Weier stated in order to be a proxy you needed to kill a person. This would show your dedication to Slenderman. Weier stated that many people do not believe Slenderman is real and she stated she wanted to prove the skeptics wrong.

Geyser was more evasive. When asked about her actions, she told investigators that Weier told her they had to kill Leutner or "he" would kill their families.[13] When asked who "he" was, Geyser initially stated that she "did not know him." But when investigators proceeded to ask her about the Slender Man, Geyser's belief in the legend and motivation became obvious:

> Geyser stated that he watches her and he can read your mind and can teleport. Geyser told Detective Casey that Slenderman has tendrolls [*sic*] on him and that they are sharp. Geyser stated she sees him in her dreams. Geyser

> stated that she sees him when no one else does and that you start to get Slender sickness because of Slender radiation. Geyser stated he is not on the computer because he doesn't like technology. It does not work around him. (Complaint, State of Wisconsin v. Morgan E. Geyser and Anissa E. Weier 2014)

The details in these interviews mixed widely known aspects of the legend cycle (e.g., proxies, tendrils, technological interference) with dyadic variations that Geyser and Weier used to motivate and rationalize their actions. The ways Geyser and Weier described their personal relationships with the character were chilling and departed from how the vast majority of users understood the legend cycle. But the Waukesha police did not know that. Detective Michelle Trussoni, who interviewed Weier, later recalled that one of her reactions to the girl's story was simply "Who the heck is Slender Man?" (*20/20* 2019). Lacking this context, the criminal complaint (as well as Jack's press conference) reflected a sense of uncertainty about the scope and scale of the problem that these local police were dealing with.

The release of the criminal complaint had two related effects. First, it associated the crime with a specific, yet nebulous online legend cycle. Even if the term "legend" was never used by institutional authorities, the way the criminal report and press conference framed the Slender Man certainly made it seem legendary—diffuse, fragmented, unsettled, and, in this case, elusive to parents. Second, because of this emerging association between digital legend and youth violence, news of the Waukesha stabbing started to garner attention beyond Wisconsin.

The incident's association with the Slender Man increased the story's perceived newsworthiness (Koven 2018, 123). That afternoon local news media included information from the criminal complaint in their coverage of the stabbing. This information was presented with little annotation or additional context and simply reiterated many of the details found in the excerpts above (Gabler 2014).[14] Around 5 p.m.,[15] stories about the stabbing began to appear on news wire services as well as in a few national news outlets like *ABC News* and *USA Today*. By that evening, users on social media were starting to share both local and national coverage of the incident. As the night progressed more news organizations—as well as blogs and online entertainment sites—started to pick up the story.

The Slender Man became an increasingly central figure as these stories spiraled outward. The earliest reports by local sources on the afternoon of June 2 mentioned the creature as part of Geyser and Weier's stated rationale, but only did so several paragraphs into the story (*FOX 6* 2014; Gabler 2014). Conversely, while the Associated Press did not name the creature in its headlines, the lede[16] of its wire story[17] highlighted the role of an online "mythological creature" as the inspiration for this crime. Immediately following the nut graph,[18] the Associated Press's story named the Slender Man as the "mythological demon-like character" and conveyed its role in the case based on the information contained in the criminal complaint (Richmond 2014). Many nonnational news outlets that covered the story on the evening of June 2 used this report as the basis for their own coverage, frequently keeping this structure and focus. By 10 p.m. that night, online entertainment sites and blogs picked up the story and elevated the role of this "mythological creature" even further, running headlines like "Girls Claim *Slender Man* Is Real, Accused of Stabbing Friend 19 Times" (Plunkett 2014).

But despite increasingly playing up the role of the Slender Man, these early reports left a lot of unanswered and implied questions. By reiterating the information about the Slender Man that was contained in the criminal complaint—and without further attempts to explain the character—these news stories began to amplify the contextual gaps contained therein. They constituted the Slender Man as a mysterious and malevolent force by using words like "demonic" and "mythological" to describe the creature and, in doing so, implied a link to preexisting societal worries about the influence of Satanism and the occult on children (see Ellis 2000; Tolbert 2018b, 98–99). Readers were informed it was a digital phenomenon, but the exact extent and form of its digital existence remained ambiguous. The newsworthiness of the story—combined with the text of the criminal complaint and Police Chief Russell P. Jack's frequently repeated warning to parents—framed the Slender Man as an imminent and mysterious threat facing parents of young children.

User responses to these early reports generally fell into one of two categories based on whether the individual user believed this to be a systemic or nonsystemic problem. Many users—especially those who were already familiar with the legend cycle—saw this as a nonsystemic problem. Their responses conveyed a belief that this was an isolated incident that didn't accurately reflect the broader folk practice. These nonsystemic responses tended to deride early news reports for their lack of context, assumptions about the character, and insinuations that Slender Man legend performances represented a pervasive danger. Some of these users saw the story as an object of ridicule and suggested that taking the Slender Man seriously as a motive was as patently laughable as blaming Bloody Mary for the crime. Users who were previously unfamiliar with the legend cycle were more split between systemic and nonsystemic responses. The latter reacted by dismissing the implied scope of these warnings—claiming that this must actually be a mental health or parenting issue—while the former began to wonder what exactly this character was, what it did, and if they should be worried about their own children.

The problem is that what was said and the exact proportion of each type of response mattered less than the fact that people were talking about it. During the night of June 2 and into the early hours of June 3, users on social networks like Twitter and Facebook shared, commented on, and debated the significance of the story. Even if users were only doing so ironically, mass irony online quickly becomes indistinguishable from sincerity, at least as far as outside observers or algorithms are concerned. The result was not only that these users served as conduits (potentially exposing connected friends and followers in their network to the story) but also that their actions—when taken in aggregate—showed both news organizations and algorithmic filters that this content had a high level of user engagement.

By the morning of June 3, "Slender Man" was beginning to trend on search engines and social media, which created a positive feedback loop. A user signing on to Facebook that afternoon, for example, might have seen friends' posts talking about the story because the algorithm had deemed that content engaging or relevant and prioritized it in their newsfeed. Alternatively, that user may have learned about the story when they saw "Slender Man" appear as a trending topic in the site's sidebar.[19] While the exact form may differ based on digital location, this type of algorithmic content filtering isn't unique to Facebook. When something becomes identified as trending, digital networks begin to expose new potential audiences to it, many of whom wouldn't have seen the trend otherwise and lack preexisting knowledge related to it. This not only draws in new users but also encourages further engagement, often in the form of rumor and other acts of discursive meaning-making. The result is that the state of "trending" exposes the story to more users, which draws more user responses, which demonstrates increasing engagement, which continues to propagate (and seemingly validates) the trend (see chapter 2).

Locating agency in this process necessitates viewing it as the product of a technological system (see Winner 1986). While it might be tempting to write off this story's shift in focus on a singular factor—a police press conference, detective interviews, news wire stories, ironic sharing, sensationalist blogs, overly worried parents, and so on—none of these explanations adequately describe how the Slender Man became amplified into a national folk devil. Instead, we have to understand not only the aggregation of these factors but also that there was something going on here beyond aggregate volition. The fact that all these parts were working together to amplify the Slender Man's role in this case wasn't an accident; it was the logical end result of a digital technological infrastructure that hypercommercializes the attention economy. The result of this system was that the Slender Man's increasingly central role in this case was something "which everybody helped to create but which nobody would take responsibility for" (Grider 1984, 137–38). Over the next several days, the creature's continuing prominence would spark a bevy of localized rumors, which ultimately culminated in associations with subsequent acts of violence.

Distortion and Rumor

By the evening of June 3, stories about the Slender Man and its role in the Waukesha stabbing were seemingly everywhere. The Slender Man continued to trend upward online, becoming a top Google search in the United States and a major trending topic on social networks like Facebook and Twitter by the late afternoon. Cable news networks like CNN aired over a dozen segments on the stabbing throughout the day. Major broadcast networks like CBS and ABC covered the story on their morning news programs and nightly newscasts. The *Washington Post* carried the story, as did *Time* magazine. Local affiliates from Minneapolis to Las Vegas reported on the incident. In total, news coverage of the Waukesha stabbing more than quadrupled from the day before. But problematically, as the story became increasingly amplified, so did the focus on the Slender Man. The creature's purported role in the crime had become so amplified by the end of the day that many news outlets had begun to refer to the events in Waukesha as the "Slender Man stabbing" (e.g., Wallace 2014).[20]

Unlike the previous day's coverage—which relied heavily on mediating material obtained from the Waukesha police department—news coverage on June 3 began to try and explain the digital cryptid to unfamiliar audiences. News organizations ran articles with headlines like "What Is Slender Man? A Meme's Possible Role in Wisconsin Stabbing," "Slender Man Stabbings: Who Is Slender Man?," and "The Origins of Slender Man, the Meme That Allegedly Drove 12-Year-Olds to Kill" (CBC News 2014; Stampler 2014; Van Oot 2014). These stories promised to explain to readers what the Slender Man was as well as its connection to the Waukesha stabbing. At the same time, they also reaffirmed and furthered that connection. These headlines frequently ascribed agency to the creature, framing it as an active participant or central figure in the case (i.e., it played a "role" or "drove" others to act). While many reports did try to contextualize the character's origins or fictional nature, those explanations were inevitably presented in light of the events in Waukesha and often followed ledes and nut graphs that uncritically reproduced accounts of the character's association with the incident. More troublingly, explanations of the Slender Man phenomenon were often frustratingly fragmentary, and this conspicuous incompleteness only served to further spread the idea of the Slender Man's culpability as well as its potential dangers.

The difficulty many of these outlets faced was in trying to encapsulate a folk practice that had become both highly diffuse and variable in the five years since its creation. Several news outlets struggled to articulate what exactly the Slender Man was, which led to varying (and sometimes contradictory) acts of distortion. A *Daily Mail* reader, for example, would have learned of the Slender Man in the following nut graph:

> Morgan Geyser and Anissa Weier face attempted murder charges after attacking their friend, saying that they did so because they wanted to join the cult of the 'Slender Man' after reading about him online. (Zennie and Associated Press Reporter 2014)

Whereas a viewer of CNN's *New Day* would have instead heard that the girls "were acting out a horror story from a web site" and then learned from the program's law enforcement analyst that the key questions from the ongoing investigation were likely:

> How many other people, especially children, are out there looking at this web site? Have there been other murders committed, you know, elsewhere in the country based on people trying to make their bones with Slender Man. So is this an isolated incident or could there be more of these that we haven't heard of.
>
> You know, maybe somebody was killed and disappeared and people assumed it was a runaway child when it could have been someone murdered by a friend of all things, and hidden in the woods or thrown in water or some other way hidden. So that's part of the investigation I'm sure. (Cuomo et al. 2014)

These examples are far from exhaustive; instead, they are meant to illustrate the disparity between explanations of the Slender Man as coverage amplified on June 3. Reports variously referred to the Slender Man as a video game character, a horror media figure, a meme, a photoshop, a fictional character, a hoax, an urban legend, a myth, a demon, an online cult, or a work of creative fiction gone both viral and awry. Multiple characterizations frequently appeared in a single story, and the disparity between these descriptions created their own dialectic tension between known (what was reported) and unknown (what else was implied to be "out there"), which made the character seem even more threatening and legendary.

But even when reports tried to offer more context or in-depth explanation, they often still inadvertently propagated a sense of conspicuous incompleteness. Journalistic descriptions of the character's history tended to follow a three-step pattern. First, they relied heavily on the Slender Man's origins on Something Awful to explain the phenomenon, thereby eliding many of the moves in performance and audience that had occurred in the intervening years (see chapters 2, 3, and 4). These descriptions tended to draw from easily available sites of vernacular curation—databases like Know Your Meme, the Creepypasta Wiki, and Wikipedia—which journalists often deferred to in order to provide a definitive interpretation, origin, and synopsis of their subject (see chapter 2). This focus on origin treated the Slender Man as a media object—it was summarized in the same way one might summarize a movie, giving details based on a singular canonical text and often privileging Victor Surge's original images.

Second, outlets tended to note that the character then "went viral" or became "popular online" but with little elaboration as to why or how that occurred. While factually correct, these ambiguous phrases left a lot to the imagination of the individual reader, and a sense of conspicuous incompleteness began to emerge. These stories began by offering readers a knowable, defined origin point for the legend cycle before informing them that it had rapidly transgressed beyond those boundaries—akin to a monster escaping from a lab. The legend cycle was now something broader and more nebulous, which the word "viral" only gestured toward. Because of the difficulty of succinctly covering a widespread and variable digital folk practice, many journalists simply acknowledged that this had happened and moved on. This frequent equivocation left further interpretation up to acts of individual assumption while also keeping the exact nature of the creature (and the extent of the potential problem) firmly in the realm of legend dialectic (see chapter 1).

Finally, these reports generally ended by acknowledging the contemporary prevalence of the creature in various digital spaces. ABC News, for instance, informed readers, "The story has been morphed and retold on amateur fiction-writing sites, in YouTube videos and on message boards. There are dozens of Twitter accounts claiming to be Slender Man, and the so-called official (yet unverified) Slender Man account has about 89,200 followers" (Lupkin 2014). While such a statement could certainly be read as an attempt to normalize the trend, it could also feed the worries of those already primed to see danger. The article's headline, "Why Did 12-Year-Olds Stab Friend for Slender Man?," likely meant that many readers who were otherwise unfamiliar with the Slender Man fell into the latter category. In practice, these framing choices meant that many discussions of prevalence functioned more as tacit warnings rather than as context. Readers were often cautioned that the Slender Man took a variety of forms and was already lurking on several popular websites that children may have been accessing. The implications of these warnings are numerous, with readers effectively being told that the potential danger to their children is everywhere, they might not recognize it, and it may already be too late.

The difficulty of reporting on a diffuse digital folk practice is significant because the distortion that emerges through amplification creates ambiguity, which hails rumor. While mass media tend to do well at summarizing discrete media texts or events, the permeable boundaries and myriad locations of digital folklore often resist easy classification and holistic summary. When the exact extent, scope, form, or nature of a digital practice is left uncertain (or glossed over with ambiguous terms like "viral" or "controversy"), then contextual gaps begin to emerge. These gaps are conspicuous in their incompleteness—they imply further questions that remain unanswered and tacitly invite acts of conjecture to fill in those gaps. Therefore, a sense of conspicuous incompleteness encourages rumor because rumor is a social tactic for discursively making sense of that which is constituted as both pressing and unsettled. And by that evening, rumors inspired by this news coverage about the Slender Man had begun to take shape in a variety of digital communities.

Late in the day on June 3, a user on The Bump, a web forum for parents and expectant mothers, posted a news story from NBC and asked other users, "Has anyone seen this? 'slender man.'" The ensuing discussion thread revealed that several others had seen the story but were still unclear about what exactly the Slender Man was. "I did see this in the news this morning," one user wrote, "I am still not understanding 100% what 'slender man' is." The original poster responded with a similar sense of uncertainty, "Me either i even tried to look it up but only skimmed and still didn't understand." The implication is that these users were turning to others in their digital community in order to discursively work through the conspicuous incompleteness present in these news reports. This specific thread benefited from a user who was previously familiar with the legend cycle and offered a more straightforward explanation:

> Basically, a discussion board had some sort of challenge for people to invent a new horror-type urban legend. One of the entries came up with this character of the Slender Man and photoshopped it into some old pictures. Then other people thought this was a cool character idea and invented other scary stories to go with it. It's the same way people have collectively told tales for thousands of years, only now we can see all the origins and contributions online.

"So—basically like a modern day Bloody Mary?" one user wrote in response to this act of clarification. This analogy resonated with other users in the thread as well, many of whom admitted familiarity with the Bloody Mary legend from their early adolescence, and it was through this familiar lens that these users began to collaboratively interpret the extent and nature of the problem.[21] But not every thread had a resident expert or discovered an identifiable analog.

It seemed that a lot of parents—the targets of these mass mediated warnings—didn't really understand what the Slender Man was, even after reading news coverage or searching Google. In light of this uncertainty, parenting forums started to become hotbeds for rumor. One of the most striking rumors was that someone had posed as the Slender Man and lured these girls into undertaking their murderous plan. When one user asked about the stabbing in a different discussion thread on The Bump, another user responded, "Some girls tried to ki[ll] there [*sic*] 12 yo friend by stabbing her 19 times and leaving her for dead. They were into the horror movie/slender man trend and some creep on the internet may or may not have told them to do it." This user has obviously engaged with news coverage of the event (correctly identifying both the ages of the girls and the number of stab wounds) but ends her description with her belief that a malicious actor—who is still at large—may be the actual driving force behind the crime.[22] On a forum for Christian parents, a similar rumor began to take shape: "They were influenced by this slenderman guy," one user explained. "Children are often easily influenced, and the full punishment should hit that guy." When another user offered a corrective—explaining the Slender Man was fictional—this user retracted their statement while qualifying that "in one source it sounded like there was a guy using that name as a handle to influence them."[23]

The nature of these rumors differed between various digital communities, as did the rumors themselves. On a forum for parents living in the Washington, DC, area, for example, users suggested that the girls' school was to blame for providing students with iPads but not with adequate supervision. One user even suggested that news coverage of the incident was actively trying to suppress that information.[24] Rumors began to coalesce on The Bump about how much the girls' parents knew before the attack. These rumors started after the *Daily Mail* published a story about a Slender Man sketch drawn by Geyser that appeared on her father's Instagram feed two months prior, which some users felt implied guilt or dereliction on the part of the girls' parents.[25] Finally, rumors began to circulate more widely about the girls themselves and their potential mental health issues.

Of all the rumors that emerged in the wake of Waukesha, it was these rumors about the girls' mental health—which had little to do with the Slender Man—that would later be proven correct. Geyser had been suffering from early-onset schizophrenia, which ran in her family (Vielmetti and Kissinger 2015). Several mental health professionals diagnosed Weier with a shared delusional disorder, which was exacerbated by her close friendship with Geyser (Kuhagen 2021a). These diagnoses explain why the girls were so deeply affected by the legend in ways that other young people simply were not (see chapter 4). However, much of this information wouldn't come to light until months or years later—well after the events in Waukesha had become defined by the Slender Man. In the absence of these definitive answers, the diverse array of rumors persisted.[26]

My goal here is not to provide an exhaustive catalog of all the rumors that circulated in response to the amplification and distortion of the Slender Man legend cycle; instead, it is to suggest that this proliferation of rumor is a natural response to news coverage of that which is legendary. What ties nearly all of these disparate rumors together is that they were all a type of sense-making that emerged from a lack of definitive information as to the nature and extent of the presented problem. They represent ways in which users not only came to understand how a pair of twelve-year-old girls could do something so heinous but also negotiated the frequently implied (and often vague) notion that the Slender Man represented an ongoing, systemic threat to children. The girls must have been misled by an adult "guy" or "creep" online. Or iPads were the culprit because technology is inherently deceptive and dangerous for young minds. Or the crime was preventable and someone must have known but lacked the courage to speak up. These were communal attempts to discursively exert control, to bring the unsettled ambiguity surrounding the case back into the realm of the familiar and to make it comprehensible by retroactively suggesting that all of this was preventable "if only." These users were struggling with the idea of blame. In doing so, they were collaboratively interpreting mass media news coverage of the event and the legend in ways that were both encouraged by that coverage yet also unintended. The common thread among these rumors came from users struggling to make sense of a senseless crime, and these rumors were becoming so ubiquitous that it wasn't long before the rumors themselves started making headlines.

On Friday, June 6, the local NBC affiliate in Cincinnati reported that another attack linked to the Slender Man had occurred. This time, a thirteen-year-old girl had attacked her mother with a knife when she arrived home from work. According to the girl's mother, she did so while wearing a hoodie and a white mask (Evans 2014). Two days later, a white supremacist couple shot and killed two police officers in Las Vegas before fleeing to a nearby Walmart, killing a bystander, and then committing suicide (Gorman and Warren 2014). Based on interviews with the couple's neighbors, this attack was also linked to the Slender Man.

In both cases, the links between violence and the Slender Man were tenuous at best. Despite this, both stories went on to receive national news coverage, and their headlines alerted readers:

> "13-Year-Old Ohio Girl Stabs Mother in 2nd 'Slenderman' Attack" (Chasmar 2014)
>
> "Mom In Ohio Says Her 13-Year-Old Daughter Stabbed Her Multiple Times Because of Slender Man" (Broderick 2014)
>
> "Las Vegas Cop Killers Were 'White Supremacists' Who Liked to Dress as Slenderman and The Joker" (Li and Network Writers 2014)
>
> "Neighbor: Vegas Gunman Dressed Up as Slenderman, Joker" (CBS Las Vegas 2014)

But in the articles themselves, these links to the Slender Man were revealed to actually be based on acts of assumption and rumor that had emerged in the wake of the Waukesha stabbing.

In the Ohio case, for instance, the mother told journalists that the attack *could have been* motivated by the Slender Man because her daughter had referenced the Slender Man in some things she had written. But, as discussed in chapters 3 and 4, this wouldn't have necessarily been unusual for someone in that age group (see also Kitta 2018b; Tucker 2018a). The mother also noted that her daughter had "even created a world for Slender Man in the game mine craft [*sic*]," possibly referencing a late-game area known as "The End," which is populated mostly by endermen (see chapter 2). This area is a standard part of the game and not an individual creation. The girl's mother also referenced the Waukesha case, which she said led her to believe that her daughter was likely under the same influence on the night of the attack, even though she had a history of mental health issues (Evans 2014).[27]

The Las Vegas case was even more tenuously linked. The couple had repeatedly expressed anti-government and anti-police sentiments and reportedly had yelled, "This is the start of a revolution!" when they opened fire. They draped their victims with a swastika and a Gadsden flag (NBC News 2014). Yet one of their neighbors had recalled during an interview that one member of the couple had dressed up as the Slender Man at some point in the past. This sliver of recollection—and the neighbor's associated belief that it was somehow essential to understanding this act of violence—was again amplified by how this story was framed. Headlines often conflated this background information with the attack, which confused readers into thinking that this individual had dressed as the Slender Man during the shooting.[28]

Although this information was shared by sources with institutional authority (newspapers, broadcast journalists, etc.), the connections in the stories themselves were presented as rumors—individual statements of belief that expressed a perceived (yet unsubstantiated) link between the Slender Man and violence. These rumors were influenced by the conspicuous incompleteness in previous reporting and demonstrate how new events become coded in terms of the existing rumor panic, both for individuals and for the news outlets that report on those beliefs (Cohen 2011). So, while these new events were only tangentially linked to the Slender Man, at this point it didn't really matter, because the rumors linking the Slender Man to acts of "inexplicable" violence had become self-sustaining.[29]

These linked attacks retroactively legitimized previous reports and rumors, lending further credence to the idea that the problem was systemic. Repeated exposure increases audience perceptions of a news story's accuracy. This holds true even in cases where the information is inaccurate or demonstrably false, and this effect is further compounded by each additional headline (Pennycook, Cannon, and Rand 2018, 1874–75). Reports of recurrence can start to rapidly erode scrutiny and skepticism, fostering belief through repetition. There now appeared to be a pattern of several separate attacks across three different states that were all linked to the Slender Man—even though that pattern only existed because new events were being interpreted through the amplified and distorted lens of the panic. While the actual links to the Slender Man were fairly tenuous, those details were often buried several paragraphs into the news coverage and were superseded by headlines like, "Slender Man Now Linked to 3 Violent Acts" (Murray 2014a).

This reporting only strengthened existing rumors. Take, for example, the following exchange from the day after the Las Vegas shooting when a user on a local parenting forum called for the Slender Man to be banned. The user shared an ABC News story about the Waukesha stabbing and wrote:

> I'm for freedom of speech and all, but this isn't speech—its a website targeting young, impressionable children.
>
> How many more kids have to face death over some adult's sick fantasy played out online? If it saves just one kid, banning it is worth it. How are we better off allowing this kind of thing?

As with many of the rumors discussed above, this post demonstrates a fundamental misunderstanding of what the Slender Man is while also echoing existing rumors about a malicious actor intentionally targeting children (in this instance, though a specific website). Other users pushed back at this suggestion and called out this post for being wrong, inaccurate, or just plain impractical. As one user wrote in response:

> The Slender Man stories are all over the internet on every kind of website. They're copied and pasted everywhere. It's just an urban myth, same as Bloody Mary when we were kids. You would have to put every message board, every chat room, Facebook and every other social networking site, Wikipedia and other wikis, and basically anything where users can submit content under an 18+ paywall. That's a patently ridiculous idea.

But despite this attempt at clarification the original poster remained undeterred. They were adamant that this wasn't just an isolated incident, and they now had evidence that it was a growing problem:

> Well, SOMETHING has to be done about this!
> ANd its not just this incident; now "slenderman" is responsible for the killing of 2 innocent police officers and linked to 4 violent acts.
> [Shares link to ABC News's "Slender Man Now Linked to 3 Violent Acts"]
> All for what?[30]

This exchange elucidates how these news reports of linked events made it more difficult to clarify rumors and dispel systemic responses. Although the clarification in this thread is similar to that in The Bump thread discussed above, the new reports of violence that emerged over the weekend seemingly rendered this nonsystemic explanation as much less persuasive. What has emerged here is a reciprocal feedback loop, wherein news is building on rumor and rumor is building on news in ways that continue to amplify and distort the exact nature and extent of the problem. In just over a week's time, sight had drifted almost entirely from the actual events in Waukesha to the widespread condemnation of a new digital bogeyman that offered easy answers wrapped up in a sense of interpretive plasticity and seemingly straightforward causality.

The Slender Man remained an issue of national fascination for several more days before finally receding from the headlines in mid-June (Bever 2014). The rumors inspired by the mass media coverage of this case persisted far longer, occasionally making new headlines well into the following year as a proposed explanation for more acts of unforeseen violence or death (Bosman 2015; Kitta 2019, 62–68; Murray 2014b). As this ongoing wariness demonstrates, the Slender Man's amplified and distorted association with the events in Waukesha never truly receded. Instead, it began to coexist with a widespread form of digital folklore that it only superficially resembled.

Sympathy for the Folk Devil

There was a story in all of this that was well-worth telling, but I remain unconvinced that it was a story about the Slender Man. Despite rumors to the contrary, there was no malicious actor luring and inducing young girls to violence in the creature's name. Costumes and iPads were merely easy signifiers that obscured more complex social issues related to mental health or ideological violence. These reports and rumors imposed a pattern where no pattern existed, because in reality the purported epidemic of legend-inspired violence was distinctly nonsystemic. Yet the most enduring legacy of the Waukesha stabbing was in the folk devil it created. In public memory the Slender Man was now inexorably linked to multiple acts of seemingly inexplicable violence.

The fact that the Slender Man became an increasingly central figure in this story wasn't a coincidence; it was the system working as designed. The communication habits of everyday users, the choices made by algorithmic filters, and the coverage and framing decisions made by mass media gatekeepers all reinforced each other in ways that amplified this story. As the story became amplified, it began to suffer from distortion that emerged from various decontextualized assumptions about the incident. Widespread news coverage of this diffuse and fragmented digital legend cycle further exacerbated this distortion by creating a sense of conspicuous incompleteness among users, which drove the emergence of rumor as a sense-making response. As those rumors proliferated, they not only influenced communal acts of interpretation but also formed the basis for subsequent news coverage. Reports and rumors of linked attacks fed back into this system, retroactively legitimizing and further strengthening the amplification loop. The result is that this type of networked amplification spreads and reifies belief genres—like legends, rumors, and conspiracy theories—while also resisting individual efforts to nuance or debunk them.

At the time, many users believed that the Waukesha stabbing effectively marked the end of the Slender Man legend cycle. These users worried that the character's amplified and distorted transmission via mass media channels had given the legend cycle negative and inauthentic associations that couldn't be overcome and that performances would dwindle as a result. After all, who would wear a Slender Man Halloween costume after news reports on the Las Vegas shooting? Who would play a prank on their parents or siblings after the reported attack in Ohio? Who could possibly create new photoshops or stories pretending the Slender Man was real after Waukesha? But we've seen similar worries before. Some users claimed the legend cycle had run its course when it expanded beyond Something Awful or when *Marble Hornets* got popular. Others declared the legend cycle dead after it was commercialized as the basis for video games and movies. In all such instances, these events didn't mark an end as much as a transition. And despite rumblings to the contrary, the Slender Man legend cycle persisted well beyond the events of June 2014.

Epilogue: The Shadow over Waukesha

Under Wisconsin law, both Geyser and Weier were charged and tried as adults (Kuhagen 2020b). Anissa Weier initially pleaded not guilty to attempted first-degree intentional homicide before ultimately pleading guilty to a lesser charge: being a party to attempted second-degree homicide (Moreno 2017). In September 2017, a jury found her not guilty by reason of mental disease or defect (Kuhagen 2020a). She received the maximum sentence of twenty-five years under the supervision of a mental health institution, including at least three years in a mental hospital (CBS News 2017; Robinson and Whipp 2017). As part of her plea deal, Weier agreed that she wouldn't petition for supervised release from that facility until July 2020 (Kuhagen 2020a; Thompson-Gee 2017). In July 2021, a judge approved Weier's request for conditional release (Casey 2021).

While awaiting trial, Morgan Geyser was diagnosed with early-onset schizophrenia (Dooley et al. 2018). Her case had been scheduled to go to trial in October 2017, but she reached a plea deal a few weeks beforehand in order to avoid jail time. Geyser pleaded guilty to attempted first-degree intentional homicide and was sentenced by the judge to forty years in a mental institution (Marcelle and Andone 2018; Moreno 2017). Geyser's attorneys attempted to appeal the case—arguing that Geyser should have been tried under a lesser charge as a juvenile—but the Wisconsin Court of Appeals upheld the Waukesha County Circuit Court's decision in 2019. In 2021, the state supreme court denied Geyser's petition to review her case, effectively upholding her sentence (Kuhagen 2021b).

Payton Leutner survived and bears scars that are slowly healing. In public interviews, she appears to be thriving (*20/20* 2019). I wish her well.

Conclusion

Lessons from the Slender Man

"What do you know about the Slender Man?" I asked.

The room went silent. My question lingered in the air as the eyes of a dozen middle schoolers fixed on the front of the room. Side conversations, under-the-table texting, and notebook doodles ceased. I suddenly had their undivided attention.

On that particular morning, I was participating in a summer journalism program for local middle schoolers in Madison, Wisconsin. Because of my research, I had been invited to serve as an expert and do an on-camera interview for their class project on internet safety. After the interview finished, I continued chatting with a few of the students. When our informal discussion turned toward internet folklore, I posed the question above and was met with a tense silence.

Their reticence was quite understandable; after all, it had only been three weeks since two girls in a nearby town had attempted to stab their friend to death and blamed the Slender Man for their actions. Most news coverage focused on this surreal twist and implored parents to monitor their children's internet use more closely (see chapter 5). As a result, this was almost certainly a question that they had been asked by the adults in their lives during the last several weeks, and it had likely been asked in a more concerned or accusatory manner.

To diffuse this tension, I assured them that I was just curious about what they knew and wouldn't be judgmental. I explained that there was a lot of misinformation spreading, and I was wondering if they wanted to talk about it. Several nodded slightly. I smiled and reiterated my question, "What do you know about the Slender Man?"

One girl, sitting in the far corner of the room, began to speak. She knew the character looked like a tall, faceless humanoid wearing a black suit. She mentioned having read some stories that other people had posted online. She knew that the character was made-up, although she didn't know where or how it had originated. Another student told me about watching his brother play one of the Slender Man video games and being scared by it. Grabbing my laptop, I showed the class an image of a Slender Man monster in a different video game—*Minecraft*. A chorus of *ahhs* suggested that most them were familiar with this iteration. Several students mentioned hearing about the Slender Man from the news or from their parents after the Waukesha stabbing. Others admitted that they had initially learned about the Slender Man from friends or from stories they had heard on the playground.

As we continued to talk, it became obvious that these different entry points were not as discrete as they initially seemed. One student, for example, told me that he had originally heard about the Slender Man through stories told by a friend at school who played the video game. This student later played the game at his friend's house, which led him to look up Slender Man videos on YouTube after he returned home. In this instance, the Slender Man legend shifted from an oral retelling (based on a commercial product), to a mediated social experience, to an exploration of digitally mediated folklore. Many of the other students also expressed that they had experienced the legend cycle through a similarly diverse—yet connected—collection of legend performances.

Talking to these young people revealed a complex web of introductory points to the Slender Man legend that included elements of oral storytelling, commercial video games, mass mediated rumors, social media posts, horror-themed wikis, and YouTube videos that had blurred over time. Much of this book has been dedicated to understanding how digital media extend and connect these varied performative modes in new ways. As I have argued, the affordances of digital media enabled these varied forms of legend performance to coalesce into a larger matrix of folk belief that stretched beyond any individual medium or discrete set of performances. Accordingly, these children didn't see the Slender Man as a predominantly oral, commercial, mass, or digital legend; to them, it was just a legend.

Online and offline communication aren't as discrete as they once were, and failing to understand the former increasingly means an incomplete understanding of the latter. Even in primarily offline contexts, the influence of the digital can be felt. This is especially true among those who have been raised among digital media and who see the digital as an extension of the everyday rather than as a separate realm. Therefore, it is not sufficient to argue that folklore exists online; instead, we must recognize that the digital medium is fundamentally extending folk culture in ways that can affect even offline interactions. This necessitates a paradigm shift that requires viewing digitally mediated legends as more than just a new type or subgenre of legend. Digitally mediated legends are simply contemporary legends, and this new technocultural paradigm challenges scholars to think more broadly about the changing nature of legends (and the beliefs they represent) in an era increasingly defined by digital media.

In this book, I have demonstrated how the affordances of digital media extend legends in new ways and, in doing so, affect nearly every aspect of the legend cycle. Digital media support the emergent nature of performance by facilitating ongoing acts of serial collaboration as well as multimediated forms of legend performance. The medium extends both the spatial and the temporal aspects of these legend performances, resulting in reshaped legend conduits that are the result of both social and algorithmic filtering. The durable trace facilitated by these digital conduits creates new visibility, thereby extending a shared sense of tradition (in the horizontal sense) and creating a constellation of potential entry points as the legend spreads. Because of this digitally mediated constellation, users become more able to see the connections between individual actions, which encourages those users to see such actions as part of a larger vernacular practice. These new forms of visibility and durability hail subsequent interaction, potentially creating feedback loops that encourage further circulation and wider participation.

If this feedback loop grows large enough, it may begin to attract attention not only from other users but also from institutional agents seeking to capitalize on the power of vernacular expression. This appropriation can take many forms, ranging from mere reference to full media texts such as video games, popular films, or news stories centered on the newest vernacular digital trend. The affordances of digital media influence not only folk culture but also the relationship between folk culture and mass media. These commercial media texts feed back into digital conversations and performances in ways that are both normative and generative. Because of the fragmented and emergent nature of legends, context is often lost or transformed through this process. In extreme cases, this intersection between folk, mass, and digital culture may result in the widespread amplification and distortion of certain aspects of the legend cycle. This amplification inspires further circulation and rumor while also reciprocally reifying that which is being amplified.

As I suggested in this book's introductory chapter, technological affordances aren't determinative, but they do make certain outcomes more likely. I have demonstrated how digital legends emerge, circulate, and gain visibility in conjunction with modern communication technologies, but it is crucial to remember that individual legend cycles are protean—as are the media technologies that carry and circulate them—so any theory of digital legend must be conceived as appropriately malleable. While it is unlikely that every legend will emerge, grow, and circulate in precisely the manner I have outlined here, the underlying nature of digital networks suggests that many of my overarching arguments regarding digital legend creation, circulation, commercialization, ostension, amplification, and distortion will likely remain applicable even when the specifics of individual cases vary. But more broadly, this book is not meant to be a yardstick; instead, it's an example of what a perspective that combines theories of folklore, media, and technology might illuminate about the changing nature of legend and belief in an age of digital networks.

In the remaining pages of this concluding chapter, I consider the wide-ranging implications of this argument not only for folklorists but also for scholars of media and technology. To do so, the following sections move beyond legend and think about the intersection between technology and folklore more generally. My goal is to demonstrate what the case of the Slender Man can tell us about the nature of digitally networked belief and to suggest what directions might prove fruitful for further research.

The Nature of Digitally Networked Belief

I began this book by arguing that a study of digital legend could elucidate how digital networks mediate belief. By looking at the case of the Slender Man, we can begin to understand broader transitions in how networked beliefs come into being, circulate, gain visibility, and become self-sustaining in the digital age. Understanding this transition is important because in our current moment concerns regarding the internet's role in facilitating several belief genres have risen to the forefront of public discourse. The proliferation and visibility of conspiracy theories, extremist rumors, anti-science social movements, and fake news have become major concerns in both political and public life. Certainly none of these genres are endemic to the internet, but scholars and citizens alike are increasingly wondering how digital communication is facilitating and extending these genres in often problematic ways. This book has several implications that respond to this conversation and offer key insights into these concerns.

Social and Technological

Belief is a fundamentally human act, but the technology that mediates belief can shape how it emerges and circulates. The internet may empower users to express themselves and share their beliefs with others, but the affordances of the medium also encourage certain modes of expression and curate those beliefs as they spread. These social and technological factors form a mutually constitutive feedback loop, wherein each factor is constantly influencing (and influenced by) the other.

This system guides the possibilities for social interaction and gives structure to digitally networked belief. The interrelationship between social and algorithmic filters dictates what is seen, what is excluded, and the order in which information is presented—all of which impact how belief circulates and becomes understood by users. While these filters are not totally determinant—a user can always make the conscious (and time-consuming) choice to try and circumvent them—in aggregate the most straightforward outcomes also tend to be the most likely. The result is a deeply imbricated system that forms what users see when they go online, whether it be searching the web or engaging with other users on a digital platform.

Understanding digitally networked beliefs, then, requires attending to both the social and technological aspects that undergird those beliefs. The consideration of factors like algorithmic filtering, ambient folksonomies, platform-specific affordances, and user-created/site-curated metadata become important ways to augment our thinking about the role of social filtering online. By doing so, we can more fully understand how belief is circulated and reinforced via digital media.

Adopting such a perspective also suggests that developing effective solutions to problems related to digitally networked belief requires viewing those problems in a similarly systemic manner. This is important because the highly individualized nature of American culture often puts a focus on correcting personal habits instead of addressing systemic problems. Fake news, for instance, is frequently framed as an individual problem that derives from faulty media literacy skills. Such a perspective isn't *wrong*, but it is incomplete, and we might come to similar conclusions regarding the role of digital networks and belief in conspiracy theories or the anti-vaccination movement. Potential solutions need to go beyond the individual and consider how the interactions between the various affordances and user habits at play might result in the spread and legitimation of beliefs that are untrue or harmful.

Proliferative and Polysemic

The affordances of digital media facilitate temporal and spatial changes to how we have previously envisioned the transmission of folklore. Digital networks enable the diffusion of belief through a vast interconnected web of strong and weak social ties, which allows belief to spread farther and faster than ever before. But while the affordances of digital networks have made belief more visible, they aren't necessarily better at conveying the deeper cultural significance of those beliefs to a casual observer. Belief is a moving target, and the durable trace is simply a reserve of potential meanings and interpretations—an algorithmically curated scrapbook that contains snapshots of moments in time that are inherently fragmented and incomplete. The result is that meanings are frequently lost, transformed, or reimagined as part of the digital circulation process. Enabled by the sociotechnical mechanisms described above, these variations derive from the ambient nature of digital communication, which presents otherwise unfamiliar users with fragments that they come to understand on their own terms.

Digital networks are good at circulating belief but not necessarily at conveying context or preserving intentionality. A specific, narrowly defined meaning inhibits wider circulation for practices that are sustained through repeated acts of individual expression. Specificity and virality are often at odds with each other, and material that circulates widely tends to be more general and adaptable—a recognizable template that others can easily adapt for their own personal expression. This suggests that the deeper or more nuanced meanings that manifest in local variants are less likely to be preserved for other users as belief goes through the wringer of virality.

Similarly, elements like irony or play may be indistinguishable from sincerity to a cultural outsider. A belief that starts as a purposeful hoax, for example, might get taken seriously as it begins to spread outward to other networked locations. When users continue to build on these new interpretations, the belief may become that which it was originally mistaken for. As the aggregation of these new understandings begins to supersede original intentionality, existing users must depart, adapt, or entrench as new users overwhelm the belief space. This process is ongoing. Those new users may find themselves overwhelmed by even newer users who have recently discovered the belief and are transforming it again by applying their own meanings and interpretations. At every level it can be said that what has occurred here bears the mark of tradition, rapidly unfolding in both the horizontal and vertical sense.

The gap between circulation and meaning helps us understand another way in which digitally networked beliefs might become problematic. While digital networks have difficulty preserving meaning, users tend to assume that they are good at it. When contextual gaps emerge, users rush to fill them based on their own knowledge and cultural values. My intention in making this observation is not to privilege original or intended meanings as more correct; instead, what I am advocating for is understanding how digital networks enable widespread and cascading assumptions that might serve to reinforce hegemonic ideas or amplify and distort belief in problematic ways.

Personalized, Self-Reinforcing, and Invisible

The filtering mechanisms that determine the visibility of digital content allow networked belief to become not only more widely accessible but also more personalized. The affordances of digital media mean that finding a belief community is no longer bound to geographic proximity; instead, the network enables a high level of fluidity, which allows users to easily find and associate with belief communities that share their values. This sense of community reinforces belief. In a positive sense, it can act as a staging area for burgeoning social movements or kindle the formation of counterpublics. In a negative sense, it can lead to enclaves or high levels of social fragmentation—and those in the latter groups will often feel as if they are part of the former.

These affordances make it easy for users to self-select into belief communities that reinforce what they already believe or want to believe. Algorithmic filters take in myriad signals to provide users with uniquely tailored online experiences. These filters are often designed to identify content relevant to a user's interests and provide that user with similar content in order to keep that user engaged and using the platform. For instance, a user with a history of engaging with far-right content may see a very different reality regarding the January 6, 2021, insurrection in the U.S. Capitol. A YouTube video shared by a friend on social media may baselessly claim that the attacks were a false flag operation. The social network's algorithm sees that content as similar to what the user has engaged with previously and ranks it high in that user's news feed. If the user clicks on the link, then YouTube's algorithm might begin to recommend similar content—videos that preach about the QAnon conspiracy theory or extol preparedness for an upcoming race war.[1] Later that day an advertisement for body armor (with an automatic rifle displayed prominently in the background) appears on their social media feed. This multisite recurrence can quickly begin to overwhelm skepticism by seemingly confirming what a user is already predisposed to believe—after all, the belief appears to be widely shared. In this scenario, what initially appears to be a rabbit hole is revealed to be quicksand.

What is even more troubling here is that these social and algorithmic filters also make it easier to ignore divergent beliefs by filtering out additional evidence, viewpoints, or context that might run contrary to the group's dominant interpretations. These may be options for users that serve a particular filtering purpose (like giving the option to mute other users), but more often these choices are made for us and without our knowledge. What each user sees as the structure of the internet is not random or arbitrary; instead, it is the product of commercial forces curating digital content in the name of fostering a sizable user base and gathering sellable data on user habits. Because many of these editing choices are invisible, it becomes easy for users to conflate their small slice of the network with the overall network. When this occurs, users may begin to think their belief is more common or "common sense" than it actually is, further legitimating that belief and stifling potential challenges to it.

Vernacular, Engaging, and Exploitable

Digitally networked beliefs aren't inherently vernacular, but users tend to perceive them as such because of their frequent association with the vernacular mode. The internet provides myriad spaces for interaction that may appear to users as separate from institutional influence, even when they are simultaneously structured and curated by a variety of institutional choices. Whether it is because these expressions are carried or conveyed through seemingly informal channels or because they emerge from a local digital community or from the aggregate volition of a nebulous digital crowd (e.g., "trending," "crowdsourced," or "viral"), users tend to perceive their own shared networked beliefs (and any associated practices) as vernacular—rooted not in institutions but in a sense of affiliation with some informal constellation of digitally networked others.

Since the vernacular is a discursive mode (as opposed to an inherent quality), these widespread perceptions of vernacularity become a communicative resource, attracting a variety of agents and purposes. Vernacular communication appeals to a sense of social trust that is positioned as existing outside of formal institutions. In doing so, such expressions cultivate a sense of authority by building on beliefs that are both informal and shared. This sense of traditionality hails further engagement and collaboration from other users. At the same time, the increased visibility provided by networked digital communication also draws the attention of a variety of institutional forces, ranging from algorithms and advertisers to propaganda and disinformation campaigns. These agents are similarly enabled to use the vernacular mode as a way to gain their own visibility, steer conversations, or sell products. In some instances, the presence of the institution is obvious—like when a piece of digital folk culture is appropriated into a movie or video game—but in other instances, the role of institutional agents is more subtle and complex.

The latter implication draws our attention to ways in which networked media perpetuate existing power imbalances while at the same time obfuscating those imbalances. The nature of social media makes it easy for bots, advertisers, brand partners, social media marketers, and propagandists to pose as everyday users and engage in vernacular discourse as a way of swaying conversations and shaping belief. These institutional agents often have a disproportionate amount of power and resources at their disposal, which allow them to coordinate and amplify ideas by interpolating other users into their efforts. The power of the vernacular mode is that it doesn't necessarily tell people what to do; instead, it convinces them that they want to participate in something that seems bigger than themselves. By creating the appearance of a controversy, trend, or underrepresented public opinion, these accounts can direct existing beliefs in ways that quickly become self-sustaining and sincere as they spread out from their point of origin. Unraveling the ensuing knot of belief and intentionality is no easy task, but at the very least it warrants a healthy skepticism on the part of the researcher as well as a resistance to lauding digital trends simply because they appear to be trends.

Far-Reaching and Pervasive

Belief doesn't stop at the edges of the medium that carries it, and the deeper implications of these new connective technologies extend well beyond the internet. When we speak of digitally networked belief, we are not speaking of a discrete entity but instead of a greater social shift. In a moment defined by the widespread adoption of networked digital communication technologies, we can't separate digital networks from belief any more than we can separate literacy from belief. This suggests that a failure to understand the role of technology in mediating belief yields an incomplete understanding of belief, even in primarily offline contexts.

Even if an individual doesn't personally use a technology, it can still affect them. In *The Whale and the Reactor*, Langdon Winner uses the example of a mechanical tomato harvester developed by researchers at the University of California in the mid-twentieth century to illustrate how technological choices spiral outward as the product of a system (1986, 26–28). These machines cost a hefty sum upfront but lowered the price of harvesting by five to seven dollars per ton compared to harvesting by hand. This apparent innovation favored large agribusinesses while also making it harder for small farms to compete because they either couldn't afford the machines, wouldn't be able to recoup their investment, or lacked the highly concentrated form of tomato growing the machines required. Thus the decade from the early 1960s to the early 1970s saw a drastic rise in tomato production, yet the number of tomato growers declined by approximately 85 percent. Even the tomatoes changed, as the "rough motion" of the harvesters required the creation of new breeds that were "hardier, studier, and less tasty than those previously grown" (26). Winner's argument makes it clear that these technological changes affected a variety of nonadopters, ranging from small-farm owners and farm workers to consumers.

Widely adopted technologies create social expectations and assumptions that incentivize their use. Digital networks have become the go-to place for sharing photos, marking milestones, checking in with loved ones, sorting resumes, conducting business, scheduling meetings, and planning hangouts. Groups ranging from friends to employers incentivize the use of these technologies by making them increasingly crucial to perform basic social functions. Like the mechanical tomato harvester, these new technologies are sold to us under the guise of efficiency and ease-of-use: the friend who eschews social media makes planning events more difficult; the employee who disconnects at 5 p.m. is seen as less dedicated than their colleague who is always on call. But what is marketed as convenience is really "an ongoing social process in which scientific knowledge, technological innovation, and corporate profit reinforce each other in deeply entrenched patterns, patterns that bear the unmistakable stamp of political and economic power" (27).

Despite this social pressure, an individual is always free to eschew the internet or to forgo some part of it—whether that be email, a smartphone, or social media. But even if an individual fully disconnects, they have not escaped from the role of digital networks in shaping belief. Friends, co-workers, and other interlocutors may still bear beliefs that are influenced in some way by networked digital communication. And even if *those* individuals are similarly disconnected, the convergence between mass media and digital media means that trending topics on social media routinely make the nightly news or provide journalists with a facsimile of public opinion. The influence of digitally networked beliefs on policy makers and social movements is even harder to avoid, enshrined in reactionary laws or local protests. At a certain point, it seems that escaping digitally networked belief becomes synonymous with an escape from modern life.

A better understanding of the relationship between digital networks and belief means a better understanding of contemporary society and culture. This book has been concerned with the analysis of legends in service of making this larger point. It is my hope that everything I have written here may be more broadly applicable and further our understanding of the nature of belief in an age of networked digital media.

"Is the Slender Man real?" I asked the group of middle schoolers near the end of our day together. The internet-savvy girl in the corner firmly shook her head, but the other students—many of whom had learned about the legend in more fragmented ways—seemed less certain. One boy, who looked a little younger than his peers, seemed unsettled by the conversation and asked me if I was *sure* the Slender Man wasn't real. He told me that his brother had shown him a picture from the internet that appeared to have the Slender Man in it. It looked very real. I raised my hand into an oath position and promised him (100 percent; on my honor as an expert; hope to die) that the Slender Man was not real. He breathed a sigh of relief and smiled.

This was the first time I had this conversation with a child, but it wouldn't be the last. In the years since, I have had several similar conversations with the children of friends and co-workers. After they discover that I research the Slender Man, they like to share all the details they can remember about the creature, often weaving fragmentary stories as they do so. When I ask if the Slender Man is real, their replies tend to express various levels of uncertainty. Most don't know where the legend came from, and none have known that it's only a couple years older than they are. The way they talk about the Slender Man always reminds me of how I talked about legends like "The Hook" and "Bloody Mary" when I was a child.[2]

At every stage of its expanding circulation, users rushed to claim that the Slender Man legend cycle had become played out or "dead." This is a common critique for a fast-moving age, levied whenever an influx of new users overwhelms the already familiar ones. But the story of the Slender Man didn't end because it was adapted into Twitter hashtags, YouTube series, or video games. It endured notoriously awful film adaptations, rampant pop culture references, and even survived the woods of Waukesha.

Legends are resilient, a product of their fragmentary and protean nature. They don't end—they aren't complete stories that wrap up neatly like books or movies—instead, their popularity waxes and wanes over time. In some instances, they go through periods of dormancy, where they are remembered but rarely performed. In other instances, they are altered for new audiences or updated to better suit new circumstances, acting as a communicative resource that sparks something recognizable yet different. The Slender Man is no longer part of my digital subculture, and it hasn't been for a very long time. But this sort of transition is not unusual. The legend persists, adapted into the folklore and expressive performances of those much younger than I. It would appear that the legend of the Slender Man doesn't end; only my role in this story does.

Appendix

Legends and Internet Culture

ALLIGATORS IN THE SEWERS: A legend about large congregations of reptilian creatures living in the sewers of urban environments (usually New York City). In some versions, these alligators have gone blind or developed albinism from long-term dwelling in sunless environments. The legend usually links the infestation of alligators to unwanted exotic pets that were flushed down toilets (see Brunvand 1981, 90–97; Kilgannon 2020).

BLOODY MARY: Both the legend of a vengeful spirit and a popular children's game to summon that spirit. In various versions, the spirit goes by names like Mary Whales, Mary Worth, or Mary Worthington. The game is often played at slumber parties and sleepovers, especially by preadolescent girls. To summon the spirit, a true believer (or simply the subject of a "dare") must enter a bathroom alone, shut the door, and turn off the lights. Facing the bathroom mirror, the summoner holds a candle (or other light source) and begins to chant. The incantation to summon the spirit varies but repeating its name three times is a common method. If done correctly, the specter's face will appear in the mirror, and there may also be a sudden appearance of blood. In my own research, the Bloody Mary legend/game was the most frequently referenced folkloric analog to the Slender Man (see Dundes 1998; Langlois 1978; see also Tucker 2005).

THE BLUE WHALE CHALLENGE: An online "game" in which participants are challenged to complete a checklist of increasingly dangerous tasks over the course of fifty days. The final task (and completion of the challenge) requires the participant to commit suicide. Although suicides in several countries were linked to the challenge in 2017, there is no conclusive evidence to support that link. Folklore scholar Alexandra Arkhipova has further suggested that the challenge itself may not have actually existed in any substantial way before newspapers began reporting on rumors of its existence and effects (see Adeane 2019; Tucker 2020).

The Boyfriend's Death: A legend about a young couple who get stuck after driving into an isolated area at night, culminating with the death of the boyfriend or husband. As a teenager, I heard the following version: A young, amorous couple is driving at night and arrives at a secluded road deep in the countryside. After parking their car under a large tree for privacy, they begin to make out. Suddenly, the young woman hears a noise outside the car and wants to leave. The young man tries to assuage her fears, but she is adamant. The boyfriend leaves the car to check on the noise and tells his date not to open the doors for any reason until he returns. She falls asleep for several hours until she is awakened by a loud noise in the middle of the night. She realizes that her boyfriend has not returned and that it has begun to rain. Assuming the noise to be thunder, she goes back to sleep. In the morning, she wakes to another loud sound. She immediately discovers that the car was covered with viscous mud while she slept and realizes that somebody is trying to break in. The window is shattered by a uniformed police officer, who bids her to follow him and not look back. She's halfway to the squad car before she glances back and sees her boyfriend hanging from the tree, rivulets of mud-red blood dripping onto the roof of the car from his slit throat (see Brunvand 1981, 5–10; see also Tucker 1999, 209).

Creepy Clown Sightings of 2016: A rumor panic about individuals who were supposedly dressing up as clowns and ominously lurking near populated areas at night. These reports coalesced from isolated rumors at an apartment complex in South Carolina and a taken-out-of-context movie promotion in Wisconsin. These reports were quickly amplified and distorted into a national news story and moral panic in the late summer and early fall of 2016 (see Laudun 2020).

The Dionaea House: A story about individuals who encounter a supernatural house that lures in its victims and seemingly exists in multiple places across the United States. The story is presented as a series of in-character blog posts, and its name comes from the scientific name for the Venus flytrap (*Dionaea muscipula*). Written by screenwriter Eric Heisserer (who adopted a variety of blogger personae for the project) from 2004 to 2006, it was sold to Warner Bros. as a movie property in 2005 but development stalled indefinitely.

DYATLOV PASS INCIDENT: An unsolved mystery about what occurred at a campsite in the northern Ural Mountains in 1959 that led to the deaths of nine Russian hikers. The inconsistent and seemingly odd injuries found on the corpses of the expedition (skull trauma, missing tongues and eyes, etc.) have led to various theories concerning their demise, which include supernatural forces, cryptozoological attacks, or the side effects of atomic testing. The most plausible explanation is that the party's fate was the result of a natural occurrence, likely an avalanche (see Gaume and Puzrin 2021).

HODAG: A fearsome cryptid said to live in the forests of northern Wisconsin. It has bovine horns, enormous fangs, sharp claws, and a row of spikes running down its back. The hodag legend was created by Eugene S. Shepard in the 1890s to spur tourism to the town of Rhinelander, Wisconsin, after the town's logging industry began to decline. In 1896, Shepard claimed to have caught a live hodag, which he then exhibited at local fairs across the state of Wisconsin. Although it was a hoax—a wooden creature controlled by wires—the ruse attracted thousands of spectators who wanted to see the mysterious creature. Today the hodag is the namesake for a yearly festival in Rhinelander and the mascot of the local high school. The town even has a large statue of the creature, located in front of the Rhinelander Chamber of Commerce (see Kortenhof 1996). My wife once took me there on a date.

THE HOOK: A legend about a young couple who have a close encounter with a dangerous hook-handed individual while out driving. After arriving at their favorite make-out spot, the couple park their car and turn on the radio to set the mood. An announcer interrupts the broadcast to inform listeners that a dangerous individual (usually a convict or a mental patient) has escaped from a nearby facility. The individual can be easily identified because his right hand has been replaced by a hook. The couple return to their activities, but after a few minutes, the young woman swears she hears a scratching noise from outside the car. Frightened, she begs to go home. The young man obliges, gunning the gas pedal. When the couple returns home, the young man circles the car to open the car door for his date, only to find a bloody hook wedged in the door handle. A fairly well-known legend among teenagers in the 1950s, the legend was further popularized after a version appeared in the Dear Abby newspaper column on the same day as the 1960 U.S. presidential election (see Brunvand 1981, 48–52).

The Kentucky Fried Rat: A legend about food contamination in which someone buys a bucket of fried chicken from a fast-food restaurant and discovers—after a few odd-tasting bites—that one of the pieces is actually a deep-fried rat (see Fine 1980).

Killswitch: A story about an eerie video game, written as a blog post in 2007 by author Catherynne M. Valente. The post documents the supposedly true history of a 1989 video game called *Killswitch*, which deletes itself upon completion. The game has two routes, each following a different character. The first route contains mysterious codes, surreal situations, and unintuitive puzzles that must be solved to complete the game. The second route is even more difficult, and the blog claims it has never been completed, leaving some mysteries from the first route open-ended. Since so few copies of the game remain, the blog leaves significant doubt as to whether the whole story will ever be known. The blog post is written in a style that evokes many contemporary legends about video games.

The Killer in the Backseat: A legend about a young woman who is terrorized while driving alone at night. After leaving a friend's home, the young woman is followed by another motorist or by a large truck. The pursuing vehicle trails her closely, occasionally hitting her rear bumper or flashing its high beams. After several fruitless attempts to lose the trailing vehicle, the woman arrives at her destination (or stops at a gas station) and runs from her car. It is then revealed that the trailing motorist had been trying to help her. The motorist had noticed someone strange in the backseat (in some versions armed with a weapon like an axe) and had bumped the car or flooded it with light whenever the intruder moved to strike. The potential assailant is thwarted, the woman is saved, and the listener's expectations are subverted (see Brunvand 1981, 52–53).

THE MOMO CHALLENGE: A hoax and moral panic from 2018 that resurged in early 2019 based on rumors of a dangerous social media trend targeting children. The 2018 panic was based around fears of a social media "game" where children and adolescents would receive images of a terrifying creature called "Momo" along with anonymous messages that contained increasingly dangerous challenges and ultimately instructed them to commit suicide. The 2019 panic added fears that images of Momo and suicide were being inserted into content aimed at children on YouTube. Despite international reporting on these rumors, the Momo Challenge was essentially a hoax that did not exist in any significant way prior to these reports (see Mikkelson 2019).

THE NEIMAN-MARCUS COOKIE RECIPE: A legend about a woman who seeks retribution after being overcharged for a confection recipe at an upscale café. A woman dining at an upscale restaurant finishes eating a delicious desert and asks the staff for the recipe. When she goes to pay her bill, the woman finds that she has been charged an exorbitant sum for the recipe (usually several hundred dollars); furthermore, since she has already seen the recipe, the staff refuse to drop the charge. The woman decides to get her revenge by copying the recipe and widely distributing it for free. This legend circulated widely via email in the 1990s (where the subject was Neiman-Marcus and cookies), but it is significantly older than that. Brunvand, for example, cataloged similar revenge recipe legends from the 1960s and 1970s that involved a red velvet cake ostensibly served by the Waldorf-Astoria in New York City (see Brunvand 1981, 154–60; Snopes Staff 1999).

QANON: A far-right conspiracy theory that developed on 4Chan (and later 8Chan) following a series of posts in 2017 by an anonymous user who claimed to be a high-level government employee with access to top secret information (Q clearance). The conspiracy claimed that the Trump administration was secretly working to counter pedophile rings, satanic cults, and other evils supposedly perpetuated by a corrupt liberal political establishment (known as "the Deep State"). The conspiracy theory is notable for integrating many other right-wing conspiracy theories and serving as a metanarrative for far-right conspiracy theorists. The conspiracy was amplified by a high level of bot activity on social networks like Twitter and ultimately became the subject of ongoing national news coverage after several individuals were spotted wearing QAnon T-shirts at a Trump rally in 2018 (see Tangherlini, Roychowdhury, and Broadwell 2020; see also Horgan 2018).

Ted the Caver: A horror story written as a series of blog posts in 2001. The blogger (Ted) documents exploring a cave with his friends over the course of several weeks in the spring of 2001. As they delve deeper into the cave on successive trips, they begin to experience unexplained (and potentially supernatural) phenomena. After a particularly unsettling excursion into the cave, Ted begins having auditory and visual hallucinations while at home. He confesses to his readers that he has become perpetually anxious and regularly experiences vivid and terrifying nightmares. Ted then informs his readers that he is going to return to the cave and find answers. The blog was never updated again.

The Tide Pod Challenge: An internet meme popular among Generation Z that jokes about eating colorful laundry detergent packets ("pods"). Although it originated as a joke, it later became amplified and taken seriously by a variety of mainstream news outlets in January 2018. Only about 130 cases of intentional exposure were documented in the United States that month, and many of those cases only occurred in the wake of the aforementioned news reports that framed the Tide Pod Challenge as a supposedly widespread and dangerous trend (see Sleight-Price, Ahlstone, and Jones 2018).

The Vanishing Hitchhiker: A legend in which a motorist picks up a ghost. The motorist is driving along an isolated country road at night when he sees a young woman by the side of the road. Worried for her safety, he stops and offers her a ride. The young woman gets in the backseat of the car and directs the motorist to her father's home, which is only a few miles up the road. The young woman remains silent for the remainder of the ride.

When the motorist arrives at her destination, he turns toward the backseat only to find that the young woman has vanished. Confused, the motorist approaches the house. An older man opens the door, and the motorist describes what has happened. The older gentleman sighs. "That was my daughter," he tells the motorist. "Ten years ago tonight she was killed by a drunk driver five miles down the road" (see Brunvand 1981, 24–40).

Notes

Introduction

1. See the appendix.

2. See the appendix.

3. Arguably, these web pages could also be considered "embryonic legends" that never grew into anything more widely expressive or dynamic (Dégh 2001, 402–3).

4. While Mikel J. Koven (2018) has suggested that the Slender Man is not an authentic legend because it lacks a sincere belief core, young adults and teens are often reluctant to candidly talk about subjects when they perceive the potential for adult disapproval (Tucker 2020). Additionally, although some scholars have suggested that a belief in the veracity of the narrative is a fundamental aspect of legends, such a criterion is difficult to apply in practice (Ellis 2001a, 5).

5. See the appendix.

6. The term "contemporary legend" has been subject to rigorous debate in the field of folkloristics, especially in the 1980s and 1990s. While some scholars suggested that urban or contemporary legends represented new folk genres (offering appropriate definitions to actively separate them from traditional legends), other scholars simply saw them as current manifestations of the legend genre. This book takes the perspective that "contemporary legend appears as the present manifestation of traditional legend, representative of the actual stage of an ongoing process that keeps the story meaningful and viable for all, but in diverse ways" (Dégh 2001, 91; see also Pettit, Smith, and Simpson 1995; Ellis 2001a, 46–47; Tangherlini 1990, 381–82).

7. For instance, the "true" story of a spectral hitchhiker who vanishes just before reaching her destination is certainly a legend, but so are stories about a working mother who finds a deep-fried rat in a bucket of Kentucky Fried Chicken she brought home to her family, alligators living in the sewers, and a woman who circulates a chocolate chip cookie recipe for free in revenge for being charged hundreds of dollars after asking for the recipe at an upscale cafe (see the appendix).

8. This choice builds on the work of Bill Ellis, who suggested the following reorientation for legend-scholarship: "What we should be trying to define is not the style of legend *texts* but rather the style of legend *performance*. In other words, legends are not folk literature but folk *behavior*" (2001a, 10).

9. Adopting the "social shaping" perspective also suggests a corollary: different groups may have very different understandings of a specific technology as well as the customs and norms related to using that technology (MacKenzie and Wajcman 1999, 21).

10. The concept of affordances can be illustrated through a common technology often found in the home—a claw hammer. As a technology, a claw hammer is especially good at pounding in or removing nails. Several aspects of the hammer make it well-suited to this task—its "preferred use." The long handle allows the user to maximize the speed of the strike more efficiently than using a rock for the same task while the metallic head provides the strike with resilience and power via mass. These affordances provide a straightforward and normative use for this technology, and it is likely that its preferred use is also its most frequent. But, in a pinch, those same affordances could make a claw hammer useful as a weapon or a doorstop. These are "modified uses." They might be unexpected (that is, they depart from the shared cultural understanding of how the technology is used), but the affordances of the technology are still well-suited for either task (even if there are likely better technologies available for both). However, try as one might, a claw hammer will never make a very good replacement for a toothbrush or a drill. It could certainly be used for either task, but the material reality of the object (hardness, bluntness) will always frustrate such attempts. In this example, the idea of "affordances" helps demonstrate both that individuals have agency over how a technology is used and that technologies have certain built-in qualities that make some uses easier than others and, as a result, make some outcomes more likely.

Chapter 1. Creation

1. While some of the earliest recorded writing comes from Mesopotamia circa 8,000 B.C.E., writing started to become more common in different cultures across the globe between 3,000 and 1,000 B.C.E.

2. Although circa 1440 marks the invention of the printing press in Germany (and the beginning steps toward widespread literacy in Western culture), it bears remembering that China invented woodblock printing several centuries earlier and that the Korea invented movable metal type similar to Gutenberg's roughly two hundred years before Western culture created their first printing press.

3. Albert Lord found something similar in his study of the singers of Serbo-Croatian epics. Lord observed that young performers who learned their repertoire

from both books and their elders had even their orally learned songs influenced by the memorization skills they had learned from reading printed books (1960, 137).

4. Gerogerigegege, "Create Paranormal Images," Something Awful, June 8, 2009, https://forums.somethingawful.com/showthread.php?threadid=3150591.

5. It is somewhat of an in-joke on the site that most Goons forget that the front page even exists. In practice, the site's forums tend to be the focus of most Something Awful culture.

6. FYAD is short for "Fuck You and Die," a forum that is more lax in rule enforcement than others and often serves as a place for "edgy" and (supposedly) ironic content. GBS is short for "General Bullshit," the forums catch-all, general interest section. PYF is short for "Post Your Favorite," a forum where users would post favorite webcomics, tweets, or memes in ongoing discussion threads, often serving as a user-curated repository of digital metacontent.

7. 4Chan itself was founded by Something Awful user Christopher "Moot" Poole in 2003 (see Phillips 2015, 18–20).

8. This book uses they/them when a user's gender is not otherwise specified or known.

9. See the appendix.

10. This user is referring to the SCP Foundation, a popular collaborative fiction project that originally spawned from users on 4Chan's paranormal board (/x/). Depending on use, SCP stands for either "Special Containment Procedures" or "Secure. Contain. Protect." (the organization's motto). As other users also noted, the SCP Foundation has many performative dynamics that are similar to those present in the Slender Man legend cycle.

11. Although Shifman is writing about memes (both pre- and postinternet), her scholarship on internet culture can be constructively applied to the study of digital legends (see Ellis 2001a, 76–83). This choice is in line with several scholars who have suggested that the Slender Man might also be viewed as an internet meme (Blank and McNeill 2015, 2018a; Chess and Newsom 2015; T. Evans 2018, 129; Tolbert 2018a, 25–26). While some scholars have suggested that the Slender Man is more meme than legend (Koven 2018, 124), it is not my intention to uphold such a dichotomy. Memes by their proper name are simply folklore and the associated concept of a "mind virus" may be better regarded "by the more objective and academically established name, which is 'contemporary legend'" (Ellis 2001a, 83).

12. BooDoug187, for example, shared a performance that took the form of an email. The email contained a transcript of a magazine interview with a Japanese manga artist who had since committed suicide. The email suggests that the manga artist's most well-known creation, the Suited Demon, is a manifestation of the "S.MAN."

13. In the omitted text, moto42 takes credit for creating the original SCP (known as SCP173) and sharing it on 4Chan's paranormal board (/x/). By writing "both," moto42 is drawing parallels between the emergence of the Slender Man and the collaborative formation of the SCP files (see note 10). This suggests that a similar process to the one presented in this chapter has led to the creation of multiple digital legend cycles.

14. This is equivalent to approximately eight hundred more posts spread out over the next eight months, which shows diminishing returns on participation over time compared to the nearly one thousand posts that occurred in June 2009.

Chapter 2. Circulation

1. Ce gars, "Create Paranormal Images," Something Awful, June 18, 2009, https://forums.somethingawful.com/showthread.php?threadid=3150591&userid=0&perpage=40&pagenumber=14.

2. Much like Victor Surge, neither ce gars nor "Jay" are this user's real name. To foster verisimilitude, Troy Wagner, the creator of *Marble Hornets*, plays the character of "Jay Merrick" in these Slender Man legend performances on Something Awful, Twitter, and YouTube. Furthering this name confusion, Wagner often referred to the character as "J" in early performative interactions. To reduce name confusion, I identify Wagner/ce gars by the name of his *Marble Hornets* character ("Jay") for most of this chapter.

3. Like many *Marble Hornet* videos, this entry is bookended by digital text written by Jay, making the total length of the video forty-seven seconds. The actual footage, which takes approximately fifteen seconds, is located in the middle of the video.

4. Some digital audio and visual file formats, like JPEG, do compress their content. These file types are referred to as "lossy" (as opposed to lossless) and can result in degradation through repeated editing and saving (often in the form of visual or sonic artifacting). This loss of quality is generally much more incremental than that seen in copylore or faxlore.

5. The material presented by using certain platforms (like a Google image search or Wiki page for the Slender Man) tends to be decontextualized performances (or an aggregation of such), meaning that such platforms tend to play more of a curatorial function rather than a directly performative one (Kaplan 2013, 128). However, learning from these digital archives is often a crucial first step to other forms of circulation, like sharing, discussing, interacting with, or performing the legend cycle (Jenkins, Ford, and Green 2013, 156–59).

6. For instance, while casually scrolling down their social media feed, a user might see that a networked acquaintance has shared a post about the threat of tainted Halloween candy or liked a video of a cryptid hunter ostensibly on the trail

of a wild hodag (Grider 1984; Peck 2020b; see also chapters 4 and 5; for "hodag," see the appendix).

7. For instance, the core innovation that helped Google become the web's most-used search engine was to harness the power of peer production in its search algorithm, treating user-created web links as "votes of confidence" when sorting through millions of search results (Benkler 2006, 76). Such tactics have become common across the web, especially on social networking sites and other forms of social media: Twitter's algorithm uses hashtags to determine the trending topics of the day; Facebook's algorithm notices what users click on and scroll past and uses that data to build individual news feeds; Reddit's algorithm accounts for user votes when determining how to order content and what makes it to the website's front page (Hess 2014; Massanari 2015; Peck 2020c). As explained in the subsequent paragraphs of this chapter, algorithmic filtering is much more complex than these straightforward input-output examples, often relying on dozens or hundreds of user-signals (many of which are supplied without the user's knowledge) to make sense of browsing habits and order content.

8. Although we can't fully account for all the intricacies of this proprietary software, we do know that they tend to be based on providing users with information that is deemed to be personally relevant—frequently functioning as a way for social media sites to give users more of what they want to see in order to keep those users actively on the site or using the service (Pariser 2012). Decoding each platform's version of "relevance" has become a distinct branch of internet marketing known as Search Engine Optimization (or SEO) where institutions and influencers attempt to manipulate the algorithm of a social network to ensure their content rises to the forefront. For a discussion of how commercial interests try to game the system, see chapter 3. For a discussion of what happens when mass media institutions enter this system, see chapter 5.

9. While the concept of gatekeeping comes from the work of sociologist Kurt Lewin (1943, 1947), influential work by scholars like White (1950), Snider (1967), Shoemaker (1991), and Livingston and Bennett (2003) has productively applied this model to the study of media, mass communication, and journalism.

10. My use of "tradition participant" (instead of the more outdated "tradition bearer") is meant to reinforce the importance of individual volition and agency in this process. "Participant" also suggests a larger variety of personal choices and potential engagements with the circulation process beyond the more binary categories associated with "active" and "passive" tradition bearers (Tangherlini 1994, 31–32; 2008, 45–46).

11. The creators originally intended to finish the story at the end of the first season. The original ending was meant to be more ambiguous and would have

ended the series on a downer note reminiscent of Ted the Caver (see the introduction and appendix). The plan was to film Jay driving down a road at night, intending to continue his investigation. The Slender Man would've shown up under each successive streetlight as Jay drove past. The account would then go silent, and no further updates would be posted ("Marble Hornets Radio Interview" 2010, 22:58–24:30).

12. The creators have stated that while making *Marble Hornets*, "There were pretty much no talks of *The Blair Witch Project.* Ever." Still, it's difficult to divorce the indirect influence of the 1999 film—which popularized the found-footage horror genre—from the aesthetic and tone of *Marble Hornets* ("Marble Hornets Radio Interview" 2010, 19:54–20:09).

13. As explained in chapter 1, early Slender Man performances would sometimes use different names for the creature to cultivate a sense of disconnection between various encounters and reports.

14. While the choice to make the Slender Man more humanlike was in line with the negotiations regarding the character's appearance in the Create Paranormal Images thread, this choice was also a practical one on the part of the filmmakers. *Marble Hornets*' first season was filmed on a shoestring budget and rapid production schedule, making a more elaborate monster costume unfeasible.

15. This was also a way for "Jay" to explain delays in production and video uploads while not breaking the performative frame of the series. In other words, if he wasn't able to get a new entry uploaded to YouTube, he could complain that he was again sick with a mysterious illness. This illness, colloquially called "Slender sickness," would go on to become a significant aspect of many digital Slender Man legend performances (Kitta 2019).

16. As I elaborate later in this chapter, *Marble Hornets* only appeared to be interactive. While the series actually changed very little based on fan input, many users assumed they were influencing the emerging series of performances.

17. Although it was never mentioned in the Create Paranormal Images thread, frequent poster KicksYouInHalf was the Something Awful username of Joseph DeLage, one of the co-creators of *Marble Hornets.*

18. This quote was amended to remove a regrettable ableist slur.

19. This entry was shared with the thread by user Crispy_Rapcakes on June 23, 2009. The linked text was appended with a single word: "NOOOOOOOOOO OOOOOOOOOOOOooooooooooooooooooooooooooooo!"

20. The main Unfiction thread, titled "[TRAILHEAD] Marble Hornets," was created on June 23, 2009, a few hours before *Marble Hornets* posted its third entry.

21. An Alternate Reality Game—commonly called an ARG—is an open-ended networked narrative that uses transmedia storytelling and interweaves ideas from both the creator and audience to create an unfolding, interactive narrative (Kinsella

2011, 61). Due to the lack of detail provided by *Marble Hornets*'s creators, many users on Unfiction (and elsewhere) assumed the series was meant to be an ARG that solicited viewer input, theories, and participation into the narrative. Given the similarity between ARGs and legends, this confusion is unsurprising. ARGs and legends tend to use similar performative frames and both genres encourage users to engage in a performance of belief and communal world-building (Kinsella 2011, 61–63; see also McNeill 2012, 88–90).

22. In this initial post, OpenClear acknowledges that, despite lurking on the Unfiction forums for some time, this is their first post. Counting this initial post, OpenClear only posted on the Unfiction forums a half dozen times. In light of this user's sparse contributions to the discussion on Unfiction, it is unclear how OpenClear discovered *Marble Hornets* and if this user had any preexisting relationship to the series, it's creators, or Something Awful; however, because this initial post subtly identifies the Slender Man by name, it is likely that one (or more) of the aforementioned possibilities is true.

23. *Marble Hornets* was not an ARG, and the series only appeared to be interactive. The series' creators would later note that user interaction had very little effect on the story they planned to tell, meaning that the series would be more accurately characterized as chaotic fiction. But while the series itself tended to be more cinematic in nature, it also inspired widespread vernacular interaction among users (Tolbert 2013). These interactions provide a useful point of analysis not only because of their place in the early circulation of the Slender Man legend but also because the assumed ARG-like nature of the series meant that users were both vocal and collaborative in trying to make sense of the Slender Man legend cycle via *Marble Hornets* ("Marble Hornets Radio Interview" 2010, 10:50–12:20).

24. Personal correspondence, July 1, 2020, in possession of the author.

25. "[IN-GAME?] Slender Man," Unfiction discussion thread, June 23, 2009, http://forums.unfiction.com/forums/viewtopic.php?t=28182.

26. Such comments were made on pages 21 and 22 of the "[TRAILHEAD] Marble Hornets" thread on Unfiction by users like xxkiriyamaxx and Chaos.

27. As the Slender Man legend began to circulate across various web spaces, growing inconsistences made it increasingly difficult for Unfiction users to discern what was and was not part of *Marble Hornets*. On the morning of July 4, 2009, for example, user Syke noted a new account called slender_hunter had started following them on Twitter. Slender_hunter seemed to know about both *Marble Hornets* and Something Awful, and, Syke noted, "He has a tumblr account with some interesting stuff. Definitely [part of the game]. He is searching for J (the cameraman and Alex's friend). . . . he wants to know where all his videos are coming from." Following Syke's post, various Unfiction users began following slender_hunter's various social media accounts. They pored over clues posted by slender_hunter,

trying to discern the significance of mysterious phone numbers and cryptic quotes from religious texts written in Arabic. Then, a week later, slender_hunter abruptly disappeared, simply telling his Twitter followers, "They've found me, need to run, need to hide, don't follow, don't contact for your own good or they will find you too." Even weeks later, Unfiction users were unsure what to make of the account and how relevant it was to understand both the Slender Man and *Marble Hornets*. These users never realized that slender_hunter was actually Ethan (a.k.a. Prodigal), who had grown annoyed at the bevy of Unfiction users messaging him for clues to *Marble Hornets*. "[They] started bugging me on Twitter about it," he later recalled. So, with the help of a few friends, Ethan created accounts for slender_hunter on various social media sites, "entirely to mess with them by creating a fake arg but not actually doing anything with it."

28. For example, the series' mysterious nature was augmented by the creators' choice to disable YouTube comments on their videos. The resulting lack of user comments meant that viewers had to go elsewhere to glean more information about what was going on or to discuss the series.

29. Quotes from Slendylvr, Watson, k-elizabeth, and Arison retrieved from "What Is the Draw to This Series?," Unfiction discussion thread, July 28, 2009, http://forums.unfiction.com/forums/viewtopic.php?t=30043.

30. My use of the term "mesoscale" is meant to suggest a knowledge domain that mediates between macroscale understandings (e.g., cultural understandings of legend as genre) and microscale actions (e.g., individual legend performances) (Tangherlini 2018, 5–6). My argument is that algorithmic filtering significantly influences the structure of the mesoscale by presenting potential performers with a certain selection of actants and relationships over others, thereby guiding the feedback loop that "leads relatively quickly to convergence on a stable narrative framework" (7).

31. A popular photoshop also suggested that the character appeared in the background of the cartoon *Gravity Falls*, but this was merely a widely believed hoax.

Chapter 3. Commercialization

1. Simply called *Slender* on its initial release, the game's developer retitled the game as *Slender: The Eight Pages* when plans for a sequel began to form. To avoid confusion between the two *Slender* games, throughout this chapter I refer to the first game by its finalized name.

2. *Slender: The Arrival* was initially released on March 26, 2013—nine months after *The Eight Pages*—and received a subsequent release on the popular video game platform Steam in October of that same year. The game was also released on videogame consoles in 2014 (Xbox 360, PlayStation 3), 2015 (Xbox One, PlayStation 4, Wii U), and 2019 (Nintendo Switch).

3. A "Let's Play" is a popular genre of digital content in which a user (or users) plays through a video game while others watch and interact (either synchronously or asynchronously). In many ways, "Let's Play" videos (or forum posts) are a precursor to the popular live-streaming of video games on websites like Twitch. Although the term was originally coined by users on Something Awful, the practice had circulated widely across the web by the early 2010s. The YouTube videos discussed in this chapter (as well as their surrounding user interactions) are examples of the "Let's Play" genre.

4. I contacted Blue Isle Studios to confirm these numbers (which came from a third-party source), but they did not respond to my request.

5. As I have argued elsewhere, when institutional appropriations of vernacular practices seem insincere, they might still hail further engagement from users, but this engagement tends to occur in ways that are unintended or oppositional (Peck 2020a). Furthermore, this engagement is often not with the practice itself but against the institution. Therefore, even when these missteps do lead to user engagement or backlash, they are still limiting when it comes to encouraging further engagement with the appropriated practice.

6. Many scholars—mainly in the European tradition—also objected to folklore that was removed from its original context (often to be sold or politicized). These scholars called such appropriations *folklorismus* (or folklorism) to distinguish them from "authentic" forms of folklore (Moser 1962; Newall 1987). Much like Dorson's flawed folklore/fakelore dichotomy, contemporary scholars have troubled this distinction for the ways in which it overly romanticizes narrow ideas of "original" and "authentic" folklore (see Bendix 1997; Buccitelli 2014; Dégh 1994, 28; Foster 2016b).

7. Similarly, the prevalence of corporate ownership, partnership, sponsorship, and advertising in mass communication often means that commercial media tread lightly when it comes to legends *about* corporations, often only emphasizing the falsity of those claims (Fine 1992, 14).

8. Admittedly, this give-and-take may be somewhat lopsided in our current media-saturated environment (Dégh 1994, 25).

9. The word "vernacular" comes from the Roman Latin word *verna*, which referred to a homeborn slave (Howard 2011, 6). In ancient Rome, most slaves were captured from acts of war or piracy and were not literate in the language of their captors (2011, 6–7). Roman law dictated that the progeny of an enslaved woman was also a slave, so these homeborn slaves, when educated in the language of Rome, became more valuable to their masters for their ability to complete more technical tasks. Therefore, "a verna was made powerful because she or he had native access to Roman institutional language and yet was explicitly defined as something which was separate from Roman institutions" (Howard 2011, 7). Over time, *verna* gave way to vernacular, which for centuries denoted informal and

localized forms of Latin that existed "alongside but apart from the formal institutional language of Latin" (Howard 2011, 5; see also Howard 2008a, 2008b).

Building on this origin, contemporary scholarship tends to conceptualize vernacular expression in one of two ways.

The first way views vernacular expression as informal, local, or traditional forms of expression. This perspective suggests that vernacular discourse is a local apparatus of public opinion formation separate from institutions, which includes "[the] mundane transactions of words and gestures that allow us to negotiate our way through our quotidian encounters" (Hauser 1999, 11). This scholarship positions the vernacular as "commonplace" (Lantis 1960), "everyday" (Burgess 2007; Burgess and Green 2009), or "folkloric" (Garlough 2011). In this view, institutional alterity is expressed in the disjunction between lived experience and institutionally encouraged rules and ways of doing.

The second way views vernacular expression in terms of the practices and discourses emerging from subaltern communities. This perspective observes that vernacular theory can illuminate how racially marginalized groups that are systemically underrepresented in technology industries and gatekeeping roles "have voluntarily subverted or remixed dominant technologies using local (cultural) practices" (Gaskins 2019, 252). In this line of scholarship, "vernacular" refers to linguistic practices, artistic and aesthetic productions, and everyday maneuvers practiced by the racially marginalized to engage with, reappropriate, and improvise uses for systems, technologies, and norms designed by the dominant group to exclude and oppress them (Fouché 2006; see also Ono and Sloop 1995, 2002). Here, institutional alterity is expressed in ways of being and communicating by groups whose marginalized identities lead them to operate simultaneously under and apart from institutional power structures (Howard 2010, 243).

While these two views diverge significantly, they both imagine the vernacular in terms of institutional alterity (Howard 2010, 243). To reconcile these two views, and because "discursive performance cannot be essentialized to a single specific intentionality, agency, or location" (509), Howard suggests a reconfiguration that imagines a dialectical vernacular. This dialectical vernacular locates vernacularity in a process that "imagines a web of intentions moving along vectors of structural power that emerge as vernacular whenever they assert their alterity from the institutional" (2008b, 497). Accordingly, this chapter uses dialectical vernacular theory to demonstrate how commercial media and influences use vernacular rhetorical tactics to appeal to their audiences.

10. The defining characteristic of an institution "is that it has been instituted or founded by some formal act" (Howard 2013, 78). Many different organizations in contemporary society might fall under this label, including corporations, nonprofits, mass media outlets, and government agencies. Institutional agents (that is,

individuals working in an official capacity that represents an institution) have the capacity to speak both in formal, institutionally prescribed ways as well as in a vernacular mode (Howard 2010). Examples of communicating via an institutional mode might include speaking to the media via a press release, addressing political constituents with a sense of official decorum, or adopting the speech codes of the cultural group(s) that dominate these institutions.

11. Foster and Tolbert (2016) offer the term "folkloresque" to suggest that many commercial media texts give the impression that they derive from a specific folk tradition or practice but in fact are closer to folklore-inspired *bricolage* (Foster 2016a, 59). Foster and Tolbert also suggest that producers and consumers of popular culture frequently mobilize the perception that something is "folkloric" as a means toward cultivating authority or authenticity, an argument that I extend in this chapter through the lens of dialectical vernacular theory.

12. It is important to recognize that a *sense* of continuity is different from actual continuity. In other words, building in a sense that a communication is building on existing vernacular practice can still be a meaningful way to cultivate vernacular authority, even if those practices don't actually exist or only exist because of prior institutional constructions.

13. By "ambiguity" I am suggesting that institutional agents can easily hide their identity and motives when communicating online and often seek to influence others by masquerading as everyday users (Peck 2020a, 92). By "diffusion," I am suggesting that the loss of context and intentionality is a common occurrence as a practice spirals away from its original source. Even if an institution is readily identifiable, diffusion might ultimately obscure their role in influencing a wider digital practice (Peck 2020c).

14. This message—which appears after several developer logos but before the game's title screen—only appears the first time the game is opened. This means that the only people likely to see this message are first-time, firsthand players and, consequently, that the message is almost always absent from gameplay footage uploaded to social media sites like YouTube.

15. The game holds an average rating of 65/100 among critics and 6.1/10 among users on the review aggregator website Metacritic. Since video games tend to be graded on a scale that skews high (generally in the 70 to 100 percent range), these ratings suggest that the general reception was somewhat lower than normal, though not egregiously so.

16. Since posting, this user has deleted their account. Their comment can be found at "/R/Horror Games Discussion—Slender: The Arrival," Reddit, 2014, https://www.reddit.com/r/Games/comments/2k5wtq/rgames_horror_game_discussion_slender_the_arrival/.

17. hellokevin, "Did Anyone Play Slender: The Arrival? What Did You Think?," Reddit, 2013, https://www.reddit.com/r/Games/comments/1e71up/did_anyone_play_slender_the_arrival_what_did_you/.

18. epicgeek, "/R/Games Horror Game Discussion—Slender: The Arrival," Reddit, 2014, https://www.reddit.com/r/Games/comments/2k5wtq/rgames_horror_game_discussion_slender_the_arrival/.

19. This comment was made by an anonymous user posting in the comments section for Thomas Grip's blog post about the game (see Grip 2013).

20. FoxyRussian, "/R/Games Horror Game Discussion—Slender: The Arrival," Reddit, 2014, https://www.reddit.com/r/Games/comments/2k5wtq/rgames_horror_game_discussion_slender_the_arrival/.

21. The high number of YouTube subscribers that PewDiePie had in March 2013 continued to grow over the next several months. By August of that year, his channel had become the most-subscribed channel on YouTube. PewDiePie maintained and expanded that popularity in the years that followed, and by 2020 his subscriber count had crested 100 million, making his channel the most-subscribed English language channel on YouTube.

22. An additional fifth part was posted a few weeks later, showing viewers a secret level in the game.

23. See, for example, Markiplier (2013) and Smosh Games (2013).

24. It should be noted that in this quote Goffman is discussing how professionals surreptitiously engage in noninstitutional forms of behavior while on the job. Here, I am suggesting that the inverse is also true—the spirited life of the performer becomes a shell that conceals official activity—and that Goffman's observation remains equally applicable.

25. This demographic data might actually skew younger when applied to our current case. First, users in the 18–26 demographic when these numbers were released would have been five to six years younger in 2012 and 2013 (when the *Slender* games were released), meaning that these numbers could reflect PewDiePie's fan base growing older over time. Second, even if these reported age demographics have stayed consistent over time, it's not unusual for users to lie about their age when creating an account. Teenagers might self-report that they are over eighteen so they can access videos that are age-restricted due to their content. Users under thirteen must lie about their age to meet the minimum age requirement for registering an account on YouTube.

26. One study found that more than 80 percent of middle schoolers were unable to tell the difference between a native advertisement—an advertisement meant to resemble the content of the medium in which it appears—and a real news story (Donald 2016). Most young adolescents in this study were also unable to distinguish commercial content from other content on the web page, even when it was labeled as "sponsored content."

27. The idea of a parasocial relationship was originally meant to recognize how audience members of mass mediated content would occasionally develop a sense of intimacy, friendship, or identification toward a celebrity or media personality that they had never met (Horton and Wohl 1956; see also Giles 2002; Hartmann and Goldhoorn 2011; Rubin and McHugh 1987). As I explain in this section, the connective and visible nature of social media challenges how we think of these types of relationships.

28. Content creators frequently encouraged this type of engagement. In the description for his *Slender: The Eight Pages* video, PewDiePie notes that he is "Proud to be the first one to Let's Play this video on YouTube. It's amazing how popular it became shortly after I played it and it shows what let's players can do to a relatively unknown game. Games are meant to be played and if anyone comments 'copy' on my behalf, please know that I'm against it" (Kjellberg 2012). In this final sentence PewDiePie is encouraging other users to make similar videos and discouraging his fans from loudly dismissing those variants as inferior or second-rate copies.

29. *Always Watching: A Marble Hornets Story* (2015) and *Slender Man* (2018) are largely forgotten (except for the occasional appearance on "worst movie" lists). In addition to coming out several years after the legend cycle's zenith, both films take significant liberties with the details of the legend cycle in order to create more film-friendly narratives and were largely panned by critics and audiences alike.

30. In September 1993 America Online began offering its users access to Usenet, beginning a period that Usenet users would go on to call "Eternal September." Before this, Usenet was mostly restricted to users at colleges, universities, and research facilities, meaning that every September (as new students entered college) a new set of users would gain access to Usenet. Because these new users were not yet aware of the etiquette of using Usenet, established users understood that a lot of posts in any given September would break from informal cultural norms for behavior and that they would need to actively work to socialize new users into the norms of communicating on Usenet. When America Online began offering access in September 1993, this influx of new users became too numerous and too ongoing for existing users to deal with, which led to significant shifts in Usenet culture. By drawing a parallel to Eternal September, I am suggesting that once a piece of digital culture (a website, a practice, a legend cycle, etc.) begins to gain mainstream popularity, the sheer influx and diversity of new users will fundamentally change cultural norms and drive away many earlier adopters.

Chapter 4. Ostension

1. Although these videos are publicly available on YouTube, in light of the low number of views and age of the subject at time of recording, I have chosen to use

a pseudonym and omit other potentially identifying information. All videos are in possession of the author.

2. Although Dégh and Vázsonyi drew on work in the field of semiotics when they introduced the term "ostension" into folklore scholarship, the contemporary use of the term in folkloristics differs appreciably from how it is used in semiotics, linguistics, and philosophy (Tolbert and Brodie 2019). Folklorists tend to view ostension as more diachronic than other fields, meaning that it is viewed "not primarily a way of communicating new, previously unknown information, but of interacting with something already communicated (the content of a traditional narrative or belief)" (Tolbert and Brodie 2019, 4). This chapter is concerned with the folkloric use of the term.

3. Inaction and avoidance are themselves choices. When such choices are made because of legends, they too are examples of ostension. An individual might decide not to shop at a certain store or eat at a certain restaurant because of a legend they heard regarding the establishment—for instance, that a friend-of-a-friend had found a deep-fried rat in her bucket of Kentucky Fried Chicken. When such acts of avoiding or inaction occur, these individuals might not be directly enacting the narrative, but they are "making choices on the basis of narrative events and thereby transmitting the narrative through their actions" (Goldstein 2004, 30). In other words, they are engaging in ostension.

4. For explanations of the legends that inspired these hypothetical examples, see the appendix.

5. A small durable trace does not mean no trace. Legend trippers walking through the woods will leave footprints and snapped branches, for example. It is very likely, however, that such a trace would be nearly bereft of context for a later observer, who might even mistake it for a sign of the supernatural (see Ellis 1996, 177). For an application of practice theory to the act of walking in natural spaces, see Schmitt 2016.

6. This hypothetical example draws from the work of Bill Ellis, who suggests that these events maintain a fairly typical pattern: "Teenagers gather together, tell spooky stories about a local site, and then travel by car to see the place for themselves" (2001a, 186; see also Ellis 1996). It also draws from my own experience as a legend-tripping teenager pre-Web 2.0 (see the introduction).

7. See the appendix.

8. Although "performance" (which I have used thus far) can be viewed as a subset of "practice" (which I advocate for in this chapter) the two are sometimes paired as opposites in the humanities, with "practice representing usual, mundane, instrumental, and constant routine while performance is the artistic, occasional, and entertaining event" (Bronner 2012, 31). However, practice and performance are actually quite compatible, and bridging this gap may be a productive way of

understanding the relationship between individual actors and collective tradition, especially in the case of digital communication (Bronner 2012; 2016, 18; see also Berger and del Negro 2016, 161; Buccitelli 2016). In line with how I have defined "performance" in this book, this chapter takes a complimentary approach to practice and performance.

9. Just as the previous example drew on the work of Bill Ellis, this example is indebted to the work of Elizabeth Tucker and her research into the role of smartphones on ghost hunts (2018b), digitally mediated ostensive play (2018a), and hypermodern ostension (2020). It also draws from my own discussions with college students about their legend-tripping experiences.

10. Locating authenticity in contemporary legend performances is often tricky. This issue is exacerbated in the case of the Slender Man, as it involves users constructing authenticity around something with a demonstrably fictitious origin point (see chapter 1). My use of "authentic" here is meant to refer to the performative elements that give the legend cycle a sense of plausibility. These elements might help the audience suspend their disbelief or facilitate a blurring of boundaries between the real and the supernatural. As I elaborate in the paragraphs that follow, although my use of "authentic" in this paragraph is juxtaposed with "play," the reality of ostensive practice is that play and authenticity are often closely linked phenomena.

11. For instance, when a user uploads a video under a name like "JAusten Productions" (2012) or includes "This video is FICTIONAL" in the description (Sam Thrower 2012), that user is acknowledging the fictional nature of the project in a way that allows the video to appear initially authentic until scrutiny is applied. Although this tactic may seem strange, one uploader comment suggests that it is meant to help stem the very common viewer comment that the video looks or seems fake (Sam Thrower 2012).

12. As of July 2021, this video has nearly 375,000 views and over 1,500 comments.

13. For more details regarding this phenomenon, see Kitta 2018a, 2018b, 2019. See also chapters 2 and 3.

14. It is very likely based on the information these commenters provided that many of them were either in elementary school or middle school. Additionally, a few seemed to be non-native English speakers.

15. Langdon Street is located one block north of State Street (the central venue for Halloween festivities near the University of Wisconsin) and home to most fraternity and sorority life on campus.

16. xXRoflFalafelXx, "Best Halloween Costume!," Reddit, 2012, http://www.reddit.com/r/funny/comments/119y40/best_halloween_costume/?sort=old&limit=500.

17. The_Bhuda_Palm, "I Know You Guys Aren't Digging Slender Costumes, but I Think My Buddy Was Able to Pull It Off Better than the Rest," Reddit, 2012,

http://www.reddit.com/r/pics/comments/12g39q/i_know_you_guys_arent_digging_slender_costumes/.

18. While commercial Slender Man costumes were widely available in 2014 (see chapter 3), I did not find any instances of them in either online or offline observations. The large amount of homemade costume submissions to this subreddit suggests the separation from commercial costuming is an important rhetorical move.

19. Javier is using "myth" in the colloquial sense of the term to mean untrue or not real.

Chapter 5. Sensation

1. Although early work on the subject often hyphenates the term (i.e., "rumor-panic"), I have chosen to use the more contemporary "rumor panic" in this book. Doing so provides a clearer parallel to "moral panic" while also matching how the term has been rendered in more recent work by scholars like Ellis (2000), Fine and Ellis (2010), and Soltero (2016).

2. Disciplinary boundaries further complicate this distinction. Citing the work of Patrick B. Mullen (1972), Patricia A. Turner notes that "rumor has traditionally been studied by social scientists while legend has fallen squarely within the disciplinary territory of folklorists" (1994, 4). This divergence in terminology helps explain why Victor, a sociologist, chose the phrase "rumor-panic" to describe what folklorists have also called a "legend-derived panic" (e.g., Ellis 1990, 32; 2001a, 202; 2002a, 22). Although Victor's term is more widely used (even among folklorists), I do wish to suggest that there is significant overlap between the idea of a "rumor panic" and a "legend-derived panic."

3. Similar to what Hall et al. suggest and to what Grider observes here, sociologist Jean-Bruno Renard argues that these sorts of warnings from institutional officials, educated elites, and other authorities frequently play a key role in the spread and legitimation of rumors and legends (1991, 13–18).

4. Socrates, for example, cautioned about the corruptive dangers of the then-new technology of writing in Plato's *Phaedrus* (ca. 370 BCE). He warned that "this invention will produce forgetfulness in the minds of those who learn to use it, because they will not practice their memory. . . . You offer your pupils the appearance of wisdom, not true wisdom, for they will read many things without instruction and will therefore seem to know many things, when they are for the most part ignorant and hard to get along with, since they are not wise, but only appear wise" (275a–b).

5. While popular use of the term "rumor" often connotes dubious veracity, Gary Alan Fine and Bill Ellis position these short, nonnarrative statements of belief more as a form of speculative discourse (2010, 4–5). Some rumors insist on their own truth while others are more ambivalent (145). What's key here, according to

Fine and Ellis, is not whether these events actually occurred but the extent to which their details, meanings, and implications become subjects for belief-based debate (146).

6. See Facebook 2020.

7. By "official or trusted source," I am referring not only to the media outlets themselves but also to the experts and authorities that those outlets choose to quote and rely on for their stories. As Grider notes, these authorities frequently play a key role in defining and sustaining legend-inspired panics (1984). See also Hall et al.'s discussion of "primary definers"—institutional officials who play a key role in defining the contours of a panic by framing information and rumors before they reach the mass media (1978, 58–59).

8. This, of course, is a contemporary version of the same syndrome that scholars like Grider (1984) and Best and Horiuchi (1985) identified decades ago, just facilitated by this new media environment.

9. This description of the events that transpired on May 31, 2014, combines information contained in the criminal complaint (Complaint, State of Wisconsin v. Morgan E. Geyser and Anissa E. Weier 2014) with excerpts of the girls' police interviews (see *20/20* 2019; Bohr and Sater 2015), televised interviews with the detectives and survivor (*20/20* 2019), and investigative reporting by ABC News in the months and years following the incident (e.g., *20/20* 2019; Dooley et al. 2018; Effron and Robinson 2014; Robinson 2019).

10. Weier, however, contradicts this story. She told investigators that Geyser kept a mental count as she stabbed Leutner and that later in the day Geyser told her she believed she had stabbed her seventeen times.

11. A press conference on Monday, June 3, 2014, placed the time of apprehension at 2:24 p.m. while a later interview with *20/20* placed it at 2:53 p.m.

12. A criminal complaint is a legal document that charges a suspect (or suspects) with a specific crime or crimes. They also contain pertinent facts about the case that led to those charges. Journalists who cover legal matters frequently obtain and use these documents in their reporting.

13. Detective Tom Casey, who interviewed Geyser, has suggested that there was "a lot of deception" in her interview and that she often tried to deflect blame onto Weier (*20/20* 2019).

14. See also *FOX 6* 2014.

15. Since the case had been mostly local before this point, previous references used local time (Central Daylight Time) to describe the order of events that had taken place. Unless specified otherwise, from this point forward I use Eastern Daylight Time to standardize the various time zones included in the growing national and international coverage of this story.

16. In journalism, the first few sentences of an article that seek to convey the most essential ideas (who, what, when, where, why) are commonly called the "lede" (sometimes erroneously spelled as "lead").

17. Wire stories are basic reports compiled and distributed to journalistic organizations by national or international news associations. They often serve as the basis for further reporting, with local reporters crediting the organization for their original reporting.

18. The nut graph is a paragraph that usually comes after the lede and establishes context for the story while also explaining to readers why the story is newsworthy. The nut graph is the story "in a nutshell."

19. From 2014 to 2018, Facebook had a sidebar for trending topics located in the top right corner of the user interface. Facebook's trending topics list mimicked a similar function on Twitter and showed users a few trending topics with a brief description of each.

20. Many news reports from the week following the stabbing (June 2–6) erroneously spelled the creature's name as a single word—Slenderman—likely because that's how the name had been misspelled in the criminal complaint. It took about a week for news organizations to standardize the correct spelling. For consistency, I use the correct two-word spelling unless citing a specific primary source that renders it otherwise.

21. JackoftheBox, "Has Anyone Seen This? 'Slender Man,'" The Bump, June 2014, https://forums.thebump.com/discussion/12358967/has-anyone-seen-this-slender-man.

22. TarheelMama202, "What Are You Doing?—The Bump," The Bump, June 2014, https://forums.thebump.com/discussion/comment/82235660#Comment_82235660.

23. jayem, "12-Year-Old Wisconsin Girl Stabbed 19 Times; Friends Arrested," Christian Forums, June 3, 2014, https://www.christianforums.com/threads/12-year-old-wisconsin-girl-stabbed-19-times-friends-arrested.7825755/.

24. Anonymous, "12-Yr-Old Milwaukee Girls Stab Friend 10 Times!," DC Urban Moms and Dads, June 3, 2014, https://www.dcurbanmom.com/jforum/posts/list/389190.page.

25. JackoftheBox, "Has Anyone Seen This? 'Slender Man,'" The Bump, June 2014, https://forums.thebump.com/discussion/12358967/has-anyone-seen-this-slender-man.

26. Once an interpretive frame becomes amplified into dominance, it is extremely hard to change that frame via in-depth reporting or fact checking. Even if news of Geyser and Weier's mental health struggles had been made public earlier, it likely would have done little to counter the burgeoning rumor panic surrounding the Slender Man (Peck 2020c).

27. An alternative explanation for the Ohio attack is that amplification reifies that which is being amplified. When young people are told by parents or media reports to stay away from a cool, dangerous, or sexy behavior that (potentially many) other young people are allegedly engaging in, they may feel compelled to try that activity for themselves. Depending on the specific behavior, these acts of imitation could occur for a variety of reasons ranging from wanting a similar level of media exposure to a youthful desire to exercise rebellion or practice autonomy.

28. For examples of users calling out these headlines for being deceptive, see amanforallsaisons, "Neighbor: Vegas Gunman Dressed Up as Slenderman, Joker—CBS Las Vegas," Reddit, 2014, https://www.reddit.com/r/news/comments/27wjje/neighbor_vegas_gunman_dressed_up_as_slenderman/.; undue-influence, "Las Vegas Cop Killers Were 'White Supremacists' Who Liked to Dress as Slenderman and The Joker," Reddit, 2014, www.reddit.com/r/news/comments/27s8ep/las_vegas_cop_killers_were_white_supremacists_who/.

29. My use of quotation marks around the term "inexplicable" is meant to suggest that these events are very much explainable. However, since these explanations are unsettling and deal with issues like mental health and white supremacy, the Slender Man presents an easier (though inaccurate) way to deal with these events while simultaneously ignoring more salient systemic problems in American culture.

30. Anonymous, "Should 'Slender Man' Be Banned?," DC Urban Moms and Dads, June 9, 2014, https://www.dcurbanmom.com/jforum/posts/list/390542.page.

Conclusion

1. See the appendix.
2. See the appendix.

References

Adeane, Ant. 2019. "Blue Whale: What Is the Truth Behind an Online 'Suicide Challenge'?" *BBC News*, January 13. https://www.bbc.com/news/blogs-trending-46505722.

American Press Institute. 2014. "How Americans Get Their News." American Press Institute, March 17. https://www.americanpressinstitute.org/publications/reports/survey-research/how-americans-get-news/.

Barzilai-Nahon, Karine. 2008. "Toward a Theory of Network Gatekeeping: A Framework for Exploring Information Control." *Journal of the American Society for Information Science and Technology* 59 (9): 1493–1512. https://doi.org/10.1002/asi.20857.

Bauman, Richard. 1984. *Verbal Art as Performance*. Prospect Heights, IL: Waveland Press.

Bauman, Zygmunt. 2007. *Liquid Times: Living in an Age of Uncertainty*. Cambridge: Polity.

Baym, Nancy K. 2010. *Personal Connections in the Digital Age*. Cambridge: Polity.

Ben-Amos, Dan. 1971. "Toward a Definition of Folklore in Context." *Journal of American Folklore* 84 (331): 3–15.

Bendix, Regina. 1997. *In Search of Authenticity: The Formation of Folklore Studies*. Madison: University of Wisconsin Press.

Benkler, Yochai. 2006. *The Wealth of Networks: How Social Production Transforms Markets and Freedom*. New Haven, CT: Yale University Press.

Berger, Harris M., and Giovanna P. Del Negro. 2002. "Bauman's Verbal Art and the Social Organization of Attention: The Role of Reflexivity in the Aesthetics of Performance." *Journal of American Folklore* 115 (455): 62–91.

———. 2016. "Reasonable Suspicion: Folklore, Practice, and the Reproduction of Institutions." *Cultural Analysis* 15 (1): 145–67.

Best, Joel. 1991. "Bad Guys and Random Violence: Folklore and Media Constructions of Contemporary Deviance." *Contemporary Legend* 1:107–22.

———. 1993. *Threatened Children: Rhetoric and Concern about Child-Victims.* Chicago: University of Chicago Press.

Best, Joel, and Kathleen A. Bogle. 2014. *Kids Gone Wild: From Rainbow Parties to Sexting, Understanding the Hype over Teen Sex.* New York: New York University Press.

Best, Joel, and Gerald T. Horiuchi. 1985. "The Razor Blade in the Apple: The Social Construction of Urban Legends." *Social Problems* 32 (5): 488–99.

Bever, Lindsey. 2014. "'Slender Man' Recedes in Wisconsin Stabbing Case as Mental Health Becomes Issue." *Washington Post,* July 3, sec. Morning Mix.

Bird, S. Elizabeth. 1992. *For Enquiring Minds: A Cultural Study of Supermarket Tabloids.* Knoxville: University of Tennessee Press.

———. 1994. "Playing with Fear: Interpreting the Adolescent Legend Trip." *Western Folklore* 53:191–209.

———. 2006. "Cultural Studies as Confluence: The Convergence of Folklore and Media Studies." In *Popular Culture Theory and Methodology: A Basic Introduction,* edited by Harold E. Hinds, Marilyn Ferris Motz, and Angela M. S. Nelson, 344–55. Madison: University of Wisconsin Press.

Blank, Trevor J. 2007. "Examining the Transmission of Urban Legends: Making the Case for Folklore Fieldwork on the Internet." *Folklore Forum* 37 (1): 15–26. http://hdl.handle.net/2022/3231.

Blank, Trevor J. 2009. "Toward a Conceptual Framework for the Study of Folklore and the Internet." In *Folklore and the Internet: Vernacular Expression in a Digital World,* edited by Trevor J. Blank, 1–20. Logan: Utah State University Press.

———. 2013. *The Last Laugh: Folk Humor, Celebrity Culture, and Mass-Mediated Disasters in the Digital Age.* Folklore Studies in a Multicultural World. Madison: University of Wisconsin Press.

———. 2018. "Folklore and the Internet: The Challenge of an Ephemeral Landscape." *Humanities* 7 (2): 50. https://doi.org/10.3390/h7020050.

Blank, Trevor J., and Lynne S. McNeill, eds. 2015. "The Slender Man." Special issue, *Contemporary Legend* 3 (5).

———. 2018a. "Introduction: Fear Has No Face; Creepypasta as Digital Legendry." In *Slender Man Is Coming: Creepypasta and Contemporary Legends on the Internet,* edited by Trevor J. Blank and Lynne S. McNeill, 3–23. Logan: Utah State University Press.

———, eds. 2018b. *Slender Man Is Coming: Creepypasta and Contemporary Legends on the Internet.* Logan: Utah State University Press.

Bohr, Nick, and Terry Sater. 2015. "Exclusive: WISN 12 Obtains Questioning of 'Slender Man' Suspects." *WISN,* February 19, sec. News. https://www.wisn.com/

article/exclusive-wisn-12-obtains-police-questioning-of-slender-man-suspects/6325578.

Bosman, Julie. 2015. "Pine Ridge Indian Reservation Struggles with Suicides among Its Young." *New York Times*, May 1, sec. U.S.

boyd, danah. 2010. "Social Network Sites as Networked Publics: Affordances, Dynamics, and Implications." In *A Networked Self: Identity, Community and Culture on Social Network Sites*, edited by Zizi Papacharissi, 39–58. New York: Routledge.

———. 2014. *It's Complicated: The Social Lives of Networked Teens.* New Haven, CT: Yale University Press.

Broderick, Ryan. 2014. "Mom in Ohio Says Her 13-Year-Old Daughter Stabbed Her Multiple Times Because of Slender Man." *BuzzFeed News*, June 9. https://www.buzzfeednews.com/article/ryanhatesthis/a-mom-in-ohio-is-claiming-her-13-year-old-daughter-stabbed-h.

Brodie, Ian. 2015. "Shira Chess and Eric Newsom. Folklore, Horror Stories, and the Slender Man: The Development of an Internet Mythology." Book review. *Contemporary Legend* 3 (5): 130–34.

Bronner, Simon J. 2009. "Digitizing and Virtualizing Folklore." In *Folklore and the Internet: Vernacular Expression in a Digital World*, edited by Trevor J. Blank, 21–66. Logan: Utah State University Press.

———. 2012. "Practice Theory in Folklore and Folklife Studies." *Folklore* 123 (1): 23–47.

———. 2016. "Toward a Definition of Folklore in Practice." *Cultural Analysis* 15 (1): 6–27.

Brunvand, Jan Harold. 1981. *The Vanishing Hitchhiker: American Urban Legends and Their Meanings.* New York: Norton.

Buccitelli, Anthony Bak. 2012. "Performance 2.0: Observations toward a Theory of the Digital Performance of Folklore." In *Folk Culture in the Digital Age: The Emergent Dynamics of Human Interaction*, edited by Trevor J. Blank, 60–84. Logan: Utah State University Press.

———. 2013. "Virtually a Local: Folk Geography, Discourse, and Local Identity on the Geospatial Web." *Western Folklore* 72 (1): 29–58.

———. 2014. "Paying to Play Digital Media, Commercialization, and the Scholarship of Alan Dundes." *Western Folklore* 73 (2/3): 235–56.

———. 2016. "Hybrid Tactics and Locative Legends: Re-reading de Certeau for the Future of Folkloristics." *Cultural Analysis* 15 (1): 78–98.

Burger, Peter. 2009. "The Smiley Gang Panic: Ethnic Legends about Gang Rape in the Netherlands in the Wake of 9/11." *Western Folklore* 68 (2/3): 275–95.

Burgess, Jean. 2007. "Vernacular Creativity and New Media." PhD diss., Queensland University of Technology. http://eprints.qut.edu.au/16378/.

Burgess, Jean, and Joshua Green. 2009. *YouTube: Online Video and Participatory Culture.* Digital Media and Society Series. Malden, MA: Polity.

Burke, Kenneth. 1950. *A Rhetoric of Motives.* Berkeley: University of California Press.

Busse, Kristina, and Jonathan Gray. 2011. "Fan Cultures and Fan Communities." In *The Handbook of Media Audiences*, edited by Virginia Nightingale, 425–43. Global Media and Communication Handbook Series (Iamcr) 1. Malden, MA: Wiley-Blackwell.

Campion-Vincent, Véronique. 1989. "Complots et avertissements: Légendes urbaines dans la ville." *Revue Française de Sociologie* 30 (1): 91–105.

———. 1997. "Organ Theft Narratives." *Western Folklore* 56:1–37.

———. 2002. "Organ Theft Narratives as Medical and Social Critique." *Journal of Folklore Research* 39 (1): 33–50.

———. 2005. *Organ Theft Legends.* Translated by Jacqueline Simpson. Jackson: University Press of Mississippi.

Carey, James W. 1989. *Communication as Culture: Essays on Media and Society.* Media and Popular Culture. Boston: Unwin Hyman.

Casey, Evan. 2021. "One of the Girls Committed to a Mental Hospital in the Slender Man Stabbing Case Has Been Granted Release." *Milwaukee Journal Sentinel*, July 1.

CBC News. 2014. "Slender Man Stabbings: Who Is Slender Man?" *CBC News*, June 3. https://www.cbc.ca/news/world/slender-man-stabbings-who-is-slender-man-1.2663012.

CBS Las Vegas. 2014. "Neighbor: Vegas Gunman Dressed Up as Slenderman, Joker." *CBS Las Vegas*, June 9.

CBS News. 2017. "Anissa Weier Sentenced in Slender Man Stabbing Case." *CBS News*, December 21. https://www.cbsnews.com/news/anissa-weier-sentenced-in-slender-man-stabbing-case/.

Chasmar, Jessica. 2014. "13-Year-Old Ohio Girl Stabs Mother In 2nd 'Slenderman' Attack." *Washington Times*, June 9.

Chen, Chih-Ping. 2016. "Forming Digital Self and Parasocial Relationships on YouTube." *Journal of Consumer Culture* 16 (1): 232–54. https://doi.org/10.1177/1469540514521081.

Chess, Shira. 2012. "Open-Sourcing Horror: The Slender Man, *Marble Hornets*, and Genre Negotiations." *Information, Communication & Society* 15 (3): 374–93. https://doi.org/10.1080/1369118X.2011.642889.

Chess, Shira, and Eric Newsom. 2015. *Folklore, Horror Stories, and the Slender Man: The Development of an Internet Mythology.* New York: Palgrave Pivot.

Chung, Siyoung, and Hichang Cho. 2017. "Fostering Parasocial Relationships with Celebrities on Social Media: Implications for Celebrity Endorsement." *Psychology & Marketing* 34 (4): 481–95. https://doi.org/10.1002/mar.21001.

City of Waukesha Police Department. 2014. "Waukesha Police June 2 2014 Press Conference." YouTube video, June 2. https://www.youtube.com/watch?v=FWIKFrKp-JU&t.

Cochrane, Timothy. 1987. "The Concept of Ecotypes in American Folklore." *Journal of Folklore Research* 24 (1): 33–55.

Cocq, Coppélie. 2015. "Indigenous Voices on the Web: Folksonomies and Endangered Languages." *Journal of American Folklore* 128 (509): 273–85.

Cohen, Stanley. 2011. *Folk Devils and Moral Panics: The Creation of the Mods and Rockers.* Routledge Classics. New York: Routledge.

Complaint, State of Wisconsin v. Morgan E. Geyser and Anissa E. Weier. 2014. Waukesha County Circuit Court.

Cuomo, Chris, Kate Bolduan, Michaela Pereira, Danny Cevallos, Rosa Flores, Tom Fuentes, and Nischelle Turner. 2014. "Twelve-Year-Old Girls Charged in Stabbing." *CNN New Day*, June 3.

Curlew, Abigail. 2017. "The Legend of the Slender Man: The Boogieman of Surveillance Culture." *First Monday* 22 (6). https://doi.org/10.5210/fm.v22i6.6901.

Davisson, Amber L., and Angela C. Leone. 2018. "From Coercion to Community Building: Technological Affordances as Rhetorical Forms." In *Theorizing Digital Rhetoric*, edited by Aaron Hess and Amber L. Davisson, 85–97. New York: Routledge.

Dégh, Linda. 1971. "The 'Belief Legend' in Modern Society: Form, Function, and Relationship to Other Genres." In *American Folk Legend*, edited by Wayland Hand, 55–68. Los Angeles: University of California Press.

———. 1994. *American Folklore and the Mass Media.* Folklore Today. Bloomington: Indiana University Press.

———. 1995. *Narratives in Society: A Performer-Centered Study of Narration.* FF Communications, no. 255. Helsinki: Suomalainen Tiedeakatemia, Academia Scientiarum Fennica

———. 1996. "What Is a Belief Legend?" *Folklore* 107:33–46.

———. 2001. *Legend and Belief: Dialectics of a Folklore Genre.* Bloomington: Indiana University Press.

Dégh, Linda, and Andrew Vázsonyi. 1975. "The Hypothesis of Multi-conduit Transmission in Folklore." In *Folklore: Performance and Communication*, edited by Dan Ben-Amos, 207–55. Paris: Den Haag.

Dégh, Linda, and Andrew Vázsonyi. 1983. "Does the Word 'Dog' Bite? Ostensive Action: A Means of Legend Telling." *Journal of Folklore Research* 20 (1): 5–34.

Dijck, José van. 2009. "Users Like You? Theorizing Agency in User-Generated Content." *Media, Culture & Society* 31 (1): 41–58. https://doi.org/10.1177/0163443708098245.

Donald, Brooke. 2016. "Stanford Researchers Find Students Have Trouble Judging the Credibility of Information Online." Stanford Graduate School of Education, November 21. https://ed.stanford.edu/news/stanford-researchers-find-students-have-trouble-judging-credibility-information-online.

Dooley, Sean, Emily Whipp, Kelley Robinson, Alexa Valiente, and Lauren Effron. 2018. "Mothers of Teens Who Pleaded Guilty in 'Slender Man' Stabbing Case Say There Were No Warning Signs of Violence." *ABC News*, January 31. https://abcnews.go.com/US/mothers-teens-pleaded-guilty-slender-man-stabbing-case/story?id=52739807.

Dorson, Richard M. 1950. "Folklore and Fake Lore." *American Mercury*, March 1950.

———. 1959. *American Folklore.* Chicago History of American Civilization 4. Chicago: University of Chicago Press.

———. 1976. *Folklore and Fakelore: Essays toward a Discipline of Folk Studies.* Cambridge, MA: Harvard University Press. https://doi.org/10.4159/harvard.9780674330207.

Dorst, John. 1990. "Tags and Burners, Cycles and Networks: Folklore in the Telectronic Age." *Journal of Folklore Research* 27 (3): 179–91.

Drake, Richard Allen. 1989. "Construction Sacrifice and Kidnapping Rumor Panics in Borneo." *Oceania* 59 (4): 269–79.

Drehs, Wayne. 2015. "How PewDiePie Became King of YouTube." *ESPN*, June 11. https://www.espn.com/espn/story/_/id/13013936/pewdiepie-how-became-king-youtube.

Dundes, Alan. 1966. "Metafolklore and Oral Literary Criticism." *Monist* 50 (4): 505–16.

———. 1998. "Bloody Mary in the Mirror: A Ritual Reflection of Pre-pubescent Anxiety." *Western Folklore* 57 (2/3): 119–35.

Dundes, Alan, and Carl R. Pagter. 1975. *Urban Folklore from the Paperwork Empire.* Publications of the American Folklore Society 62. Austin, TX: American Folklore Society.

Effron, Lauren, and Kelley Robinson. 2014. "Slender Man Stabbing Survivor's Parents: 'She's Meant to Do Something Special.'" *ABC News*, September 26. http://abcnews.go.com/US/slender-man-stabbing-survivors-parents-describe-horrific-ordeal/story?id=25787516.

Eisenstein, Elizabeth L. 1980. *The Printing Press as an Agent of Change: Communications and Cultural Transformations in Early-Modern Europe.* Combined paperback ed. Cambridge: Cambridge University Press.

Ellis, Bill. 1981. "The Camp Mock-Ordeal *Theater as Life*." *Journal of American Folklore* 94 (374): 486–505.

———. 1989. "Death by Folklore: Ostension, Contemporary Legend, and Murder." *Western Folklore* 48 (3): 201–20.

———. 1990. "The Devil-Worshippers at the Prom: Rumor-Panic as Therapeutic Magic." *Western Folklore* 49 (1): 27–49.

———. 1996. "Legend-Trips and Satanism: Adolescents' Ostensive Traditions as 'Cult' Activity." In *Contemporary Legend: A Reader*, edited by Gillian Bennett and Paul Smith, 167–86. New Perspectives in Folklore 4. London: Routledge, Taylor & Francis Group.

———. 2000. *Raising the Devil: Satanism, New Religions, and the Media.* Lexington: University Press of Kentucky.

———. 2001a. *Aliens, Ghosts, and Cults: Legends We Live.* Jackson: University Press of Mississippi.

———. 2001b. "A Model for Collecting and Interpreting World Trade Center Disaster Jokes." *New Directions in Folklore* 5. https://scholarworks.iu.edu/journals/index.php/ndif/article/view/19881.

———. 2002a. "Hitler's Birthday: Rumor-Panics in the Wake of the Columbine Shootings." *Children's Folklore Review* 24 (1/2): 21–32.

———. 2002b. "Making a Big Apple Crumble: The Role of Humor in Constructing a Global Response to Disaster." *New Directions in Folklore* 6. https://scholarworks.iu.edu/journals/index.php/ndif/article/view/19883.

———. 2018. "'Fake News' in the Contemporary Legend Dynamic." *Journal of American Folklore* 131 (522): 398–404.

Evans, Brad. 2014. "Hamilton Co. Mom: Daughter's Knife Attack Influenced by Slender Man." *WLWT*, June 6, sec. News. https://www.wlwt.com/article/hamilton-co-mom-daughter-s-knife-attack-influenced-by-slender-man/3543596.

Evans, Timothy H. 2018. "Slender Man, H. P. Lovecraft, and the Dynamics of Horror Cultures." In *Slender Man Is Coming: Creepypasta and Contemporary Legends on the Internet*, edited by Trevor J. Blank and Lynne S. McNeill, 128–40. Logan: Utah State University Press.

Facebook. 2020. "What 'The Social Dilemma' Gets Wrong." https://about.fb.com/wp-content/uploads/2020/10/What-The-Social-Dilemma-Gets-Wrong.pdf.

Fägersten, Kristy Beers. 2017. "The Role of Swearing in Creating an Online Persona: The Case of YouTuber PewDiePie." *Discourse, Context & Media* 18:1–10.

Fernback, J. 2003. "Legends on the Net: An Examination of Computer-Mediated Communication as a Locus of Oral Culture." *New Media & Society* 5 (1): 29–45. https://doi.org/10.1177/1461444803005001902.

Fine, Gary Alan. 1979. "Folklore Diffusion through Interactive Social Networks: Conduits in a Preadolescent Community." *New York Folklore* 5 (1): 87–126.

———. 1980. "The Kentucky Fried Rat: Legends and Modern Society." *Journal of the Folklore Institute* 17 (2/3): 222–43.

———. 1991. "Redemption Rumors and the Power of Ostension." *Journal of American Folklore* 104 (412): 179–81.
———. 1992. *Manufacturing Tales: Sex and Money in Contemporary Legends*. Publications of the American Folklore Society, New Series. Knoxville: University of Tennessee Press.
Fine, Gary Alan, and Bill Ellis. 2010. *The Global Grapevine: Why Rumors of Terrorism, Immigration, and Trade Matter.* Oxford: Oxford University Press.
Finlayson, Rob. 2014. Personal Interview via Skype. Interview in possession of author.
Foley, John Miles. 2012. *Oral Tradition and the Internet: Pathways of the Mind.* Urbana: University of Illinois Press.
Foote, Monica. 2007. "Userpicks: Cyber Folk Art in the Early 21st Century." *Folklore Forum* 37 (1): 27–38.
Foster, Michael Dylan. 2016a. "The Folkloresque Circle: Toward a Theory of Fuzzy Allusion." In *The Folkloresque: Reframing Folklore in a Popular Culture World*, edited by Michael Dylan Foster and Jeffrey A. Tolbert, 41–63. Logan: Utah State University Press.
———. 2016b. "Introduction: The Challenge of the Folkloresque." In *The Folkloresque: Reframing Folklore in a Popular Culture World*, edited by Michael Dylan Foster and Jeffrey A. Tolbert, 3–33. Logan: Utah State University Press.
Foster, Michael Dylan, and Jeffrey A. Tolbert, eds. 2016. *The Folkloresque: Reframing Folklore in a Popular Culture World.* Logan: Utah State University Press.
Fouché, Rayvon. 2006. "Say It Loud, I'm Black and I'm Proud: African Americans, American Artifactual Culture, and Black Vernacular Technological Creativity." *American Quarterly* 58 (3): 639–61.
FOX 6 Now Milwaukee. 2014. "Two Girls Accused of Plotting to Kill Friend, Victim Stabbed 19 Times," June 2. https://www.fox6now.com/news/two-girls-accused-of-plotting-to-kill-friend-victim-stabbed-19-times.
Frank, Russell. 2004. "When the Going Gets Tough, the Tough Go Photoshopping: September 11 and the Newslore of Vengeance and Victimization." *New Media & Society* 6 (5): 633–58. https://doi.org/10.1177/146144804047084.
———. 2009. "The Forward as Folklore: Studying E-Mailed Humor." In *Folklore and the Internet: Vernacular Expression in a Digital World*, edited by Trevor J. Blank, 98–122. Logan: Utah State University Press.
———. 2011. *Newslore: Contemporary Folklore on the Internet.* Jackson: University Press of Mississippi.
———. 2015. "Caveat Lector: Fake News as Folklore." *Journal of American Folklore* 128 (509): 315–32.
Gabielkov, Maksym, Arthi Ramachandran, Augustin Chaintreau, and Arnaud Legout. 2016. "Social Clicks: What and Who Gets Read on Twitter?" In *Proceedings of the 2016 ACM SIGMETRICS International Conference on Measurement*

and Modeling of Computer Science—SIGMETRICS '16, 179–92. Antibes Juan-les-Pins, France: ACM Press. https://doi.org/10.1145/2896377.2901462.

Gabler, Ellen. 2014. "Charges Detail Waukesha Pre-Teens' Attempt to Kill Classmate." *Milwaukee Journal Sentinel*, June 2.

Garcia, Denise. 2017. "Social Media Mavens Wield 'Influence,' and Rake in Big Dollars." *CNBC*, August 12. https://www.cnbc.com/2017/08/11/social-media-influencers-rake-in-cash-become-a-billion-dollar-market.html.

Garlough, Christine. 2011. "Folklore and Performing Political Protest: Calls of Conscience at the 2011 Wisconsin Labor Protests." *Western Folklore* 70 (3/4): 337–70.

Gaskins, Nettrice. 2019. "Techno-Vernacular Creativity and Innovation across the African Diaspora and Global South." In *Captivating Technology: Race, Carceral Technoscience, and Liberatory Imagination in Everyday Life*, edited by Ruha Benjamin, 252–74. Durham, NC: Duke University Press.

Gaume, Johan, and Alexander M. Puzrin. 2021. "Mechanisms of Slab Avalanche Release and Impact in the Dyatlov Pass Incident in 1959." *Communications Earth & Environment* 2 (1): 10. https://doi.org/10.1038/s43247-020-00081-8.

Geertz, Clifford. 1973. *The Interpretation of Cultures: Selected Essays.* New York: Basic Books.

Gencarella, Stephen Olbrys. 2009. "Constituting Folklore: A Case for Critical Folklore Studies." *Journal of American Folklore* 122 (484): 172–96.

Genova, Vincent. 2018. "PewDiePie Reveals His Channel Statistics after Alinity Suggested All His Fans Were 9 Year Olds." *Dexerto*, July 1. https://www.dexerto.com/entertainment/pewdiepie-reveals-his-channel-statistics-after-alinity-suggested-all-his-fans-were-9-year-olds-110491/.

Georges, Robert A., and Michael Owen Jones. 1995. *Folkloristics: An Introduction.* Bloomington: Indiana University Press.

Giddens, Anthony. 1984. *The Constitution of Society: Outline of the Theory of Structuration.* Berkeley: University of California Press.

———. 1991. *Modernity and Self-Identity: Self and Society in the Late Modern Age.* Stanford, CA: Stanford University Press.

Giles, David C. 2002. "Parasocial Interaction: A Review of the Literature and a Model for Future Research." *Media Psychology* 4 (3): 279–305. https://doi.org/10.1207/S1532785XMEP0403_04.

Gillespie, Tarleton. 2018. *Custodians of the Internet: Platforms, Content Moderation, and the Hidden Decisions That Shape Social Media.* New Haven, CT: Yale University Press.

Goffman, Erving. 1959. *The Presentation of Self in Everyday Life.* New York: Anchor Books Doubleday.

———. 1974. *Frame Analysis: An Essay on the Organisation of Experience.* New York: Harper & Row.

Goldstein, Diane E. 2004. *Once upon a Virus: AIDS Legends and Vernacular Risk Perception*. Logan: Utah State University Press.

———. 2007a. "Scientific Rationalism and Supernatural Experience Narratives." In *Haunting Experiences: Ghosts in Contemporary Folklore*, edited by Diane E. Goldstein, Sylvia Ann Grider, and Jeannie B. Thomas, 60–78. Logan: Utah State University Press.

———. 2007b. "The Commodification of Belief." In *Haunting Experiences: Ghosts in Contemporary Folklore*, edited by Diane E. Goldstein, Sylvia Ann Grider, and Jeannie B. Thomas, 171–205. Logan: Utah State University Press.

Gonzalez-Martin, Rachel V. 2016. "Digitizing Cultural Economies: 'Personalization' and U.S. Quinceanera Practice Online." *Cultural Analysis* 15 (1): 57–77.

Gorman, Ryan, and Lydia Warren. 2014. "White Supremacist Couple Who Killed Two Cops and an Innocent Walmart Shopper 'Wanted to Overthrow the Government and Liked to Dress Up as the Slender Man.'" *Daily Mail*, June 8.

Grider, Sylvia. 1984. "The Razor Blades in the Apples Syndrome." In *Perspectives on Contemporary Legend: Proceedings of the Conference of Contemporary Legend*, edited by Paul Smith, 128–40. Sheffield, UK: CECTAL.

Grip, Thomas. 2013. "Thoughts on Slender; The Arrival." *In the Games of Madness* (blog), May 12. https://frictionalgames.blogspot.com/2013/05/thoughts-on-slender-arrival.html.

Grundberg, Sven, and Jens Hansegard. 2014. "YouTube's Biggest Draw Plays Games, Earns $4 Million a Year." *Wall Street Journal*, June 16, sec. Tech.

Gunn, Joshua. 2005. "Prime-Time Satanism: Rumor-Panic and the Work of Iconic Topoi." *Visual Communication* 4 (1): 93–120. https://doi.org/10.1177/1470357205048939.

Halavais, Alexander M. Campbell. 2009. *Search Engine Society*. Digital Media and Society Series. Malden, MA: Polity.

Hall, Stuart, Chas Critcher, Tony Jefferson, John Clarke, and Brian Roberts. 1978. *Policing the Crisis: Mugging, the State, and Law and Order*. Critical Social Studies. London: Macmillan.

Hand, Martin. 2012. *Ubiquitous Photography*. Cambridge, UK: Polity Press.

Hartmann, Tilo, and Charlotte Goldhoorn. 2011. "Horton and Wohl Revisited: Exploring Viewers' Experience of Parasocial Interaction." *Journal of Communication* 61 (6): 1104–21. https://doi.org/10.1111/j.1460-2466.2011.01595.x.

Hauser, Gerard A. 1999. *Vernacular Voices: The Rhetoric of Publics and Public Spheres*. Columbia: University of South Carolina Press.

Hess, Aaron. 2010. "Democracy through the Polarized Lens of the Camcorder: Argumentation and Vernacular Spectacle on YouTube in the 2008 Election." *Argumentation and Advocacy* 47:106–22.

Hindman, Matthew Scott. 2009. *The Myth of Digital Democracy.* Princeton, NJ: Princeton University Press.

Horgan, Colin. 2018. "QAnon, Slender Man, and Our Paranoid Surveillance Society." *Medium,* August 28. https://gen.medium.com/qanon-slender-man-and-our-paranoid-surveillance-society-b3d44075ba87.

Horton, Donald, and Richard R. Wohl. 1956. "Mass Communication and Para-Social Interaction: Observations on Intimacy at a Distance." *Psychiatry* 19 (3): 215–29. https://doi.org/10.1080/00332747.1956.11023049.

Howard, Robert Glenn. 2005. "Toward a Theory of World Wide Web Vernacular: The Case for Pet Cloning." *Journal of Folklore Research* 42 (3): 323–60.

———. 2008a. "Electronic Hybridity: The Persistent Processes of the Vernacular Web." *Journal of American Folklore* 121 (480): 192–218.

———. 2008b. "The Vernacular Web of Participatory Media." *Critical Studies in Media Communication* 25 (5): 490–513. https://doi.org/10.1080/15295030802468065.

———. 2009. "Enacting a Virtual 'Ekklesia': Online Christian Fundamentalism as Vernacular Religion." *New Media & Society* 12 (5): 729–44. https://doi.org/10.1177/1461444809342765.

———. 2010. "The Vernacular Mode: Locating the Non-institutional in the Practice of Citizenship." In *Public Modalities: Rhetoric, Culture, Media, and the Shape of Public Life,* edited by Daniel C Brouwer and Robert Asen, 240–61. Tuscaloosa: University of Alabama Press.

———. 2011. *Digital Jesus: The Making of a New Christian Fundamentalist Community on the Internet.* The New and Alternative Religions Series. New York: New York University Press.

———. 2013. "Vernacular Authority: Critically Engaging 'Tradition.'" In *Tradition in the Twenty-First Century: Locating the Role of the Past in the Present,* edited by Trevor J. Blank and Robert Glenn Howard, 72–99. Logan: Utah State University Press.

———. 2017. "GunNets: Why a Theory of Heterogeneous Volition Is Necessary in the Study of Digital Communication." *Cultural Analysis* 16 (1): 116–33.

Howard, Robert Glenn, and Trevor J. Blank. 2013. "Living Traditions in a Modern World." In *Tradition in the Twenty-First Century: Locating the Role of the Past in the Present,* edited by Trevor J. Blank and Robert Glenn Howard, 1–21. Logan: Utah State University Press.

Hufford, David. 1982. *The Terror That Comes in the Night: An Experience-Centered Study of Supernatural Assault Traditions.* Philadelphia: University of Pennsylvania Press.

Ingraham, Chris, and Joshua Reeves. 2016. "New Media, New Panics." *Critical Studies in Media Communication* 33 (5): 455–67. https://doi.org/10.1080/15295036.2016.1227863.

JAusten Productions. 2012. "HIKER KILLED BY THE SLENDER MAN!!!!! MUST WATCH!!!" YouTube video, September 12. https://www.youtube.com/watch?v=DHp_XteuLEM.

Jenkins, Henry, Sam Ford, and Joshua Green. 2013. *Spreadable Media: Creating Value and Meaning in a Networked Culture.* Postmillennial Pop. New York: New York University Press.

Jensen, Ethan. 2014. Personal interview. Interview in possession of author.

Kaplan, Merrill. 2013. "Curation and Tradition on Web 2.0." In *Tradition in the Twenty-First Century: Locating the Role of the Past in the Present,* edited by Trevor J. Blank and Robert Glenn Howard, 123–48. Logan: Utah State University Press.

Kibby, M. D. 2005. "Email Forwardables: Folklore in the Age of the Internet." *New Media & Society* 7 (6): 770–90. https://doi.org/10.1177/1461444805058161.

Kilgannon, Corey. 2020. "The Truth about Alligators in the Sewers of New York." *New York Times,* February 26.

Kinsella, Michael. 2011. *Legend-Tripping Online: Supernatural Folklore and the Search for Ong's Hat.* Jackson: University Press of Mississippi.

Kirshenblatt-Gimblett, Barbara. 1998. "Folklore's Crisis." *Journal of American Folklore* 111 (441): 281–327.

Kitta, Andrea. 2018a. "Alternative Health Websites and Fake News: Taking a Stab at Definition, Genre, and Belief." *Journal of American Folklore* 131 (522): 405–12.

———. 2018b. "'What Happens When the Pictures Are No Longer Photoshops?': Slender Man, Belief, and the Unacknowledged Common Experience."" In *Slender Man Is Coming: Creepypasta and Contemporary Legends on the Internet,* edited by Trevor J. Blank and Lynne S. McNeill, 77–90. Logan: Utah State University Press.

———. 2019. *The Kiss of Death: Contagion, Contamination, and Folklore.* Logan: Utah State University Press.

Kjellberg, Felix. 2012. "SLENDER—Part 1 (+Download Link) Reaction Facecam." YouTube video, July 1. https://www.youtube.com/watch?v=OZMBG4Pn3Sg.

———. 2013. "Slender: The Arrival—Part 1 ORIGINAL SLENDER GAME RELEASED!" YouTube video, March 27. https://www.youtube.com/watch?v=EDYQnhLxjJU.

———. 2014. "The Most Powerful Swede in the World." Interview by Maria Lindholm. *ICON.* http://iconmagazine.se/portfolio/the-most-powerful-swede-in-the-world/.

Kortenhof, Kurt Daniel. 1996. *Long Live the Hodag! The Life and Legacy of Eugene Simeon Shepard: 1854–1923.* Rhinelander, WI: Hodag Press.

Koven, Mikel J. 1999. "*Candyman* Can: Film and Ostension." *Contemporary Legend,* n.s. 2:155–73.

———. 2003. "Folklore Studies and Popular Film and Television: A Necessary Critical Survey." *Journal of American Folklore* 116 (460): 176–95.

———. 2007. "*Most Haunted* and the Convergence of Traditional Belief and Popular Television." *Folklore* 118 (2): 183–202. https://doi.org/10.1080/00155870701337403.

———. 2008. *Film, Folklore, and Urban Legends.* Lanham, MD: Scarecrow.

———. 2018. "The Emperor's New Lore; or, Who Believes in the Big Bad Slender Man?" In *Slender Man Is Coming: Creepypasta and Contemporary Legends on the Internet,* edited by Trevor J. Blank and Lynne S. McNeill, 113–27. Logan: Utah State University Press.

Kuhagen, Christopher. 2020a. "Anissa Weier, Convicted in the Slender Man Stabbing Case, Has Petitioned for Release from a State Mental Health Hospital." *Milwaukee Journal Sentinel,* November 20.

———. 2020b. "Timeline: How the Waukesha Slender Man Stabbing Case Played Out over the Years." *Milwaukee Journal Sentinel,* September 2.

———. 2021a. "Anissa Weier, One of the Women in the Slender Man Stabbing, Should Be Released from a State Mental Hospital, Her Attorneys Say." *Milwaukee Journal Sentinel,* April 15.

———. 2021b. "Wisconsin Supreme Court Denies Morgan Geyser's Petition to Review Her Case in the 2014 Slender Man Stabbing." *Milwaukee Journal Sentinel,* February 9.

Kuipers, Giselinde. 2005. "'Where Was King Kong When We Needed Him?': Public Discourse, Digital Disaster Jokes, and the Functions of Laughter after 9/11." *Journal of American Culture* 28 (1): 70–84. https://doi.org/10.1111/j.1542-734X.2005.00155.x.

Langlois, Janet. 1978. "'Mary Whales, I Believe in You': Myth and Ritual Subdued." *Indiana Folklore* 11 (1): 5–33.

Lantis, Margaret. 1960. "Vernacular Culture." *American Anthropologist* 62:202–16.

Laudun, John. 2020. "The Clown Legend Cascade of 2016." In *Folklore and Social Media,* edited by Trevor J. Blank and Andrew Peck, 188–208. Logan: Utah State University Press.

Lee, Junghee, and Hyunjoo Lee. 2010. "The Computer-Mediated Communication Network: Exploring the Linkage between the Online Community and Social Capital." *New Media & Society* 12 (5): 711–27. https://doi.org/10.1177/1461444809343568.

Lessig, Lawrence. 2008. *Remix: Making Art and Commerce Thrive in the Hybrid Economy.* New York: Penguin Press.

Lewin, Kurt. 1943. "Forces behind Food Habits and Methods of Change." *Bulletin of the National Research Council* 108:35–65.

———. 1947. "Frontiers in Group Dynamics: Concept, Method and Reality in Social Science; Social Equilibria and Social Change." *Human Relations* 1 (1): 5–41. https://doi.org/10.1177/001872674700100103.

Li, David K., and Network Writers. 2014. "Las Vegas Cop Killers Were 'White Supremacists' Who Liked to Dress as Slenderman and The Joker." *Herald Sun*, June 9. https://www.heraldsun.com.au/news/law-order/true-crime-scene/las-vegas-cop-killers-were-white-supremacists-who-liked-to-dress-as-slenderman-and-the-joker/news-story/018fb3933d65bbc81d5174684a4db15b.

Lindahl, Carl. 2005. "Ostensive Healing: Pilgrimage to the San Antonio Ghost Tracks." *Journal of American Folklore* 118 (468): 164–85.

Livingston, Steven, and W. Lance Bennett. 2003. "Gatekeeping, Indexing, and Live-Event News: Is Technology Altering the Construction of News?" *Political Communication* 20 (4): 363–80. https://doi.org/10.1080/10584600390244121.

Lord, Albert Bates. 1960. *The Singer of Tales*. Cambridge, MA: Harvard University Press.

Lorenz, Taylor. 2019. "Momo Is Not Trying to Kill Children." *The Atlantic*, February 28.

Lowthorp, Leah. 2018. "#CRISPRfacts, Gene Editing, and Joking in the Twittersphere." *Journal of American Folklore* 131 (522): 482–92.

Lupkin, Sydney. 2014. "Why Did 12-Year-Olds Stab Friend for Slender Man?" *ABC News*, June 3. https://abcnews.go.com/Health/12-year-olds-stab-friend-slender-man/story?id=23979903.

MacKenzie, Donald, and Judy Wajcman. 1999. "Introductory Essay: The Social Shaping of Technology." In *The Social Shaping of Technology*, edited by Donald MacKenzie and Judy Wajcman, 3–27. 2nd ed. Buckingham, UK: Open University Press.

Maddox, Jessica. 2018. "Of Internet Born: Idolatry, the Slender Man Meme, and the Feminization of Digital Spaces." *Feminist Media Studies* 18 (2): 235–48. https://doi.org/10.1080/14680777.2017.1300179.

Magliocco, Sabina. 2012. "Beyond Belief: Context, Rationality and Participatory Consciousness." *Western Folklore* 71 (1): 5–24.

Manning, Paul. 2018. "Monstrous Media and Media Monsters: From Cottingly to Waukesha." In *Slender Man Is Coming: Creepypasta and Contemporary Legends on the Internet*, edited by Trevor J. Blank and Lynne S. McNeill, 155–81. Logan: Utah State University Press.

"Marble Hornets Q&A: Connecticon." 2014. YouTube video, July 14. https://www.youtube.com/watch?v=tLax_MaimDo.

"Marble Hornets Radio Interview (Full Audio)." 2010. YouTube video, November 24, 2012. https://www.youtube.com/watch?v=tcZO8dZ3edY.

Marcelle, Joy, and Dakin Andone. 2018. "2nd Teen in 'Slenderman' Stabbing Gets 40 Years in Mental Institution." *CNN*, February 1.

Markiplier. 2013. "Slender: The Arrival | Part 1 | SLENDER HAS ARRIVED." YouTube video, March 27. https://www.youtube.com/watch?v=RsIcF3-MTsk.

Marwick, A. E., and d. boyd. 2011. "I Tweet Honestly, I Tweet Passionately: Twitter Users, Context Collapse, and the Imagined Audience." *New Media & Society* 13 (1): 114–33. https://doi.org/10.1177/1461444810365313.

Marwick, Alice. 2008. "To Catch a Predator? The MySpace Moral Panic." *First Monday* 13 (6). https://firstmonday.org/article/view/2152/1966.

Marwick, Alice, and danah boyd. 2011. "To See and Be Seen: Celebrity Practice on Twitter." *Convergence: The International Journal of Research into New Media Technologies* 17 (2): 139–58. https://doi.org/10.1177/1354856510394539.

Massanari, Adrienne Lynne. 2015. *Participatory Culture, Community, and Play: Learning from Reddit.* Digital Formations 75. New York: Peter Lang.

Mauney, Matt. 2014. "Florida Teen Obsessed with 'Slender Man' Sets Fire to Home as Family Sleeps." *Orlando Sentinel*, September 5.

McLuhan, Marshall. 1962. *The Gutenberg Galaxy: The Making of Typographic Man.* Reprint, Toronto: University of Toronto Press.

McNeill, Lynne S. 2009. "The End of the Internet: A Folk Response to the Provision of Infinite Choice." In *Folklore and the Internet: Vernacular Expression in a Digital World*, edited by Trevor J. Blank, 80–97. Logan: Utah State University Press.

———. 2012. "Real Virtuality: Enhancing Locality by Enacting the Small World Theory." In *Folk Culture in the Digital Age: The Emergent Dynamics of Human Interaction*, edited by Trevor J. Blank, 85–97. Logan: Utah State University Press.

———. 2013. "And the Greatest of These Is Tradition: The Folklorist's Toolbox in the Twenty-First Century." In *Tradition in the Twenty-First Century: Locating the Role of the Past in the Present*, edited by Trevor J. Blank and Robert Glenn Howard, 174–85. Logan: Utah State University Press.

———. 2018. "'My Friend Posted It and That's Good Enough for Me!': Source Perception in Online Information Sharing." *Journal of American Folklore* 131 (522): 493–99.

———. 2020. "Classifying #BlackLivesMatter: Genre and Form in Digital Folklore." In *Folklore and Social Media*, edited by Trevor J. Blank and Andrew Peck, 179–87. Logan: Utah State University Press.

McNeill, Lynne S., and Elizabeth Tucker. 2018a. "Introduction." In *Legend Tripping: A Contemporary Legend Casebook*, edited by Lynne S. McNeill and Elizabeth Tucker, 3–30. Logan: Utah State University Press.

———. 2018b. *Legend Tripping: A Contemporary Legend Casebook.* Logan: Utah State University Press.

Meraz, S., and Z. Papacharissi. 2013. "Networked Gatekeeping and Networked Framing on #Egypt." *International Journal of Press/Politics* 18 (2): 138–66. https://doi.org/10.1177/1940161212474472.

Meyrowitz, Joshua. 1985. *No Sense of Place: The Impact of Electronic Media on Social Behavior.* New York: Oxford University Press.

Mikkelson, David. 2019. "How Much of a Threat Is the Purported 'Momo Challenge' Suicide Game?" *Snopes*, February 26. https://www.snopes.com/news/2019/02/26/momo-challenge-suicide-game/.

Milner, Ryan M. 2016. *The World Made Meme: Public Conversations and Participatory Media.* The Information Society Series. Cambridge, MA: MIT Press.

Milspaw, Yvonne J., and Wesley K. Evans. 2010. "Variations on Vampires: Live Action Role Playing, Fantasy and the Revival of Traditional Beliefs." *Western Folklore* 69 (2): 211–50.

Moran, Robert. 2019. "Who Is PewDiePie, YouTube's Record-Setting Personality?" *Sydney Morning Herald*, August 27. https://www.smh.com.au/entertainment/celebrity/who-is-pewdiepie-youtube-s-record-setting-personality-20190827-p52l7a.html.

Moreno, Ivan. 2017. "Teen Pleads Guilty to Lesser Charge in Slender Man Attack." *Associated Press*, August 21. https://apnews.com/article/us-news-wisconsin-milwaukee-wi-state-wire-homicide-a08f33cbf7eb402c9355794fa3f0ebcb.

Morris, Jeremy Wade. 2014. "Artists as Entrepreneurs, Fans as Workers." *Popular Music and Society* 37 (3): 273–90. https://doi.org/10.1080/03007766.2013.778534.

Moser, Hans. 1962. "Vom Folklorismus in Unserer Zeit." *Volkskunde* 58:177–209.

Motz, Marilyn. 1998. "The Practice of Belief." *Journal of American Folklore* 111 (441): 339–55.

Mould, Tom. 2018a. "A Doubt-Centered Approach to Contemporary Legend and Fake News." *Journal of American Folklore* 131 (522): 413–20.

———. 2018b. "Introduction to the Special Issue on Fake News: Definitions and Approaches." *Journal of American Folklore* 131 (522): 371–78.

Mullen, Patrick B. 1972. "Modern Legend and Rumor Theory." *Journal of the Folklore Institute* 9 (2/3): 95–109. https://doi.org/10.2307/3814160.

———. 2000. "Belief and the American Folk." *Journal of American Folklore* 113 (448): 119–43.

Murray, Rheana. 2014a. "Slender Man Now Linked to 3 Violent Acts." *ABC News*, June 9. http://abcnews.go.com/US/slender-man-now-linked-violent-acts/story?id=24058562.

———. 2014b. "Teen Inspired by 'Slender Man' Set House on Fire: Police." *ABC News*, September 5. https://abcnews.go.com/US/teen-inspired-slender-man-set-house-fire-police/story?id=25262814.

NBC News. 2014. "Two Cops, Three Others Killed in Las Vegas Shooting Spree." *NBC News*, June 8. https://www.nbcnews.com/storyline/vegas-cop-killers/two-cops-three-others-killed-las-vegas-shooting-spree-n125766.

Nelson, Jacob L, and Harsh Taneja. 2018. "The Small, Disloyal Fake News Audience: The Role of Audience Availability in Fake News Consumption." *New Media & Society* 20 (10): 3720–37. https://doi.org/10.1177/1461444818758715.

Newall, Venetia J. 1987. "The Adaptation of Folklore and Tradition (Folklorismus)." *Folklore* 98 (2): 131–51.

Noble, Safiya Umoja. 2018. *Algorithms of Oppression: How Search Engines Reinforce Racism*. New York: New York University Press.

Noyes, Dorothy. 2009. "Tradition: Three Traditions." *Journal of Folklore Research* 46 (3): 233–68.

O'Connor, Bonnie Blair. 1995. *Healing Traditions: Alternative Medicine and the Health Professions*. Studies in Health, Illness, and Caregiving. Philadelphia: University of Pennsylvania Press.

Ong, Walter J. 1982. *Orality and Literacy: The Technologizing of the Word*. New Accents. London: Routledge.

Ono, Kent A, and John M Sloop. 1995. "The Critique of Vernacular Discourse." *Communication Monographs* 62 (1): 19–46.

———. 2002. *Shifting Borders: Rhetoric, Immigration, and California's Proposition 187*. Mapping Racisms. Philadelphia: Temple University Press.

Orland, Kyle. 2018. "Valve Leaks Steam Game Player Counts; We Have the Numbers." *Ars Technica*, July 6. https://arstechnica.com/gaming/2018/07/steam-data-leak-reveals-precise-player-count-for-thousands-of-games/.

Papacharissi, Zizi. 2010. *A Private Sphere: Democracy in a Digital Age*. Digital Media and Society. Cambridge, UK: Polity.

Pariser, Eli. 2012. *The Filter Bubble: How the New Personalized Web Is Changing What We Read and How We Think*. London: Penguin Books.

Peck, Andrew. 2014. "A Laugh Riot: Photoshopping as Vernacular Discursive Practice." *International Journal of Communication* 8:1638–62.

———. 2015a. "At the Modems of Madness: The Slender Man, Ostension, and the Digital Age." *Contemporary Legend* 3 (5): 14–37.

———. 2015b. "Tall, Dark, and Loathsome: The Emergence of a Legend Cycle in the Digital Age." *Journal of American Folklore* 128 (509): 333–48.

———. 2017. "Capturing the Slender Man: Online and Offline Vernacular Practice in the Digital Age." *Cultural Analysis* 16 (1): 30–48.

———. 2018. "The Cowl of Cthulhu: Ostensive Practice in the Digital Age." In *Slender Man Is Coming: Creepypasta and Contemporary Legends on the Internet*, edited by Trevor J. Blank and Lynne S. McNeill, 51–76. Logan: Utah State University Press.

———. 2020a. "The Death of Doge: Institutional Appropriations of Internet Memes." In *Folklore and Social Media*, edited by Trevor J. Blank and Andrew Peck, 83–107. Logan: Utah State University Press.

———. 2020b. "Introduction: Old Practices, New Media." In *Folklore and Social Media*, edited by Trevor J. Blank and Andrew Peck, 3–23. Logan: Utah State University Press.

———. 2020c. "A Problem of Amplification: Folklore and Fake News in the Age of Social Media." *Journal of American Folklore* 133 (529): 329–51.

Peck, Andrew, and Katie Day Good. 2020. "When Paper Goes Viral: Handmade Signs as Vernacular Materiality in Digital Space." *International Journal of Communication* 14:626–48.

Pennington, Rosemary, and Jessica Birthisel. 2016. "When New Media Make News: Framing Technology and Sexual Assault in the Steubenville Rape Case." *New Media & Society* 18 (11): 2435–51. https://doi.org/10.1177/1461444815612407.

Pennycook, Gordon, Tyrone D. Cannon, and David G. Rand. 2018. "Prior Exposure Increases Perceived Accuracy of Fake News." *Journal of Experimental Psychology: General* 147 (12): 1865–80. https://doi.org/10.1037/xge0000465.

Pettitt, Thomas. 2007. "Before the Gutenberg Parenthesis: Elizabethan-American Compatibilies." Paper presented at Media in Transition 5: Creativity, Ownership and Collaboration in the Digital Age, Massachusetts Institute of Technology, Cambridge, April 27–29.

Pettitt, Thomas, Paul Smith, and Jacqueline Simpson. 1995. "Contemporary Legend—The Debate Continues." *Folklore* 106:96–100.

Phillips, Whitney. 2015. *This Is Why We Can't Have Nice Things: Mapping the Relationship between Online Trolling and Mainstream Culture.* The Information Society Series. Cambridge, MA: MIT Press.

Phillips, Whitney, and Ryan M. Milner. 2017. *The Ambivalent Internet: Mischief, Oddity, and Antagonism Online.* Cambridge, UK: Polity.

———. 2018. "Ghosts in the Machines: How Centuries of Technological Play with Death Has Helped Make Sense of Life." In *A Networked Self and Birth, Life, Death*, edited by Zizi Papacharissi, 240–56. New York: Routledge, Taylor & Francis Group.

———. 2020. "The Vernacular Vortex: Analyzing the Endless Churn of Donald Trump's Twitter Orbit." In *Folklore and Social Media*, edited by Trevor J. Blank and Andrew Peck, 67–82. Logan: Utah State University Press.

Plato. 1925. *Plato: In Twelve Volumes. 1: Euthyphro. Apology. Crito. Phaedo. Phaedrus.* Translated by Harold North Fowler. Vol. 9. The Loeb Classical Library 36. Reprint, Cambridge, MA: Harvard University Press.

Plunkett, Luke. 2014. "Girls Claim Slender Man Is Real, Accused of Stabbing Friend 19 Times." *Kotaku*, June 2. https://kotaku.com/girls-claim-slender-man-is-real-stab-classmate-19-time-1585164160.

Preston, Michael J. 1974. "Xerox-Lore." *Keystone Folklore* 19:11–26.

———. 1994. "Traditional Humor from the Fax Machine: 'All of a Kind.'" *Western Folklore* 53 (2): 147–69.

Prizer, Tim. 2018. "'Shame Old Roads Can't Talk': Narrative, Experience, and Belief in the Framing of Legend Trips as Performance." In *Legend Tripping: A Contemporary Legend Casebook*, edited by Lynne S. McNeill and Elizabeth Tucker, 129–52. Logan: Utah State University Press.

Radford, Benjamin. 2019. "The Rise and Fall of the 'Momo Challenge' Online Suicide Game Conspiracy." *Skeptical Inquirer* 43 (3). https://skepticalinquirer.org/2019/05/the-rise-and-fall-of-the-momo-challenge-online-suicide-game-conspiracy/.

Rambukkana, Nathan. 2015. "From #RaceFail to #Ferguson: The Digital Intimacies of Race-Activist Hashtag Publics." In *Hashtag Publics: The Power and Politics of Discursive Networks*, edited by Nathan Rambukkana, 29–46. Digital Formations 103. New York: Peter Lang.

Renard, Jean-Bruno. 1991. "LSD Tattoo Transfers: Rumor from North America to France." *Folklore Forum* 24 (2): 3–26.

Reyman, Jessica. 2018. "The Rhetorical Agency of Algorithms." In *Theorizing Digital Rhetoric*, edited by Aaron Hess and Amber L. Davisson, 112–25. New York: Routledge.

Richmond, Todd. 2014. "12-Year-Old Wisconsin Girls Charged in Stabbing." *Associated Press*, June 2. https://apnews.com/article/ed892d67a63347718b5353aba8b689a3.

Robinson, Kelley. 2019. "'Slender Man' Stabbing Victim Speaks Publicly for First Time: 'Without the Whole Situation, I Wouldn't Be Who I Am.'" *ABC News*, October 24. https://abcnews.go.com/US/slender-man-stabbing-victim-speaks-publicly-time-situation/story?id=66268385.

Robinson, Kelley, and Emily Whipp. 2017. "Teen Who Pleaded Guilty in Slender Man Stabbing Case to Remain in Institutional Care for 25 Years, Judge Says." *ABC News*, December 21. https://abcnews.go.com/US/teen-pleaded-guilty-slender-man-stabbing-case-remain/story?id=51909413.

Rojecki, Andrew, and Sharon Meraz. 2016. "Rumors and Factitious Informational Blends: The Role of the Web in Speculative Politics." *New Media & Society* 18 (1): 25–43. https://doi.org/10.1177/1461444814535724.

Rubin, Rebecca B., and Michael P. McHugh. 1987. "Development of Parasocial Interaction Relationships." *Journal of Broadcasting & Electronic Media* 31 (3): 279–92. https://doi.org/10.1080/08838158709386664.

Sam Thrower. 2012. "FRIGHTENING Slender Man Sighting (MOVIE) Hunting in the Woods." YouTube video, December 21. https://www.youtube.com/watch?v=ubT51oyo7NU.

Sawin, Patricia E. 2002. "Performance at the Nexus of Gender, Power, and Desire: Reconsidering Bauman's Verbal Art from the Perspective of Gendered Subjectivity as Performance." *Journal of American Folklore* 115 (455): 28–61.

Schmitt, Casey R. 2016. "The Tactical Trail: Sense of Place and Place of Practice." *Cultural Analysis* 15 (1): 128–44.

Schomer, Audrey. 2019. "Influencer Marketing: State of the Social Media Influencer Market in 2020." *Business Insider*, December 17. https://www.businessinsider.com/influencer-marketing-report.

Shibutani, Tamotsu. 1966. *Improvised News: A Sociological Study of Rumor.* New York: Bobbs-Merrill.

Shifman, Limor. 2014. *Memes in Digital Culture.* MIT Press Essential Knowledge. Cambridge, MA: MIT Press.

Shoemaker, Pamela J. 1991. *Gatekeeping.* Communication Concepts 3. Newbury Park, CA: Sage.

Shoemaker, Pamela J., and Tim P. Vos. 2009. *Gatekeeping Theory.* New York: Routledge. https://doi.org/10.4324/9780203931653.

Sleight-Price, Camille, Daisy Ahlstone, and Michelle W. Jones. 2018. "Forbidden Foodways: Tide Pods, Ostensive Practice, and Intergenerational Conflict." *Contemporary Legend* 3 (8): 1–27.

"Slender: The Arrival." n.d. *Metacritic.* https://www.metacritic.com/game/pc/slender-the-arrival.

Smosh Games. 2013. "SLENDER MAN HAS ARRIVED (Backseat Gaming)." YouTube video, April 2. https://www.youtube.com/watch?v=T5H_eJM4syg.

Snider, Paul B. 1967. "'Mr. Gates' Revisited: A 1966 Version of the 1949 Case Study." *Journalism Quarterly* 44 (3): 419–27. https://doi.org/10.1177/107769906704400301.

Snopes Staff. 1999. "Is the Neiman Marcus Cookie Story True?" *Snopes*, November 3. https://www.snopes.com/fact-check/neiman-marcus-cookies/.

Soltero, Gonzalo. 2016. "The Mexican Transmission of 'Lights Out!'" *Journal of Folklore Research* 53 (3): 115–35.

Stampler, Laura. 2014. "The Origins of Slender Man, the Meme That Allegedly Drove 12-Year-Olds to Kill." *Time*, June 3.

Sydow, C. W. von. 1977. *Selected Papers on Folklore.* International Folklore. New York: Arno Press.

Tangherlini, Timothy R. 1990. "'It Happened Not Too Far from Here . . .': A Survey of Legend Theory and Characterization." *Western Folklore* 49 (4): 371–90.

———. 1994. *Interpreting Legend: Danish Storytellers and Their Repertoires.* New York: Routledge.

———. 2008. "'Where Was I?': Personal Experience Narrative, Crystallization and Some Thoughts on Tradition Memory." *Cultural Analysis* 7:41–65.

———. 2018. "Toward a Generative Model of Legend: Pizzas, Bridges, Vaccines, and Witches." *Humanities* 7 (1). https://doi.org/10.3390/h7010001.

Tangherlini, Timothy R., Vwani Roychowdhury, and Peter M. Broadwell. 2020. "Bridges, Sex Slaves, Tweets, and Guns: A Multi-domain Model of Conspiracy Theory." In *Folklore and Social Media*, edited by Trevor J. Blank and Andrew Peck, 39–66. Logan: Utah State University Press.

Taylor, T. L. 2018. *Watch Me Play: Twitch and the Rise of Game Live Streaming*. Princeton Studies in Culture and Technology. Princeton, NJ: Princeton University Press.

The Slender Man. 2013. "Scariest Real Slender Man Attack Caught on Tape Disturbing NSFW!" YouTube video, January 18. https://www.youtube.com/watch?v=nYH7bmFgCkY.

Thomas, Jeannie Banks. 2018. "#BlackLivesMatter: Galvanizing and Oppositional Narratives." In *Race and Ethnicity in Digital Culture: Our Changing Traditions, Impressions, and Expressions in a Mediated World*, edited by Anthony Bak Buccitelli, 95–114. Santa Barbara, CA: Praeger.

Thompson, Tok. 2020. "The Beauty, the Beast, and the Fanon: The Vernacularization of the Literary Canon and an Epilogue for Modernity." In *Folklore and Social Media*, edited by Trevor J. Blank and Andrew Peck, 161–78. Logan: Utah State University Press.

Thompson-Gee, Justin. 2017. "UPDATE: Anissa Weier Sentenced to 25 Years in Mental Hospital in Slender Man Stabbing Case." *WDJT Milwaukee*, December 21. https://cbs58.com/news/anissa-weier-to-be-sentenced-thursday-in-slender-man-stabbing-case.

Toelken, Barre. 1996. *The Dynamics of Folklore*. Rev. and expanded ed. Logan: Utah State University Press.

Tolbert, Jeffrey A. 2013. "'The Sort of Story That Has You Covering Your Mirrors': The Case of Slender Man." *Semiotic Review*, no. 2 (November). https://www.semioticreview.com/ojs/index.php/sr/article/view/19/19.

———. 2016. "Introduction." In *The Folkloresque: Reframing Folklore in a Popular Culture World*, edited by Michael Dylan Foster and Jeffrey A. Tolbert, 123–24. Logan: Utah State University Press.

———. 2018a. "'Dark and Wicked Things': Slender Man, the Folkloresque, and the Implications of Belief." In *Slender Man Is Coming: Creepypasta and Contemporary Legends on the Internet*, edited by Trevor J. Blank and Lynne S. McNeill, 91–112. Logan: Utah State University Press.

———. 2018b. "'The Sort of Story That Has You Covering Your Mirrors': The Case of Slender Man." In *Slender Man Is Coming: Creepypasta and Contemporary Legends on the Internet*, edited by Trevor J. Blank and Lynne S. McNeill, 25–50. Logan: Utah State University Press.

Tolbert, Jeffrey A., and Ian Brodie. 2019. "Ostension." In *SAGE Research Methods Foundations*, edited by Paul Anthony Atkinson, Sara Delamont, Richard A. Williams, Alexandru Cernat, and Joseph Sakshaug. https://methods.sagepub.com/foundations.

Toma, C. L., and J. T. Hancock. 2013. "Self-Affirmation Underlies Facebook Use." *Personality and Social Psychology Bulletin* 39 (3): 321–31. https://doi.org/10.1177/0146167212474694.

Tucker, Elizabeth. 1999. "Tales and Legends." In *Children's Folklore: A Source Book*, edited by Brian Sutton-Smith, Jay Mechling, Thomas W. Johnson, and Felicia R. McMahon, 193–211. Logan: Utah State University Press.

———. 2005. "Ghosts in Mirrors: Reflections of the Self." *Journal of American Folklore* 118 (468): 186–203.

———. 2008. "'Go to Bed, Now You're Dead': Suffocation Songs and Breath Control Games." *Children's Folklore Review* 31:45–58.

———. 2014. "The Endangered Child: Choking and Fainting Games in the Online Underground of YouTube." *Children's Folklore Review* 36:19–34.

———. 2018a. "Slender Man Is Coming to Get Your Little Brother or Sister: Teenagers' Pranks Posted on YouTube." In *Slender Man Is Coming: Creepypasta and Contemporary Legends on the Internet*, edited by Trevor J. Blank and Lynne S. McNeill, 141–54. Logan: Utah State University Press.

———. 2018b. "'There's an App for That': Ghost Hunting with Smartphones." In *Legend Tripping: A Contemporary Legend Casebook*, edited by Lynne S. McNeill and Elizabeth Tucker, 192–206. Logan: Utah State University Press.

———. 2020. "The Blue Whale Suicide Challenge: Hypermodern Ostension on a Global Scale." In *Folklore and Social Media*, edited by Trevor J. Blank and Andrew Peck, 209–225. Logan: Utah State University Press.

Tufekci, Zeynep. 2017. *Twitter and Tear Gas: The Power and Fragility of Networked Protest.* New Haven, CT: Yale University Press.

Turner, Patricia A. 1994. *I Heard It through the Grapevine: Rumor in African-American Culture.* Berkeley: University of California Press.

———. 2018. "Respecting the Smears: Anti-Obama Folklore Anticipates Fake News." *Journal of American Folklore* 131 (522): 421–25.

20/20. "The Wicked." 2019. Aired on October 25. https://abc.com/shows/2020/episode-guide/2019–10/25–102519-the-wicked.

Van Doorn, N. 2010. "The Ties That Bind: The Networked Performance of Gender, Sexuality and Friendship on MySpace." *New Media & Society* 12 (4): 583–602. https://doi.org/10.1177/1461444809342766.

Van Oot, Torey. 2014. "What Is Slender Man? A Meme's Possible Role in Wisconsin Stabbing." *NBC4 Washington*, June 3. https://www.nbcwashington.com/

news/national-international/what-is-slenderman-the-story-behind-the-meme-wisconsin-stabbing/74834/.

Victor, Jeffrey S. 1989. "A Rumor-Panic about a Dangerous Satanic Cult in Western New York." *New York Folklore* 15 (1/2): 23–49.

———. 1990. "Satanic Cult Rumors as Contemporary Legend." *Western Folklore* 49 (1): 51–81.

———. 1993. *Satanic Panic: The Creation of a Contemporary Legend.* Chicago: Open Court.

———. 1998. "Moral Panics and the Social Construction of Deviant Behavior: A Theory and Application to the Case of Ritual Child Abuse." *Sociological Perspectives* 41 (3): 541–65.

Vielmetti, Bruce, and Meg Kissinger. 2015. "Family History of Mental Illness Revealed in Slender Man Case." *Milwaukee Journal Sentinel*, June 17.

Wallace, Kelly. 2014. "Slenderman Stabbing Case: When Can Kids Understand Reality vs. Fantasy?" *CNN*, June 3. https://www.cnn.com/2014/06/03/living/slenderman-stabbing-questions-for-parents/index.html.

Wallsten, Kevin. 2010. "'Yes We Can': How Online Viewership, Blog Discussion, Campaign Statements, and Mainstream Media Coverage Produced a Viral Video Phenomenon." *Journal of Information Technology & Politics* 7 (2/3): 163–81. https://doi.org/10.1080/19331681003749030.

Westerman, William. 2009. "Epistemology, the Sociology of Knowledge, and the *Wikipedia* Userbox Controversy." In *Folklore and the Internet: Vernacular Expression in a Digital World*, edited by Trevor J. Blank, 123–58. Logan: Utah State University Press.

White, David Manning. 1950. "The 'Gate Keeper': A Case Study in the Selection of News." *Journalism Quarterly* 27 (4): 383–90. https://doi.org/10.1177/107769905002700403.

Willsey, Kristiana. 2020. "Dear David: Affect and Belief in Twitter Horror." In *Folklore and Social Media*, edited by Trevor J. Blank and Andrew Peck, 145–60. Logan: Utah State University Press.

Willson, Michele. 2014. "The Politics of Social Filtering." *Convergence: The International Journal of Research into New Media Technologies* 20 (2): 218–32. https://doi.org/10.1177/1354856513479761.

Winner, Langdon. 1986. *The Whale and the Reactor: A Search for Limits in an Age of High Technology.* Chicago: University of Chicago Press.

Wojcik, Daniel. 1996. "'Polaroids from Heaven': Photography, Folk Religion, and the Miraculous Image Tradition at a Marian Apparition Site." *Journal of American Folklore* 109 (432): 129–48. https://doi.org/10.2307/541832.

———. 2009. "Spirits, Apparitions, and Traditions of Supernatural Photography." *Visual Resources* 25 (1/2): 109–36. https://doi.org/10.1080/01973760802674390.

Yolen, Jane. 1988. "America's Cinderella." In *Cinderella, a Casebook*, edited by Alan Dundes, 294–306. Madison: University of Wisconsin Press.

Zappavigna, Michele. 2011. "Ambient Affiliation: A Linguistic Perspective on Twitter." *New Media & Society* 13 (5): 788–806. https://doi.org/10.1177/1461444810385097.

Zelizer, Barbie. 2010. *About to Die: How News Images Move the Public.* New York: Oxford University Press.

Zennie, Michael, and Associated Press Reporter. 2014. "Two 12-Year-Olds Obsessed with Online Ghost Stories 'Lured Classmate into Woods and Stabbed Her 19 Times' to Prove Slender Man Myth Was Real." *Daily Mail*, June 3.

Zipes, Jack. 1997. *Happily Ever After: Fairy Tales, Children, and the Culture Industry.* New York: Routledge.

———. 2001. *Sticks and Stones: The Troublesome Success of Children's Literature from Slovenly Peter to Harry Potter.* New York: Routledge.

Index

Page references in italics refer to illustrations.